Picnics · Potlucks & PRIZEWINNERS

About the cover:

A bountiful autumn picnic is set in Memorial Park, Lebanon, Indiana, with the Abigail J. Herr log cabin in the background. Built in 1839, the cabin was given to the James Hill Chapter of the Daughters of the American Revolution by John Herr as a memorial to his mother. In 1935 the cabin was moved to this location and restored by W.P.A. workers.

Foods featured: Buttermilk Picnic Chicken, The Butcher's Ham Loaf, Hoosier Chili, South-of-the-Border Bread, Whole Wheat Onion Buns, Classic Macaroni & Cheese, Calico Jam, Bacon & Egg Potato Salad, Layered Taco Dip, Spiced Berry Cider, Cherry Berry Pie, Pecan Pie, Chocolate Zucchini Cake, Chocolate Chip Tofu Bars, Persimmon Spice Cookies, Honey Pecan Snaps, Pecan Frosties, German Chocolate Brownies, Lemon-Glazed Persimmon Bars, Peanut Blossoms.

Foods prepared by Recipe Book Committee members; Food Styling by Annie Watts. Pumpkins and mums complements of Altum's Horticultural Center & Gardens, Zionsville.

Special thanks to Lebanon Parks & Recreation.

Copyright © 1999
Indiana 4-H Foundation
225 South East Street, Suite 760
Indianapolis, IN 46202-4042

Designed, Edited, and Manufactured by
Favorite Recipes® Press
an imprint of

FRP™

P.O. Box 305142
Nashville, TN 37230
1-800-358-0560

Library of Congress Number: 99-094057

ISBN: 0-9669065-0-0

Book Design: Jim Scott
Art Director: Steve Newman
Project Manager: Susan Larson

Manufactured in the
United States of America

First Printing: 1999
15,000 copies

Dedication

The Indiana 4-H Foundation dedicates this book to Mary Frances Smith, for her many years of leadership, service, and commitment to Indiana 4-H. A native of Monroe County, Miss Smith was a 4-H'er and Junior Leader for 10 years and adult leader for nearly 20 years. She joined the state 4-H staff in 1950 and for 26 years was instrumental in the development and growth of many statewide 4-H programs. She was actively involved in the establishment of the Indiana 4-H Foundation and the Hoosier 4-H Leadership Center. In 1974 Miss Smith was the first woman on the state staff to achieve the rank of full professor. She received both her bachelor's and master's degrees from Indiana University. For many 4-H'ers of the 1950s, 1960s and 1970s, Mary Frances Smith was the quiet mentor who by word and deed was a shining example of the 4-H pledge, "To Make the Best Better." Her lifelong interest in Indiana 4-H youth continues today.

The Indiana 4-H Foundation

The Indiana 4-H Foundation, Inc., chartered in 1961, is a not-for-profit organization that supports 4-H at the county, regional, and state levels. Begun in 1906, Indiana 4-H is the largest youth development program in the state, providing young men and women with informal educational opportunities in leadership, citizenship, and life skills development. With its nearly 100-year history of developing successful citizens, Indiana 4-H is a tradition worth continuing into the next century! The Foundation is committed to that vision. Your purchase of this recipe book supports that effort.

Special Thanks

The Indiana 4-H Foundation appreciates the support, hard work, and involvement of the many individuals who have contributed to the creation of *Picnics • Potlucks & Prizewinners*. Without their commitment of time, talents, expertise, and energy, this publication would not have been possible.

The Recipe Book Committee
Fancheon Resler, *Chair*
Kathy Budreau, Nancy King, Judi Merkel, Sydney Pontius, Nancy J. Sala, Pat Stahly, Annie Watts

Photographer
René Stanley, Photography by René, Lebanon

Editorial Consultant
Annie Watts, Food Marketing Services, Roachdale

Marion County Cooperative Extension Service

State 4-H Department, Purdue University

1998 Indiana State Fair 4-H Exhibit Hall and Marsh Agriculture-Horticulture Building staff

Indiana 4-H Foundation Board Of Directors
President Richard L. Butler
Vice President Danita Rodibaugh
Treasurer James A. Balas
Noel Callahan, Linda Chezem, Bill Dull, Kenda Resler Friend, Gregory J. Gwaltney, John Hardin, Robert Kalton, Stan Knafel, Karen Koester-Ade, Victor L. Lechtenberg, Ted McKinney, Joe A. Milner, Michelle Moore, Stanley E. Poe, Stanley L. Pugh, MaryAnn Schlegel Ruegger, John Swisher, Chris Wirthwein, Eric Wolfe

Indiana 4-H Foundation Staff
Nancy J. Sala, Tina Wiley

And all the 4-H'ers, leaders, alumni, families, and friends of Indiana 4-H who shared their favorite recipes and photographs.

Contents

In Appreciation

The dictionary defines "circle" as "a group of people sharing an interest, activity, or achievement; a sphere of influence or interest."

The Indiana 4-H Foundation extends special appreciation to The Clover Circle. These organizations' generous financial gifts and in-kind contributions for the production and marketing of *Picnics • Potlucks & Prizewinners* allow the Foundation to devote more dollars to the statewide 4-H programs and activities it supports.

The Clover Circle

Marsh Supermarkets, LLC

Alltrista Consumer Products Company
Marketers of Ball and Kerr Brand Home Canning Products

A.E. Staley Manufacturing Co.

Indiana Beef Council

Indiana Farm Bureau, Inc.

Indiana Pork Producers Association

Indiana State Fair Board

Introduction

We Hoosiers are known for our own brand of hospitality, filled with warmth and friendliness, an easy-going style of entertaining and frequent get-togethers—church suppers, firehouse bean dinners, family reunions, neighborhood block parties, Fourth of July barbecues, and tailgate picnics. Indiana 4-H families and friends also enjoy the special camaraderie of county fair celebrations and always-anticipated annual treks to the State Fair. All these gatherings mean good food!

In *Picnics • Potlucks & Prizewinners*, we have screened, tested, and selected the best of more than 2,000 recipes, from appetizers to desserts. We've included family favorites, regional specialties that feature native foods, wonderful ways to use our state's agricultural bounty, and, of course, prizewinning recipes from 4-H'ers' foods projects and open-class recipe contests. In the tradition of learning that is part of 4-H, we've shared cooking hints and tips and nutrition information, as well as tidbits about Indiana products and our Hoosier heritage.

Cooking and food preparation have always been important skills taught in 4-H food projects. As times changed, the foods, recipes, and cooking techniques have changed too. What hasn't changed is the unique role that foods and cooking have in our personal expressions of hospitality, our celebrations of family, heritage, and culture. In that spirit, we offer *Picnics • Potlucks & Prizewinners*. Enjoy!

The Recipe Book Committee

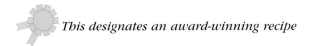 *This designates an award-winning recipe*

It's up, up and away for the hot air balloons on opening day of the Indiana State Fair in this photo by 4-H'er Martha Spaetti of Gibson County. And it's up, up and away for any get-together with the great party starter ideas in "Finger Foods & Fizz." This appealing array of appetizers and beverages includes dips and spreads of every kind, savory snacks, and tantalizing tidbits that invite a celebration.

FINGER FOODS

& FIZZ

AN APPEALING ARRAY OF APPETIZERS AND BEVERAGES

Southwest Artichoke Dip   *Yield: 12 servings*

1 (12-ounce) can artichoke
  hearts, drained, chopped

1 (4-ounce) can diced green
  chiles

3/4 cup grated Parmesan
  cheese

3/4 cup mayonnaise

1 teaspoon garlic powder

1/2 cup shredded medium or
  sharp Cheddar cheese

Preheat oven to 350 degrees. Combine the artichoke hearts, chiles, Parmesan cheese, mayonnaise and garlic powder in a bowl and mix well. Spoon into a shallow baking dish. Sprinkle the Cheddar cheese over the top. Bake for 10 to 15 minutes or until hot and bubbly. Serve with tortilla chips.

Approx Per Serving: Cal 162; Prot 5 g; Carbo 3 g; T Fat 14 g; 81% Calories from Fat; Chol 20 mg; Fiber <1 g; Sod 414 mg

Slow-Cook Bean Dip   *Yield: 18 servings*

1 (16-ounce) can refried beans

1 cup salsa

1 cup shredded Monterey Jack
  cheese

1 cup shredded Cheddar cheese

3/4 cup sour cream

3 ounces cream cheese,
  softened

1 tablespoon chili powder

1/4 teaspoon ground cumin

Combine the beans, salsa, Monterey Jack cheese, Cheddar cheese, sour cream, cream cheese, chili powder and cumin in a slow cooker and mix well. Cook on High for 2 hours or Low for 4 hours, stirring occasionally. Serve with tortilla chips.

Approx Per Serving: Cal 115; Prot 5 g; Carbo 6 g; T Fat 8 g; 62% Calories from Fat; Chol 24 mg; Fiber 2 g; Sod 234 mg

Oriental Cabbage Dip   *Yield: 24 servings*

2 cups sour cream

1 cup prepared slaw dressing

2 teaspoons instant
   beef bouillon

1 teaspoon Worcestershire
   sauce

1 teaspoon garlic powder

2 cups finely shredded
   green cabbage

1 cup finely shredded
   red cabbage

1 (8-ounce) can sliced water
   chestnuts, finely chopped

3/4 cup sliced green onions

1 tablespoon sesame seeds,
   toasted

This unusual dip combines traditional coleslaw ingredients with savory Oriental seasonings for a creamy, crunchy accompaniment to potato chips or fresh vegetables. For a spectacular presentation, use the large outer cabbage leaves to line the serving bowl.

Combine the sour cream, slaw dressing, instant bouillon, Worcestershire sauce and garlic powder in a bowl and mix well. Add the green cabbage, red cabbage, water chestnuts, green onions and sesame seeds and mix well. Refrigerate, covered, for 2 hours or longer. Line the serving bowl with red and green cabbage leaves. Stir the dip. Spoon into the serving bowl. Garnish with additional green onions. Serve with potato chips or carrots.

Approx Per Serving: Cal 101; Prot 1 g;
Carbo 5 g; T Fat 8 g; 74% Calories from Fat;
Chol 17 mg; Fiber 1 g; Sod 228 mg

After adding cheese

to a hot mixture,

stir the mixture constantly

to speed melting.

Creamy Chili Dip   *Yield: 6 servings*

1 (15-ounce) can chili with
   beans

8 ounces cream cheese

1 (16-ounce) package tortilla
   chips

Combine the chili and cream cheese in a saucepan. Cook over medium-low heat until the cream cheese is melted and the mixture is well blended, stirring constantly. Pour into a serving bowl. Serve with tortilla chips.

Approx Per Serving: Cal 590; Prot 12 g;
Carbo 57 g; T Fat 37 g; 55% Calories from Fat;
Chol 54 mg; Fiber 8 g; Sod 881 mg

Pumpkin Dip   *Yield: 16 servings*

*2 teaspoons cinnamon or
   to taste*

1/2 teaspoon nutmeg

4 cups powdered sugar, sifted

*16 ounces cream cheese,
   softened*

1 (16-ounce) can pumpkin

Combine the cinnamon, nutmeg and powdered sugar in a bowl and mix well. Place the cream cheese in a bowl. Add the sugar mixture gradually, beating until smooth. Add the pumpkin and beat until smooth. Serve with gingersnaps, graham crackers or apple slices.

Approx Per Serving: Cal 225; Prot 3 g;
Carbo 33 g; T Fat 10 g; 39% Calories from Fat;
Chol 31 mg; Fiber 1 g; Sod 85 mg

Fresh Garden Salsa   *Yield: 32 servings*

*4 large firm tomatoes, cored,
   chopped, drained*

*1 large sweet onion, coarsely
   chopped*

*1 large green bell pepper,
   coarsely chopped*

*1 large red bell pepper, coarsely
   chopped*

1/4 cup chopped fresh cilantro

*1 (4-ounce) can chopped
   green chiles*

*1 envelope taco salad or fresh
   salsa seasoning mix*

1 teaspoon ground cumin

1/2 teaspoon garlic powder

*1 to 2 teaspoons sugar
   (optional)*

Here's a great idea for any summer gathering. This recipe combines the bounty of the garden with zesty seasonings for a refreshing salsa that can serve as salad, side dish or appetizer.

Combine the tomatoes, onion, green pepper, red pepper, cilantro, chiles, seasoning mix, cumin, garlic powder and sugar in a large bowl and mix well. Let stand at room temperature for 30 minutes or longer. Serve with tortilla chips.

Variation: For a hotter, spicier salsa, add chopped jalapeños, chili powder or hot sauce to taste.

Approx Per Serving: Cal 13; Prot 1 g;
Carbo 3 g; T Fat <1 g; 9% Calories from Fat;
Chol 0 mg; Fiber 1 g; Sod 92 mg

Salsa Cheese Dip in Bread Bowl   *Yield: 15 servings*

1 (2-pound) round bread loaf

½ cup sour cream

8 ounces cream cheese,
   softened

¼ cup salsa

1½ cups shredded
   Cheddar cheese

Cut the top off of the bread loaf. Cut the top into pieces and place on a baking sheet. Hollow out the center of the bread, placing the removed bread pieces on the baking sheet. Bake the bread pieces at 400 degrees for 5 minutes. Combine the sour cream, cream cheese, salsa and Cheddar cheese in a bowl and mix well. Pour into the bread shell. Wrap in aluminum foil. Bake at 400 degrees for 1 hour. Remove the foil and place on a serving plate. Arrange baked bread pieces around the bread round.

Approx Per Serving: Cal 282; Prot 10 g; Carbo 32 g; T Fat 13 g; 41% Calories from Fat; Chol 34 mg; Fiber 1 g; Sod 437 mg

Layered Seafood Spread   *Yield: 12 servings*

16 ounces cream cheese,
   softened

2 tablespoons lemon juice

1 teaspoon Worcestershire
   sauce

¼ teaspoon garlic powder

2 tablespoons chopped
   green onions

¾ cup cocktail sauce

8 ounces peeled, cooked
   shrimp, chopped, or 4 ounces
   crab meat

Beat cream cheese, lemon juice, Worcestershire sauce and garlic powder in a bowl until light and fluffy. Stir in the green onions. Spread cheese mixture into a circle on a serving plate. Refrigerate, covered, until completely chilled. Pour the cocktail sauce over the cream cheese mixture. Arrange the shrimp over the top. Serve with assorted crackers.

Variation: Omit the lemon juice, decrease the cream cheese to 1 (8-ounce) package, add ½ cup sour cream and ½ cup mayonnaise. Top with cocktail sauce and shrimp, then 2 cups of shredded mozzarella cheese and chopped fresh tomatoes.

Approx Per Serving: Cal 167; Prot 7 g; Carbo 5 g; T Fat 14 g; 72% Calories from Fat; Chol 78 mg; Fiber <1 g; Sod 359 mg

Layered Taco Dip *Yield: 60 servings*

12 to 16 ounces ground turkey
  or lean ground beef

2 teaspoons minced garlic

1 teaspoon chili powder

1 teaspoon ground cumin

1 large onion, chopped

1 red bell pepper, chopped

1 green bell pepper, chopped

1 (4-ounce) can chopped green
  chiles, drained

1 (31-ounce) can fat-free
  refried beans

3 avocados, cut into halves,
  pitted, peeled

1 teaspoon garlic powder

1 teaspoon seasoned salt

1 to 2 tablespoons lemon juice

1 envelope taco seasoning mix

2 cups sour cream

This is a festive make-ahead appetizer that's great for a large holiday party or family reunion. It's likely to become your "signature" dish—one that you're always asked to bring!

Brown the ground turkey with the next 6 ingredients in a large skillet coated with vegetable cooking spray, stirring until the ground turkey is crumbly. Stir in the green chiles. Line a colander with paper towels. Spoon the turkey mixture into the colander. Let stand until cooled. Spread the beans on the bottom of a 10-inch springform pan or large platter. Spoon the cooled turkey mixture evenly over the beans. Mash the avocados in a bowl. Stir in the garlic powder, seasoned salt and enough lemon juice to make of a spreading consistency. Spread over the turkey layer. Combine the taco seasoning mix and sour cream in a bowl and mix well. Spread over the avocado layer.

Refrigerate, covered with plastic wrap, until ready to serve. Place the springform pan on a serving platter. Remove the plastic wrap and the side of the pan. Garnish with tomatoes, green onions, olives, shredded Monterey Jack cheese or Cheddar cheese. Serve with tortilla chips.

Variations: May substitute light sour cream for the sour cream. May add jalapeños, hot pepper sauce or additional chili powder for a hotter, spicier dip. May substitute two 6-ounce containers frozen avocado dip, thawed for the avocados, garlic powder, seasoned salt and lemon juice.

Approx Per Serving: Cal 63; Prot 3 g; Carbo 4 g; T Fat 4 g; 55% Calories from Fat; Chol 9 mg; Fiber 1 g; Sod 131 mg

Baked Mexican Dip *Yield: 40 servings*

1 pound lean ground beef

1 (15-ounce) can refried beans

1 (8-ounce) can tomato sauce

1 envelope taco seasoning mix

1 medium onion, chopped

2 cups sour cream

2 cups shredded Cheddar
   cheese

Brown the ground beef in a skillet, stirring until crumbly; drain. Add the beans, tomato sauce, seasoning mix and onion and mix well. Spoon into a 9x13-inch baking dish. Refrigerate, covered, for 8 to 12 hours. Preheat oven to 350 degrees. Bake for 15 minutes. Combine the sour cream and cheese and mix well. Spread over the top. Bake for 5 minutes. Serve with tortilla chips.

Approx Per Serving: Cal 110; Prot 6 g;
Carbo 3 g; T Fat 8 g; 64% Calories from Fat;
Chol 26 mg; Fiber 1 g; Sod 188 mg

Easy Tex-Mex Dip *Yield: 26 servings*

1 (16-ounce) can refried beans

1/4 cup sour cream

2 tablespoons taco
   seasoning mix

1 (2½-ounce) can sliced black
   olives, drained

1 cup finely chopped cooked
   chicken

1 medium tomato, chopped

1 green onion, sliced

2 cups shredded iceberg lettuce

1 cup shredded Mexican blend
   cheese

Spread the beans on a 10-inch round serving platter. Combine the sour cream and taco seasoning mix in a bowl and mix well. Spread evenly over the beans. Sprinkle the olives, chicken, tomato, green onion, lettuce and cheese over the sour cream layer. Refrigerate, covered, for 2 hours or longer. Serve with tortilla chips.

Approx Per Serving: Cal 51; Prot 4 g;
Carbo 4 g; T Fat 3 g; 45% Calories from Fat;
Chol 11 mg; Fiber 1 g; Sod 125 mg

Party Planning Pointers

(1) Make a detailed list of everything from whom to invite to foods to serve and when each step should be completed.
(2) Plan the menu and select easy recipes that can be prepared at least partially in advance.
(3) Keep it simple and stick to what you're comfortable with.
(4) Gather your serving pieces ahead of time.

Hot Spinach Dip   *Yield: 12 servings*

8 ounces cream cheese,
  softened

2 tablespoons milk

2 tablespoons finely chopped
  green onions

1/2 teaspoon garlic powder

1/4 teaspoon salt

1/4 teaspoon pepper

1 (10-ounce) package frozen
  chopped spinach

1 (6-ounce) can chunk ham,
  drained

1 cup sour cream

3/4 cup chopped pecans
  (optional)

Combine the cream cheese, milk, green onions, garlic powder, salt and pepper in a microwave-safe bowl and mix well. Cook the spinach using the package directions until partially cooked; drain. Press the spinach between paper towels to remove excess moisture. Stir the spinach and ham into the cream cheese mixture. Microwave on Medium for 4 minutes, stirring once after 2 minutes. Fold in the sour cream and pecans. Serve with crackers and chips.

Approx Per Serving: Cal 135; Prot 5 g; Carbo 2 g; T Fat 12 g; 77% Calories from Fat; Chol 35 mg; Fiber 1 g; Sod 314 mg

Skinny Spinach Cheese Dip   *Yield: 20 servings*

1 (10-ounce) package frozen
  chopped spinach, thawed

1 1/2 cups 1% low-fat cottage
  cheese

2 cups fat-free sour cream

1 (8-ounce) can sliced water
  chestnuts, drained, chopped

1/2 cup light or fat-free salad
  dressing or mayonnaise

1 envelope vegetable soup mix

2 to 3 teaspoons prepared
  horseradish

1/2 teaspoon garlic powder

Press the spinach between paper towels to remove excess moisture. Purée the cottage cheese in a blender. Combine the spinach, puréed cottage cheese, sour cream, water chestnuts, salad dressing, soup mix, horseradish and garlic powder in a bowl and mix well. Refrigerate, covered, for 8 to 12 hours. Serve with melba rounds, low-fat crackers or fresh vegetables.

Approx Per Serving: Cal 69; Prot 4 g; Carbo 9 g; T Fat 2 g; 21% Calories from Fat; Chol 1 mg; Fiber 1 g; Sod 278 mg

Tofu Ranch Dip
Yield: 8 servings

1¼ cups soft silken tofu

1 envelope ranch salad
   dressing mix

¾ cup light salad dressing or
   mayonnaise

Combine the tofu, salad dressing
mix and salad dressing in a blender
container. Process until smooth.
Refrigerate until completely chilled.
Serve with fresh vegetables or
crackers.

Approx Per Serving: Cal 91; Prot 2 g;
Carbo 8 g; T Fat 6 g; 57% Calories from Fat;
Chol 0 mg; Fiber <1 g; Sod 462 mg

Braunschweiger Ball
Yield: 16 servings

8 ounces braunschweiger

3 tablespoons salad dressing
   or mayonnaise

2 tablespoons Worcestershire
   sauce

1 small onion, chopped

½ teaspoon cracked pepper

½ teaspoon garlic powder

8 ounces cream cheese,
   softened

10 olives, sliced

Combine the braunschweiger, salad
dressing, Worcestershire sauce,
onion, pepper and garlic powder in
a bowl and mix well. Shape into a
ball. Frost with the cream cheese.
Arrange the sliced olives over the
cream cheese.

Approx Per Serving: Cal 118; Prot 3 g;
Carbo 3 g; T Fat 10 g; 82% Calories from Fat;
Chol 39 mg; Fiber <1 g; Sod 303 mg

Indiana is the fourth
largest producer of soybeans
in the U.S. Soybeans are a
major source of domestic
and international trade for
Indiana agriculture. Soybeans
are low in saturated and
total fat, cholesterol free
and high in fiber, and are
being increasingly recognized
for their disease prevention
role in the diet. Soybeans
are used in margarine,
vegetable oil, salad dressing
and mayonnaise. Other soy
foods include tofu, tempeh,
and meat alternatives
such as vegetable burgers,
soy milk and soy flour.

Deviled Ham Cheese Ball   *Yield: 16 servings*

8 ounces cream cheese,
softened

1 (5-ounce) jar pimiento
cheese spread

1 (5-ounce) jar Old English
cheese spread

1 (4-ounce) can deviled ham

1/2 medium onion, finely
chopped

1/4 teaspoon salt (optional)

1 teaspoon Worcestershire
sauce

4 drops hot pepper sauce
(optional)

1/2 to 1 cup crushed pecans

Combine the cream cheese, pimiento cheese spread, Old English cheese spread, ham, onion, salt, Worcestershire sauce and hot pepper sauce in a bowl and mix until well blended. Refrigerate until firm. Shape into a ball. Roll in the pecans in a shallow dish to coat.

Variation: Substitute 1 cup shredded Cheddar cheese and 1/2 cup finely chopped green bell pepper for the pimiento cheese spread and Old English cheese spread.

Approx Per Serving: Cal 200; Prot 6 g; Carbo 4 g; T Fat 21 g; 81% Calories from Fat; Chol 34 mg; Fiber 1 g; Sod 337 mg

Pineapple Pecan Cheese Ball   *Yield: 16 servings*

16 ounces cream cheese,
softened

1 (8-ounce) can crushed
pineapple, drained

1/4 cup chopped green
bell pepper

2 tablespoons chopped sweet
onion or celery

3/4 teaspoon Beau Monde
seasoning

1 cup chopped pecans

Combine the cream cheese, pineapple, green pepper, onion and Beau Monde seasoning in a bowl and mix well. Refrigerate for 30 minutes. Shape into a ball. Roll in the pecans in a shallow dish to coat. Serve with crackers.

Approx Per Serving: Cal 157; Prot 3 g; Carbo 4 g; T Fat 15 g; 83% Calories from Fat; Chol 31 mg; Fiber 1 g; Sod 112 mg

Fruited Brie Bake   *Yield: 16 servings*

1 (8- to 15-ounce) wheel Brie
cheese
½ cup whole cranberry sauce
½ cup apricot preserves
¼ to ½ cup sliced almonds

Here's an easy and out-of-the-ordinary appetizer that's perfect for holiday entertaining. Prepare the Brie wheel in advance then just heat at party time. The scooped-out cheese can be added to other cheeses when making a spread or cheese ball.

Preheat oven to 350 degrees. Cut the top ¼ inch off of the Brie. Hollow out the center of the wheel, leaving a 1-inch shell; reserve the scooped-out cheese for another use. Place wheel in a shallow ovenproof dish. Spoon the cranberry sauce into the cheese shell. Cover with the top of the cheese. Spread the preserves over the top. Sprinkle with the almonds. Bake for 8 to 10 minutes or until soft and slightly melted. Serve with crackers.

Approx Per Serving: Cal 143; Prot 6 g;
Carbo 10 g; T Fat 9 g; 55% Calories from Fat;
Chol 27 mg; Fiber 1 g; Sod 173 mg

Low temperatures
and short cooking times
are the secrets to
successfully cooking with
cheese. Also, use a pan
with a heavy bottom
to distribute heat
more evenly.

Party Salmon Spread   *Yield: 12 servings*

1 (16-ounce) can salmon,
drained, flaked
8 ounces cream cheese,
softened
1 tablespoon lemon juice
1 teaspoon prepared
horseradish
2 teaspoons grated onion
¼ teaspoon liquid smoke
½ cup chopped pecans

Combine the salmon, cream cheese, lemon juice, horseradish, onion and liquid smoke in a bowl and mix well. Shape into a ball. Roll in the pecans in a shallow dish to coat. Refrigerate, covered, for 3 hours or longer. Garnish with parsley. Serve with crackers.

Approx Per Serving: Cal 154; Prot 10 g;
Carbo 2 g; T Fat 12 g; 70% Calories from Fat;
Chol 36 mg; Fiber <1 g; Sod 241 mg

Shrimp Cocktail Strata Tart   *Yield: 16 servings*

2¹/₂ cups fresh bread crumbs

1 cup half-and-half

4 eggs, beaten

2 (4-ounce) cans shrimp, drained

¹/₂ cup cocktail or hot seafood sauce

¹/₄ cup chopped green onions

2 tablespoons lemon juice

1¹/₂ teaspoons instant chicken bouillon

¹/₄ teaspoon pepper

Preheat oven to 350 degrees. Combine the crumbs and half-and-half in a large bowl and mix well. Let stand for 10 minutes. Add the eggs, shrimp, cocktail sauce, green onions, lemon juice, instant bouillon and pepper and mix well. Pour into an oiled 10-inch tart pan or quiche dish. Bake for 30 to 35 minutes or until set. Cool. Cut into wedges. Serve warm or chilled with additional cocktail sauce.

Approx Per Serving: Cal 84; Prot 6 g; Carbo 7 g; T Fat 4 g; 40% Calories from Fat; Chol 84 mg; Fiber <1 g; Sod 290 mg

 # Crab Cheese Melts   *Yield: 12 servings*

1 (1-pound) loaf Vienna bread

¹/₂ cup butter, softened

3 ounces cream cheese, softened

1 (7-ounce) can crab meat, drained, chopped

8 ounces shredded mozzarella cheese

1 cup chopped green onions

Cut the bread in half lengthwise. Combine the butter and cream cheese in a bowl and mix well. Stir in the crab meat. Spread on the cut side of each half of the bread. Sprinkle with the mozzarella cheese and green onions. Place on a baking sheet. Bake at 350 degrees for 15 to 20 minutes or until cheese is melted. Cut into 2-inch slices.

Approx Per Serving: Cal 268; Prot 11 g; Carbo 21 g; T Fat 16 g; 52% Calories from Fat; Chol 58 mg; Fiber 1 g; Sod 456 mg

Crab-Stuffed Mushrooms   *Yield: 12 servings*

12 large fresh mushrooms

¼ cup margarine or butter

2 tablespoons finely
    chopped onion

1 to 4 cloves garlic, finely
    chopped

1 tablespoon chopped parsley

¼ cup dry bread crumbs or
    cracker crumbs

1 (6-ounce) can crab meat,
    drained

Seafood seasoning blend or
    seasoned salt to taste

Preheat oven to 350 degrees. Remove the stems from the mushrooms and chop finely. Brown the mushroom caps lightly in the margarine in a skillet. Remove the mushroom caps and place in an 8- or 9-inch square baking pan. Add the chopped mushroom stems, onion, garlic and parsley to the skillet. Cook until lightly browned. Stir in the crumbs and crab meat. Fill the mushroom caps with the crab mixture. Bake for 8 to 10 minutes or until heated through. Serve immediately.

Approx Per Serving: Cal 65; Prot 4 g; Carbo 3 g; T Fat 4 g; 57% Calories from Fat; Chol 13 mg; Fiber <1 g; Sod 112 mg

Teriyaki Scallop Roll-Ups   *Yield: 24 servings*

12 sea scallops (about
    8 ounces), cut into halves

24 fresh pea pods

12 water chestnuts,
    cut into halves

12 slices bacon, partially
    cooked, drained, cut into
    halves crosswise

⅓ cup lime juice

¼ cup soy sauce

¼ cup vegetable oil

1 tablespoon brown sugar

2 cloves garlic, finely chopped

½ teaspoon pepper

Wrap 1 scallop half, 1 pea pod and 1 water chestnut half with 1 bacon slice half and secure with a wooden pick. Place in a shallow dish. Repeat with remaining scallop halves. Combine the lime juice, soy sauce, oil, brown sugar, garlic and pepper in a bowl and mix well. Pour over the scallop roll-ups. Refrigerate, covered, for 4 hours or longer, turning occasionally. Preheat the oven to 450 degrees. Place the scallop roll-ups on a rack in an aluminum foil-lined shallow baking dish. Bake for 6 minutes; turn. Bake for 6 minutes longer or until bacon is crisp.

Approx Per Serving: Cal 63; Prot 4 g; Carbo 2 g; T Fat 4 g; 61% Calories from Fat; Chol 8 mg; Fiber <1 g; Sod 334 mg

Picnic Packing Pointers

For carrying most picnic foods, choose sturdy plastic containers with tight-sealing lids. They protect foods from getting crushed and from leaking.

Some foods, including salads, meats, cheeses, and dairy products, need to be kept chilled. Pack these cold foods with an ice pack in an insulated bag or cooler. You also can freeze cold juices to act as ice. By picnic time, the drinks will still be cold but thawed enough for drinking.

Consume perishable foods within two hours of preparation; one hour if outside in temperatures above 90 degrees.

Tortilla Roll-Ups Garden-Style   *Yield: 60 servings*

16 ounces cream cheese, softened

1 envelope ranch salad dressing mix

10 flour tortillas

1/2 cup finely chopped carrot

1/2 cup finely chopped green onions or sweet onion

1/2 cup finely chopped green bell pepper or red bell pepper

2 cups shredded Cheddar cheese

Refrigerated flour tortillas can form the wraps for a variety of tasty fillings. These make-ahead snacks are perfect party fare. Be creative and try different additions to the cream cheese base. How about pimiento, pineapple and chives? Or go Oriental with water chestnuts, green onions and alfalfa sprouts spiked with a touch of soy or teriyaki sauce. Just finely chop ingredients and be sure to taste as you create.

Beat the cream cheese in a bowl until light and fluffy. Stir in the salad dressing mix. Spread over the tortillas. Sprinkle the carrot, green onions, green pepper and Cheddar cheese over the cream cheese layer. Roll each tortilla up jelly roll fashion. Cut into slices. Secure slices with a wooden pick if desired. Refrigerate, covered, until serving time.

Variation: Decrease the cream cheese to 8 ounces and Cheddar cheese to 1 cup. Substitute 1 cup sour cream, 1 (4-ounce) can chopped green chiles, 1 (4-ounce) can chopped black olives, drained, 1/2 cup chopped green onions and garlic powder to taste for the ranch salad dressing mix, carrots, green onions and green pepper. Combine the cream cheese, Cheddar cheese, sour cream, green chiles, olives, green onions and garlic powder in a bowl and mix well. Spread onto the tortillas. Serve with salsa.

Approx Per Serving: Cal 83; Prot 3 g; Carbo 7 g; T Fat 5 g; 52% Calories from Fat; Chol 12 mg; Fiber <1 g; Sod 141 mg

Funny Face Franks   *Yield: 1 serving*

1 slice American cheese

2 slices bread

1 hot dog, cut into halves
   lengthwise

1 tablespoon butter, melted

1 cup shredded lettuce, divided

2 olives

1 carrot slice

1 tomato slice

1 hat made from cardboard
   (optional)

A great kid's snack—fun for the babysitter too.

Place the cheese between the 2 bread slices. Cut the cheese sandwich into a circle or square, removing the crusts. Wrap the hot dog halves around the sandwich and fasten with wooden picks. Place on a buttered baking sheet. Brush the bread and hot dog with melted butter. Bake at 400 degrees for 5 minutes. Sprinkle ¾ cup of the lettuce on a plate. Place the sandwich over the lettuce. Arrange the olives on the sandwich for eyes. Place the carrot slice on the sandwich for the nose. Place the tomato slice on the sandwich for the mouth. Place the remaining lettuce on the sandwich for hair. Place the hat at the top of the sandwich.

Nutritional analysis is not available for this recipe.

Fruit & Nut Mix   *Yield: 20 (½-cup) servings*

2 (12-ounce) cans mixed nuts

1 (15-ounce) package
   seedless raisins

1 (8-ounce) package dates,
   chopped

½ cup banana chips or
   to taste

8 ounces sunflower kernels

½ cup chopped fresh coconut
   or flaked coconut or to taste

Combine the nuts, raisins, dates, banana chips, sunflower kernels and coconut in a bowl and mix well. Store in an airtight container.

Approx Per Serving: Cal 394; Prot 9 g; Carbo 36 g; T Fat 27 g; 58% Calories from Fat; Chol 0 mg; Fiber 6 g; Sod 8 mg

Backpack Fruit Snack

Yield: 15 (¹/₂-cup) servings

2 cups dried apple rings
2 cups banana chips
1¹/₂ cups dried pineapple
1 cup raisins
1 cup honey-roasted peanuts

Combine the apple rings, banana chips, pineapple, raisins and peanuts in a bowl and mix well. Store in an airtight container for 8 to 12 hours or longer.

Approx Per Serving: Cal 213; Prot 2 g; Carbo 37 g; T Fat 7 g; 29% Calories from Fat; Chol 0 mg; Fiber 3 g; Sod 54 mg

Sunshine Snack Mix

Yield: 20 (¹/₂-cup) servings

4 ounces dried apples, chopped
10 ounces dried apricots, chopped
3 ounces banana chips, chopped
4 ounces dried blueberries or cranberries
8 ounces yogurt-covered raisins
10 ounces honey-roasted sunflower kernels
18 ounces salted mixed nuts, chopped

Combine the apples, apricots, banana chips, blueberries, raisins, sunflower kernels and nuts in a large bowl and mix well. Store in an airtight container.

Approx Per Serving: Cal 292; Prot 6 g; Carbo 34 g; T Fat 17 g; 50% Calories from Fat; Chol 1 mg; Fiber 5 g; Sod 178 mg
Nutritional analysis does not include honey-roasted sunflower kernels.

Sunflower Seeds

Yield: 4 (¹/₂-cup) servings

2 cups sunflower seeds
Salt to taste

Cover the seeds with boiling water in a saucepan. Let stand for 5 minutes; drain. Pat the seeds dry. Arrange in a thin layer on a shallow baking pan. Sprinkle with salt. Bake at 350 degrees for 20 minutes.

Approx Per Serving: Cal 410; Prot 16 g; Carbo 14 g; T Fat 36 g; 73% Calories from Fat; Chol 0 mg; Fiber 8 g; Sod 2 mg

Squash and Pumpkin Seeds   *Yield: 4 (¹/₂-cup) servings*

2 cups squash or
*   pumpkin seeds*
1 to 2 tablespoons
*   vegetable oil*
1¹/₄ teaspoons salt

Remove fibers from the seeds; do
not wash. Mix the seeds, oil and salt
in a bowl. Spread the seeds in a
shallow baking pan. Bake at 250
degrees until crisp and light brown.

Approx Per Serving: Cal 418; Prot 17 g;
Carbo 12 g; T Fat 37 g; 74% Calories from Fat;
Chol 0 mg; Fiber 3 g; Sod 739 mg

Party Popcorn   *Yield: 20 (¹/₂-cup) servings*

8 cups popped popcorn
¹/₂ cup pretzels
¹/₂ cup mixed nuts
¹/₂ cup snack crackers
¹/₂ cup potato shoestrings
¹/₃ cup butter, melted
1 teaspoon soy sauce
1 to 2 drops of hot
*   pepper sauce*
¹/₂ envelope bacon and
*   onion dip mix*

Combine the popcorn, pretzels, nuts,
crackers and potato shoestrings in a
bowl and mix well. Combine the
butter, soy sauce and hot pepper
sauce in a bowl and mix well. Pour
over the popcorn mixture. Toss to
coat. Sprinkle the dip mix over the
popcorn mixture. Toss to coat. Spread
on a baking sheet. Bake at 350
degrees for 8 to 10 minutes, stirring
occasionally. Cool completely.

Approx Per Serving: Cal 80; Prot 2 g;
Carbo 6 g; T Fat 6 g; 62% Calories from Fat;
Chol 8 mg; Fiber 1 g; Sod 186 mg

Like other cereal grains,
popcorn is a high
carbohydrate food furnishing
heat and energy to the
body. Popcorn is high in
fiber and has more protein
than many other foods. One
cup of plain popcorn has
between 25 and 50 calories.

Christmas Fruit Punch

Yield: 32 (¹/₂-cup) servings

2 cups cranberry juice

2 cups pineapple juice

1 (6-ounce) can frozen
  lemonade concentrate,
  thawed

1 (6-ounce) can frozen orange
  juice concentrate, thawed

1 (10-ounce) package frozen
  sweetened strawberries or
  raspberries, thawed

1 large lime, sliced

4 cups ginger ale, chilled

30 ice cubes

Combine the cranberry juice, pineapple juice, lemonade concentrate, orange juice concentrate, strawberries and lime slices in a large bowl and mix well. Refrigerate until completely chilled. Pour into a punch bowl. Stir in the ginger ale and ice cubes.

Approx Per Serving: Cal 55; Prot <1 g; Carbo 14 g; T Fat <1 g; 1% Calories from Fat; Chol 0 mg; Fiber <1 g; Sod 3 mg

Golden Celebration Punch

Yield: 60 (¹/₂-cup) servings

1 (12-ounce) can frozen
  orange juice concentrate,
  thawed

1 (46-ounce) can apricot
  nectar, chilled

1 (46-ounce) can pineapple
  juice, chilled

8 cups cold water

1 cup lemon juice

2 (1-liter) bottles ginger ale,
  chilled

Fruited Ice Ring (optional)

Created for a golden wedding anniversary reception, this punch could be spiked with vodka or rum if a spirited version is desired.

Combine the orange juice concentrate, apricot nectar, pineapple juice, water, lemon juice and ginger ale in a large punch bowl and mix well. Add the Fruited Ice Ring, fruit side up.

Approx Per Serving: Cal 46; Prot <1 g; Carbo 12 g; T Fat <1 g; 1% Calories from Fat; Chol 0 mg; Fiber <1 g; Sod 3 mg

Fruited Ice Ring

3¹/₂ cups ginger ale or water,
  divided

Fruits of choice

Mint leaves

Pour 3 cups of the ginger ale into a 1-quart ring mold; freeze. Arrange the fruits and mint leaves over the frozen ginger ale. Pour the remaining ¹/₂ cup of ginger ale over the fruit and mint leaves; freeze. May use fruits such as orange slices, lemon slices, strawberries or apricot halves.

Mocha Cappuccino Punch

Yield: 24 (1/2-cup) servings

2 tablespoons instant
   coffee granules

1/4 teaspoon cinnamon

1 cup hot water

1 (14-ounce) can fat-free
   sweetened condensed milk

1/2 cup chocolate-flavored
   syrup

4 cups milk or half-and-half

1/4 cup coffee-flavored
   liqueur (optional)

1 quart chocolate or coffee
   ice cream

2 cups club soda, chilled

Here's a refreshing punch that combines the goodness of milk and ice cream with two increasingly popular flavors—coffee and chocolate. Great for a festive gathering any time of year!

Dissolve the coffee granules and cinnamon in the hot water in a bowl. Stir in the condensed milk and chocolate-flavored syrup. Refrigerate until completely chilled. Combine the coffee mixture, milk and liqueur in a punch bowl and mix well. Scoop the ice cream into the punch. Stir in the club soda. Garnish with a sprinkling of cocoa or cinnamon.

Variation: Substitute 4 cups of dairy eggnog for the milk and add 1/4 cup brandy or bourbon if desired.

Approx Per Serving: Cal 137; Prot 4 g;
Carbo 22 g; T Fat 4 g; 25% Calories from Fat;
Chol 14 mg; Fiber <1 g; Sod 62 mg

Sugar-Free Lemon Strawberry Punch

Yield: 24 (1/2-cup) servings

3 cups sliced strawberries

1 (3-ounce) package artificially
   sweetened sugar-free
   lemonade mix

8 cups cold water, divided

Sugar substitute equivalent to
   1/4 cup sugar

4 cups lemon-lime carbonated
   beverage, chilled

Purée the strawberries in a blender. Add the lemonade mix, 2 cups of the water and sugar substitute. Process until smooth. Pour into a punch bowl. Add the remaining 6 cups of water and the carbonated beverage and mix well. Garnish with additional strawberries, lemon slices or mint leaves.

Approx Per Serving: Cal 34; Prot <1 g;
Carbo 6 g; T Fat <1 g; 3% Calories from Fat;
Chol 0 mg; Fiber <1 g; Sod 5 mg

The Strawberry Calendar

Locally grown strawberries brighten our gardens and produce stands in mid-May and June. Fortunately, sunny California, Florida and other areas around the world supply our supermarkets with fresh berries nearly year round. Over 75% of all strawberries grown in the United States come from California. California strawberries are most abundant and of the highest quality from April through June.

Use a coffee filter to hold whole spices when making hot spiced beverages. Just gather the edge of the filter and fasten with a plastic twist tie. Make a pin hole to release air.

4-H Punch   *Yield: 100 servings*

4 envelopes unsweetened lemon-lime drink mix

2 (46-ounce) cans pineapple juice

1 cup lemon juice

4 cups sugar

1 gallon water

1 (2-liter) bottle ginger ale, chilled

Combine the drink mix, pineapple juice, lemon juice, sugar and water in a large bowl and mix well. Refrigerate until completely chilled. Stir in the ginger ale.

Approx Per Serving: Cal 72; Prot <1 g; Carbo 19 g; T Fat <1 g; 0% Calories from Fat; Chol 0 mg; Fiber <1 g; Sod 2 mg

Spiced Berry Cider   *Yield: 32 (½-cup) servings*

4 cups water

1 (12-ounce) can frozen orange juice concentrate, thawed

1 cup lemon juice

1½ cups packed brown sugar

8 whole cloves

6 cinnamon sticks

6 cardamom pods, or 1 teaspoon whole allspice

1 whole nutmeg (optional)

8 cups apple cider or apple juice, chilled

4 cups cranberry juice, chilled

Here's a refreshing punch to serve for any fall or winter gathering. This spiced cider can be served hot or cold—perfect for a Halloween party or to welcome the family for Thanksgiving.

Combine the water, orange juice concentrate, lemon juice, brown sugar, cloves, cinnamon, cardamom and nutmeg in a saucepan. Bring to a boil. Reduce the heat. Simmer for 10 to 15 minutes. Refrigerate until completely chilled. Remove the cloves, cinnamon, cardamom and nutmeg. Pour into a large punch bowl. Add the apple cider and cranberry juice and mix well. Serve over ice. Garnish with apple or orange slices.

Variation: To serve warm, add the apple cider and cranberry juice to the spiced mixture in the saucepan and simmer for 15 to 20 minutes.

Approx Per Serving: Cal 105; Prot <1 g; Carbo 27 g; T Fat <1 g; 1% Calories from Fat; Chol 0 mg; Fiber <1 g; Sod 7 mg

Sparkling Spiced Tea   *Yield: 12 (1-cup) servings*

6 cups water

1 cup packed brown sugar

6 cinnamon sticks

8 whole cloves

8 tea bags

1 cup orange juice

½ cup lemon juice

1 (1-liter) bottle ginger ale, chilled

Iced tea is a favorite year 'round beverage for many Hoosiers. Here's a lightly spiced version for those who prefer "sweet" tea. For a party, double the ingredients and serve from a punch bowl with a few orange slices for garnish.

Combine the water, brown sugar, cinnamon and cloves in a saucepan. Bring to a boil. Reduce the heat. Simmer for 10 minutes. Add the tea bags. Steep for 5 minutes. Remove the tea bags, cinnamon and cloves. Stir in the orange juice and lemon juice. Refrigerate, covered, until completely chilled. Stir in the ginger ale. Serve over ice.

Approx Per Serving: Cal 111; Prot <1 g; Carbo 29 g; T Fat <1 g; 0% Calories from Fat; Chol 0 mg; Fiber <1 g; Sod 17 mg

Westfield Cloverleaves Fruit Slush   *Yield: 16 (1-cup) servings*

2 cups sugar

4 cups warm water

2 bananas

6 ¼ cups cold water, divided

1 (46-ounce) can pineapple juice

2 envelopes unsweetened cherry-flavored drink mix

Dissolve the sugar in the warm water in a 1-gallon freezer container. Purée the bananas and ½ cup of the cold water in a blender. Add the banana mixture, pineapple juice and drink mix to the sugar water and mix well. Stir in the remaining 5¾ cups cold water. Freeze for 24 hours. Remove from freezer. Let stand until mixture begins to melt. Stir until smooth and slushy.

Approx Per Serving: Cal 156; Prot <1 g; Carbo 40 g; T Fat <1 g; 1% Calories from Fat; Chol 0 mg; Fiber 1 g; Sod 83 mg

If you're watching your fat intake, don't cut milk from your diet. Fat-free and ½% low-fat milk have all the nutrients of whole milk with little or no fat and are certified by the American Heart Association as part of a healthy, well-balanced diet.

B & B Orange Frost   *Yield: 4 (1-cup) servings*

1 (6-ounce) can frozen orange
   juice concentrate
1 cup water
1 cup milk
½ cup sugar
1 teaspoon vanilla extract
10 ice cubes

Combine the orange juice concentrate, water, milk, sugar, vanilla and ice cubes in a blender container. Process until smooth.

Approx Per Serving: Cal 202; Prot 3 g;
Carbo 44 g; T Fat 2 g; 9% Calories from Fat;
Chol 8 mg; Fiber <1 g; Sod 31 mg

Strawberry Watermelon Slush
Yield: 5 (1-cup) servings

2 cups cubed seeded
   watermelon
1 pint fresh strawberries,
   rinsed, hulled
½ cup sugar
⅓ cup lemon juice
2 cups ice cubes

Here's a fruity, refreshing cooler for a hot summer day!

Purée the watermelon, strawberries, sugar and lemon juice in a blender. Add the ice gradually, blending until smooth. Garnish with mint and additional strawberries.

Approx Per Serving: Cal 118; Prot 1 g;
Carbo 30 g; T Fat <1 g; 3% Calories from Fat;
Chol 0 mg; Fiber 2 g; Sod 2 mg

Orange Dream   *Yield: 1 serving*

³/₄ cup fat-free milk

*1¹/₂ tablespoons frozen
   unsweetened orange juice
   concentrate*

*¹/₄ cup fat-free vanilla
   frozen yogurt*

Shake up a milk cooler for a refreshing treat anytime and create a milk mustache while you're at it!

Combine the milk, orange juice concentrate and frozen yogurt in a shaker and shake until well blended.

Approx Per Serving: Cal 161; Prot 8 g; Carbo 30 g; T Fat <1 g; 2% Calories from Fat; Chol 3 mg; Fiber <1 g; Sod 133 mg

Apple Pie in a Glass   *Yield: 1 serving*

³/₄ cup fat-free milk

*1¹/₂ tablespoons frozen apple
   juice concentrate*

*¹/₄ cup fat-free vanilla
   frozen yogurt*

¹/₈ teaspoon cinnamon

Combine the milk, apple juice concentrate, frozen yogurt and cinnamon in a shaker and shake until well blended.

Approx Per Serving: Cal 163; Prot 8 g; Carbo 31 g; T Fat <1 g; 2% Calories from Fat; Chol 3 mg; Fiber <1 g; Sod 139 mg

Purple Cow   *Yield: 1 serving*

³/₄ cup fat-free milk

*1¹/₂ tablespoons frozen grape
   juice concentrate*

*¹/₄ cup fat-free vanilla frozen
   yogurt*

Combine the milk, grape juice concentrate and frozen yogurt in a shaker and shake until well blended.

Approx Per Serving: Cal 157; Prot 8 g; Carbo 29 g; T Fat <1 g; 3% Calories from Fat; Chol 3 mg; Fiber <1 g; Sod 133 mg

Indiana was home to one of the first commercially successful vineyards in the U.S. in the early 1800s. The Indiana grape and wine industry survived disease and severe weather, but Prohibition (1919–1934) finally ended its progress until the small winery law passed in 1971, allowing wineries to sell directly to the public. Today, many of the state's 19 wineries offer tours and tastings. Many of these wineries are showcased in the annual "Taste of Indiana Agriculture" preceding the state fair. For more information about Indiana wine, contact the Indiana Wine Grape Council at 1-800-832-WINE.

Wine Slush   *Yield: 20 (¹/₂-cup) servings*

1 cup sugar

2 cups water

1 (3-ounce) package red raspberry gelatin

¹/₂ cup lemon juice

1 (750-ml) bottle red wine, such as Zinfandel

1 (46-ounce) can pineapple juice

Combine the sugar and water in a saucepan. Bring to a boil. Remove from heat. Dissolve the gelatin in the sugar water. Stir in the lemon juice. Let stand until cooled. Stir in the wine and pineapple juice. Pour into a freezer container; freeze. Turn into a punch bowl. Let stand until mixture begins to melt. Stir until smooth and slushy.

Approx Per Serving: Cal 119; Prot 1 g; Carbo 24 g; T Fat <1 g; 0% Calories from Fat; Chol 0 mg; Fiber <1 g; Sod 12 mg

Lemon Shake-Up   *Yield: 20 servings*

2 cups sugar

1 cup water

1 cup lemon juice

You don't have to wait for the state fair to enjoy this perennial favorite!

Combine the sugar and water in a saucepan. Bring to a boil. Boil for 5 minutes; cool. Stir in the lemon juice. To serve, add 2 tablespoons of the lemon syrup to a glass of ice water and mix well. Repeat for the remaining lemon syrup. Store unused syrup, covered, in the refrigerator.

Approx Per Serving: Cal 80; Prot <1 g; Carbo 21 g; T Fat 0 g; 0% Calories from Fat; Chol 0 mg; Fiber <1 g; Sod <1 mg

Fruit Smoothie   *Yield: 2 (1-cup) servings*

1 banana

*1 (12-ounce) package low-fat
  firm silken tofu*

*1 (10-ounce) package frozen
  sweetened strawberries or
  raspberries, partially thawed*

¼ cup apple juice

Process the banana, tofu, strawberries and apple juice in a blender until smooth. Add additional apple juice to make of the desired consistency. May be stored in the refrigerator for 1 to 2 days.

Approx Per Serving: Cal 267; Prot 12 g; Carbo 56 g; T Fat 3 g; 8% Calories from Fat; Chol 0 mg; Fiber 4 g; Sod 120 mg

Hot Cocoa Mix   *Yield: 16 servings*

1 cup nondairy creamer

1 cup nonfat dry milk

¾ to 1 cup sugar

½ cup unsweetened cocoa

Make a double batch and tuck a jar into a holiday gift basket.

Combine the creamer, dry milk, enough sugar to make of the desired sweetness and cocoa in a bowl and mix well. Store in an airtight container. Spoon 3 heaping tablespoons into a mug. Pour ¾ cup boiling water over the mix. Stir until dissolved.

Variations: Mocha—Add ¼ cup instant coffee granules; Mexican—Add 1 teaspoon cinnamon; Low Calorie—Substitute 15 envelopes of aspartame sweetener for the sugar. Spoon 2 heaping tablespoons into a mug.

Approx Per Serving: Cal 100; Prot 2 g; Carbo 20 g; T Fat 2 g; 20% Calories from Fat; Chol 1 mg; Fiber 1 g; Sod 24 mg

Cantaloupe and cabbage, peppers and potatoes, sweet corn and snap beans— every year 4-H'ers bring the best of their garden produce to the State Fair— hoping for a blue ribbon to honor the fruits of their labor. In "Garden Goodness & Grains," here's a cornucopia of recipes that celebrate the bounty of the harvest—colorful salads, rice and pasta side dishes, vegetables of every variety, ready for picking.

GARDEN GOODNESS & GRAINS

A CORNUCOPIA OF RECIPES THAT CELEBRATE THE BOUNTY OF THE HARVEST

Minted Fruit   *Yield: 4 servings*

2 cups fresh blueberries or raspberries

2 cups cut-up cantaloupe or watermelon

2 cups fresh strawberry halves

2 cups cut-up honeydew melon

1/2 cup sugar

1/3 cup lemon juice

1/3 cup orange juice

1/3 cup water

1/4 teaspoon peppermint extract

Lettuce leaves (optional)

2 cups lemon or pineapple sherbet or frozen yogurt

Here's a light summer fruit salad or dessert to serve for your next Extension Homemakers gathering. Marinating the fruit in citrus juices spiked with a hint of peppermint extract adds a refreshing flavor twist. Choose your favorite seasonal fruits and try other flavors of sherbet.

Combine the blueberries, cantaloupe, strawberries and honeydew in a large bowl. Combine the sugar, lemon juice, orange juice, water and peppermint extract in a bowl. Stir until the sugar dissolves. Pour over the fruit. Marinate, covered, in the refrigerator for 3 to 4 hours; drain. Arrange on 4 lettuce-lined plates. Top with scoops of sherbet. Garnish with mint.

Approx Per Serving: Cal 369; Prot 3 g; Carbo 89 g; T Fat 3 g; 7% Calories from Fat; Chol 6 mg; Fiber 5 g; Sod 67 mg

Blueberries and Cream Salad   *Yield: 12 servings*

2 (3-ounce) packages concord grape gelatin

2 cups boiling water

1 (20-ounce) can crushed pineapple

1 (20-ounce) can blueberry pie filling

8 ounces cream cheese, softened

1/2 cup sugar

1 cup sour cream

1/2 cup chopped pecans (optional)

1 teaspoon vanilla extract

Dissolve the gelatin in boiling water in a bowl. Stir in the pineapple and pie filling. Spoon into a 9x13-inch dish. Refrigerate until set. Beat the cream cheese in a mixer bowl until fluffy. Beat in the sugar. Stir in the sour cream, pecans and vanilla until well blended. Spread over the blueberry layer. Refrigerate, covered, for 8 to 10 hours or longer. Cut into squares.

Approx Per Serving: Cal 276; Prot 4 g; Carbo 44 g; T Fat 11 g; 34% Calories from Fat; Chol 29 mg; Fiber 1 g; Sod 107 mg

Christmas Ribbon Salad   *Yield: 30 servings*

2 (3-ounce) packages
  lime gelatin

1 (20-ounce) can crushed
  pineapple

1 (3-ounce) package
  lemon gelatin

1 cup boiling water

1/2 cup miniature
  marshmallows

8 ounces cream cheese,
  softened

1 cup mayonnaise or
  salad dressing

1 cup whipping cream,
  whipped

2 (3-ounce) packages cherry or
  cranberry gelatin

Prepare the lime gelatin using package directions. Pour into a 9x13-inch dish and an 8-inch square dish. Refrigerate until almost set. Drain the pineapple, reserving the liquid. Add enough water to the reserved pineapple juice to measure 1 cup. Dissolve the lemon gelatin in boiling water in a bowl. Add the marshmallows and stir until melted. Beat in the cream cheese and 1 cup pineapple liquid. Stir in pineapple; cool. Fold in the mayonnaise and whipped cream. Refrigerate until thickened. Spread over the lime gelatin layer in each dish. Refrigerate until almost set. Prepare the cherry gelatin using package directions. Refrigerate until partially set. Spoon over the pineapple layer in each dish. Refrigerate, covered, until firm. Cut into squares. Serve on lettuce leaves.

4th of July Ribbon Salad
Substitute grape gelatin for the lime gelatin.

Springtime Ribbon Salad
Substitute strawberry or peach gelatin for the cherry gelatin.

Citrus Ribbon Salad
Substitute orange gelatin for the cherry gelatin.

Approx Per Serving: Cal 175; Prot 2 g; Carbo 17 g; T Fat 11 g; 57% Calories from Fat; Chol 24 mg; Fiber <1 g; Sod 109 mg

Did you know that peppermint and spearmint are profitable commercial crops in northern Indiana? The state ranks fourth in peppermint production, fifth in spearmint. Two primary uses of mint oils are dental hygiene products and chewing gum.

Strawberry Luscious Salad   *Yield: 16 servings*

1 (6-ounce) package
  strawberry gelatin
2 cups boiling water
1 (10-ounce) package
  frozen sliced sweetened
  strawberries, thawed
1 (20-ounce) can crushed
  pineapple
2 large bananas, mashed
½ cup sour cream

Dissolve the gelatin in boiling water in a large bowl. Stir in the strawberries, pineapple and bananas until well blended. Spoon half the mixture into a 9x13-inch dish. Refrigerate until set. Spread the sour cream evenly over the gelatin. Spoon the remaining gelatin mixture over the sour cream. Refrigerate until firm.

Approx Per Serving: Cal 116; Prot 2 g; Carbo 26 g; T Fat 2 g; 12% Calories from Fat; Chol 3 mg; Fiber 1 g; Sod 29 mg

Melon Mint Gelatin   *Yield: 8 servings*

1 (3-ounce) package lemon
  gelatin
1 (3-ounce) package lime
  gelatin
1½ cups boiling water
¾ cup plus 1 tablespoon lime
  juice, divided
½ cup cold water
⅛ teaspoon peppermint extract
⅔ cup cantaloupe balls
⅔ cup watermelon balls
⅔ cup honeydew balls
½ cup sour cream
1 tablespoon honey
3 tablespoons flaked coconut

Combine the lemon gelatin and lime gelatin in a bowl. Pour the boiling water over the gelatin. Stir until the gelatin is dissolved. Add ¾ cup of the lime juice, cold water and peppermint extract and mix well. Refrigerate until partially set. Fold in the cantaloupe, watermelon and honeydew balls. Spoon into a lightly oiled 5-cup ring mold. Refrigerate, covered, for 3 hours or until set. Unmold onto a serving plate. Combine the sour cream, honey and remaining 1 tablespoon lime juice in a bowl and mix well. Stir in the coconut. Serve over the gelatin.

Approx Per Serving: Cal 146; Prot 3 g; Carbo 28 g; T Fat 4 g; 21% Calories from Fat; Chol 6 mg; Fiber <1 g; Sod 81 mg

Bacon and Egg Potato Salad   *Yield: 12 servings*

2 pounds red potatoes

1/2 cup water

1/3 cup cider vinegar

1/3 cup olive oil

1 1/2 teaspoons celery salt

1 to 2 tablespoons
    Dijon mustard

2 teaspoons sugar

1/2 teaspoon pepper

1/2 cup sliced green onions

6 slices bacon, cooked,
    crumbled

3 hard-cooked eggs, chopped

1/4 cup grated Parmesan
    cheese

3 tablespoons chopped parsley

Here's a French-style potato salad dressed with vinaigrette instead of mayonnaise.

Combine the potatoes with enough water to cover in a saucepan. Bring to a boil. Boil until tender; drain. Refrigerate for 10 minutes or until cool enough to handle. Combine the water, vinegar, oil, celery salt, mustard, sugar and pepper in a bowl and mix well. Cut the potatoes into cubes. Combine the potatoes, green onions and vinegar mixture in a bowl and mix well. Refrigerate, covered, for 8 to 10 hours or longer. Let stand at room temperature for 30 minutes. Stir in the bacon, eggs, Parmesan cheese and parsley. Garnish with additional hard-cooked eggs.

Approx Per Serving: Cal 176; Prot 5 g; Carbo 17 g; T Fat 10 g; 50% Calories from Fat; Chol 57 mg; Fiber 2 g; Sod 360 mg

Ham and Cheese Potato Salad   *Yield: 15 servings*

2 1/2 to 3 pounds potatoes

1 cup mayonnaise or
    salad dressing

1/2 cup sour cream

2 tablespoons Dijon mustard

1 teaspoon celery seeds

1/2 teaspoon salt

1/4 teaspoon pepper

8 ounces each Cheddar and
    Monterey Jack cheese, cubed

2 cups chopped cooked ham

3/4 cup chopped, seeded,
    drained tomato

1/4 cup chopped green onions

1/4 cup chopped parsley

Peel the potatoes if desired. Combine the potatoes with enough water to cover in a saucepan. Bring to a boil. Boil until tender; drain. Cool. Combine the mayonnaise, sour cream, mustard, celery seeds, salt and pepper in a bowl and mix well. Cut the potatoes into cubes. Add to the mayonnaise mixture and toss to coat. Add the Cheddar cheese, Monterey Jack cheese, ham, tomato, green onions and parsley and mix well. Refrigerate, covered, for 2 hours or longer.

Approx Per Serving: Cal 355; Prot 14 g; Carbo 20 g; T Fat 24 g; 61% Calories from Fat; Chol 54 mg; Fiber 2 g; Sod 642 mg

Historically speaking, native strawberries, like other fruits and nuts that grew wild, were widely used in colonial and frontier homesteads, either fresh during their brief spring season or carefully preserved in jams and jellies. Development of hybrid strawberry plants has led to the big, plump berries we enjoy today.

California Triple-A Tossed Salad   *Yield: 8 servings*

1 envelope Italian salad
   dressing mix
¼ cup balsamic vinegar
½ cup olive oil
½ to ¾ teaspoon
   garlic powder
Freshly ground pepper
1 (14-ounce) can artichoke
   hearts, drained, cut
   into halves
2 heads romaine lettuce, torn
   into bite-size pieces
1 firm avocado, chopped
Fresh asparagus spears,
   steamed, cut into bite-size
   pieces (optional)
1 cup grated Romano cheese
4 ounces blue cheese,
   crumbled

This sophisticated green salad combines artichokes, avocado and asparagus with the savory goodness of romano and blue cheeses—a sensational blend of flavors and textures.

Prepare salad dressing using the vinegar and oil following the package directions. Add the garlic powder and pepper and mix well. Combine the artichokes and dressing in a sealable plastic bag. Marinate, in the refrigerator, for 8 to 10 hours or longer. Combine the romaine, avocado, asparagus, Romano cheese, blue cheese and artichoke mixture in a large bowl and mix well. Garnish with croutons.

Tip: An easy way to chop an avocado is to hold the pitted avocado half in your hand. Cut through the avocado flesh several times vertically and horizontally using a sharp knife and being careful not to cut into the peel. Scoop out the flesh with a spoon.

Approx Per Serving: Cal 303; Prot 10 g; Carbo 11 g; T Fat 25 g; 73% Calories from Fat; Chol 24 mg; Fiber 3 g; Sod 821 mg

Orange and Almond Green Salad   *Yield: 8 servings*

*½ cup sliced or slivered
  almonds*

¼ cup sugar

*8 to 12 cups torn mixed greens
  such as romaine, iceberg
  lettuce, spinach or leaf lettuce*

1 to 2 cups chopped celery

*½ cup sliced green onions, or
  1 sweet red onion, sliced,
  separated into rings*

*1 (11-ounce) can mandarin
  orange segments, drained*

1 avocado, chopped (optional)

*1 to 2 cups fresh strawberry
  halves (optional)*

Vinaigrette Dressing

Combine the almonds and sugar in a small skillet. Cook over medium heat until almonds are well coated and golden, stirring constantly. Remove to waxed paper. Cool completely, stirring to separate. Combine the greens, celery and onions in a large bowl and mix well. Add the oranges, avocado and strawberries. Shake the Vinaigrette Dressing. Pour over the salad and toss to coat. Sprinkle sugared almonds over the top.

Approx Per Serving: Cal 252; Prot 3 g; Carbo 24 g; T Fat 17 g; 59% Calories from Fat; Chol 0 mg; Fiber 3 g; Sod 199 mg

Vinaigrette Dressing

½ cup vegetable or olive oil

¼ cup red wine vinegar

¼ cup sugar

½ teaspoon salt

⅛ teaspoon pepper

⅛ teaspoon hot pepper sauce

*2 tablespoons chopped parsley
  or poppy seeds*

Combine the vegetable oil, red wine vinegar, sugar, salt, pepper, hot pepper sauce and parsley in a 1-pint jar and shake to mix. Refrigerate until chilled.

Heartland Spinach Salad   *Yield: 4 servings*

1 pound fresh spinach leaves, torn into bite-size pieces

1 (16-ounce) can bean sprouts, drained, or 8 ounces mushrooms, sliced

1 (8-ounce) can sliced water chestnuts, drained

1/4 cup sliced green onions, or 1 small red onion, sliced

2 to 4 hard-cooked eggs, chopped

8 ounces bacon, cooked, crumbled

1/2 cup canola or vegetable oil

1/4 cup sugar

1/4 cup tangy ketchup

1/4 cup red wine vinegar

2 teaspoons Worcestershire sauce

Combine the spinach, bean sprouts, water chestnuts, onions, eggs and bacon in a large bowl and mix well. Combine the oil, sugar, ketchup, vinegar and Worcestershire sauce in a saucepan. Cook until heated through; do not boil. Pour over salad and toss to coat.

Approx Per Serving: Cal 567; Prot 18 g; Carbo 32 g; T Fat 42 g; 66% Calories from Fat; Chol 228 mg; Fiber 7 g; Sod 827 mg

Broccoli Cauliflower Salad   *Yield: 10 servings*

1 bunch broccoli, trimmed, cut into florets

1 head cauliflower, cut into small florets

1 red onion, chopped or sliced

1/2 to 1 cup raisins

1 cup mayonnaise

1/4 to 1/2 cup sugar

2 tablespoons vinegar

8 ounces bacon, cooked, crumbled

Combine the broccoli, cauliflower, onion and raisins in a bowl and mix well. Combine the mayonnaise, sugar and vinegar in a bowl and mix well. Pour over the broccoli mixture and toss to coat. Sprinkle bacon over the top.

Variations: May add 1 carrot, coarsely shredded; 1 1/2 cups sliced mushrooms; 2 cups shredded Cheddar cheese; 1 cup chopped, seeded, drained tomato and 2 hard-cooked eggs, sliced; or 1/2 cup sour cream and garnish with cherry tomatoes.

Approx Per Serving: Cal 314; Prot 5 g; Carbo 27 g; T Fat 21 g; 60% Calories from Fat; Chol 22 mg; Fiber 3 g; Sod 269 mg

Oriental Shrimp Salad in Puff Bowl   *Yield: 6 servings*

3/4 cup mayonnaise or
   salad dressing

1/4 cup lemon juice

1 tablespoon prepared
   horseradish

1/4 to 1/2 teaspoon garlic salt

1 pound small shrimp, peeled,
   deveined, cooked

4 ounces fresh pea pods, or
   1 (6-ounce) package frozen
   pea pods, thawed

1 (8-ounce) can sliced water
   chestnuts, drained

1 cup sliced mushrooms

2 ounces fresh bean sprouts

1/4 cup sliced green onions

Puff Bowl or lettuce leaves
   (optional)

Serve this zesty shrimp salad in its own bread bowl for a spectacular luncheon main dish.

Combine mayonnaise, lemon juice, horseradish and garlic salt in a large bowl and mix well. Stir in shrimp, pea pods, water chestnuts, mushrooms, bean sprouts and green onions. Refrigerate, covered, until chilled. Spoon into Puff Bowl or over lettuce leaves.

Approx Per Serving: Cal 284; Prot 11 g; Carbo 9 g; T Fat 23 g; 72% Calories from Fat; Chol 110 mg; Fiber 3 g; Sod 419 mg

Raw shrimp in the shell (sometimes called green shrimp) are available fresh or frozen. Peeled and deveined raw shrimp are also available. Shrimp are sold by the pound—the bigger the shrimp, the higher the price and fewer per pound.

Puff Bowl

2 eggs

1/2 cup flour

1/2 cup milk

2 tablespoons butter or
   margarine, melted

1/4 teaspoon salt

Preheat oven to 425 degrees. Beat eggs until frothy in a mixer bowl. Beat in the flour gradually, until smooth. Add the milk, butter and salt and mix well. Pour into a greased 9-inch pie plate. Bake for 15 minutes. Reduce oven temperature to 350 degrees. Bake for 10 to 15 minutes or until browned.

Buttermilk—A commercial dairy product made by adding special bacterial cultures to milk (usually skim milk). Salt also is usually added. Buttermilk is a smooth and fairly thick liquid, with a distinctive, slightly sour, tangy flavor. It is used as a beverage and as an ingredient in baking and other recipes. Dry buttermilk powder also is available.

Marinated Vegetable Salad   *Yield: 6 servings*

2 (16-ounce) cans French-style green beans, drained

1 (16-ounce) can tiny green peas, drained

1 cup chopped celery

1 cup chopped onion

1 (2-ounce) jar diced pimiento, drained

1¹/₂ cups sugar

1 cup vinegar

¹/₂ cup vegetable oil

1 tablespoon salt

1 tablespoon water

Make this tasty vegetable medley for your next summer cookout or pitch-in supper.

Combine the green beans, peas, celery, onion and pimiento in a large bowl. Combine the sugar, vinegar, oil, salt and water in a separate bowl. Stir until sugar dissolves. Pour over the vegetables and mix well. Refrigerate, covered, for 6 to 8 hours or longer. May be drained before serving.

Variation: Substitute 1 (16-ounce) can white corn kernels, drained and 1 cup chopped green bell pepper for the green beans. Decrease sugar to 1 cup, vinegar to ³/₄ cup and salt to 1 teaspoon.

Approx Per Serving: Cal 458; Prot 6 g; Carbo 72 g; T Fat 19 g; 35% Calories from Fat; Chol 0 mg; Fiber 7 g; Sod 1770 mg

Herbed Buttermilk Dressing   *Yield: 8 (¹/₄-cup) servings*

1 cup buttermilk

1 cup mayonnaise or salad dressing

1 teaspoon dried basil leaves

¹/₂ teaspoon garlic salt

¹/₂ teaspoon dried thyme leaves

¹/₄ teaspoon onion powder

¹/₄ teaspoon pepper

Combine the buttermilk, mayonnaise, basil, garlic salt, thyme, onion powder and pepper in a bowl and mix well. Refrigerate, covered, until completely chilled. Serve with green salads or as a vegetable dip.

Approx Per Serving: Cal 213; Prot 1 g; Carbo 2 g; T Fat 22 g; 95% Calories from Fat; Chol 21 mg; Fiber 0 g; Sod 295 mg

Lemon Vinaigrette
Yield: 16 (¹/₄-cup) servings

¹/₂ cup chopped onion

¹/₄ cup chopped parsley

1 cup red wine vinegar

¹/₄ cup fresh lemon juice

1 teaspoon dry mustard

2 cups olive oil

Salt and freshly ground pepper

Process the onion, parsley, vinegar, lemon juice and dry mustard in a blender until smooth. Add the oil gradually, processing constantly at high speed until well blended. Season with salt and pepper. Refrigerate, covered, until ready to use.

Approx Per Serving: Cal 248; Prot <1 g; Carbo 1 g; T Fat 27 g; 98% Calories from Fat; Chol 0 mg; Fiber <1 g; Sod 2 mg

Onion Vinaigrette Dressing
Yield: 7 (¹/₄-cup) servings

1 medium onion, chopped

1 cup vegetable oil, divided

¹/₂ cup sugar

¹/₃ cup distilled vinegar

1 teaspoon each celery seeds, dry mustard and salt

¹/₈ teaspoon garlic powder

Process the onion and ¹/₂ cup of the oil in a blender container until smooth. Add the remaining ¹/₂ cup oil, sugar, vinegar, celery seeds, dry mustard, salt and garlic powder and blend well. Refrigerate, covered, until ready to use.

Approx Per Serving: Cal 340; Prot <1 g; Carbo 16 g; T Fat 31 g; 81% Calories from Fat; Chol 0 mg; Fiber <1 g; Sod 333 mg

Sugar-Free Slaw Dressing
Yield: 8 (¹/₄-cup) servings

1 cup or 24 packets aspartame sweetener

³/₄ cup distilled vinegar

¹/₄ cup sunflower oil

¹/₈ teaspoon pepper

Combine the sweetener, vinegar, oil and pepper in a blender container. Process until smooth. Refrigerate, covered, until ready to use.

Approx Per Serving: Cal 159; Prot 0 g; Carbo 25 g; T Fat 7 g; 38% Calories from Fat; Chol 0 mg; Fiber 0 g; Sod <1 mg

Sweet French Dressing
Yield: 8 (¹/₄-cup) servings

¹/₂ cup vegetable oil

1 small onion, chopped

¹/₂ cup sugar

¹/₃ cup ketchup

¹/₄ to ¹/₃ cup vinegar

Juice of 1 lemon

¹/₂ teaspoon each paprika and salt

Combine the oil and onion in a blender container. Process until smooth. Add the sugar, ketchup, vinegar, lemon juice, paprika and salt. Process until well blended. Refrigerate, covered, until ready to use.

Approx Per Serving: Cal 186; Prot <1 g; Carbo 17 g; T Fat 14 g; 64% Calories from Fat; Chol 0 mg; Fiber <1 g; Sod 267 mg

Taking deviled eggs to a picnic or pitch-in? Here's a sure way to have them look great when you arrive—Use your favorite deviled egg recipe. Arrange whites in plastic container or serving plate; cover. Place yolks in small sealable plastic bag; knead with fingers to mash yolks. Add remaining ingredients to bag; knead until mixed. Keep whites, yolk mixture and any garnish cold until serving time. At picnic site, cut corner from plastic bag of yolk mixture; pipe into whites. Garnish.

Barbecue Green Beans *Yield: 12 servings*

4 to 6 strips bacon

1 medium onion, chopped

3 (14-ounce) cans green beans, drained

1 cup packed brown sugar

1 cup ketchup

1 (8-ounce) can water chestnuts, drained, sliced

Cut the bacon into pieces. Cook in a skillet until crisp. Remove bacon to paper towels, reserving drippings. Brown the onion in the bacon drippings. Combine the bacon, onion, green beans, brown sugar, ketchup and water chestnuts in a large baking dish and mix well. Bake at 250 degrees for 2 hours.

Approx Per Serving: Cal 186; Prot 3 g; Carbo 31 g; T Fat 7 g; 31% Calories from Fat; Chol 8 mg; Fiber 3 g; Sod 590 mg

Quick Pickled Beets and Eggs *Yield: 8 servings*

8 eggs

1 (14-ounce) can sliced beets

1 cup cider vinegar

¼ cup sugar

6 peppercorns

4 whole cloves

1 teaspoon salt

½ bay leaf

Combine the eggs with enough water to cover in a saucepan. Cook until eggs are hard-cooked. Peel eggs while warm. Drain the beets reserving the liquid. Combine the reserved liquid, vinegar, sugar, peppercorns, cloves, salt and bay leaf in a saucepan. Bring to a boil. Simmer for 5 minutes. Alternate layers of 2 beet slices and 1 hard-cooked egg in a 1-quart jar until all ingredients are used. Pour the hot liquid mixture over the layers. Refrigerate, covered, for 24 hours or longer.

Approx Per Serving: Cal 115; Prot 7 g; Carbo 11 g; T Fat 5 g; 38% Calories from Fat; Chol 313 mg; Fiber <1 g; Sod 447 mg

Skillet Green Beans   *Yield: 4 servings*

1 pound green beans, trimmed

1 cup chicken broth

2 tablespoons butter

2 garlic cloves, minced

1 medium red bell pepper, chopped

1/4 teaspoon salt

Combine the green beans and chicken broth in a skillet. Bring to a boil over high heat. Cook for 6 to 8 minutes or until beans are tender-crisp and liquid has evaporated. Remove the beans from the skillet. Melt the butter in the skillet over high heat. Add the garlic. Cook for 2 to 3 minutes, stirring constantly. Add the cooked green beans, red pepper and salt. Cook for 2 to 3 minutes or until heated through, stirring constantly.

Approx Per Serving: Cal 106; Prot 4 g; Carbo 11 g; T Fat 6 g; 50% Calories from Fat; Chol 16 mg; Fiber 4 g; Sod 406 mg

Broccoli Rice Bake   *Yield: 8 servings*

2 (10-ounce) packages frozen chopped broccoli, thawed

3/4 cup instant rice

1 (12-ounce) can evaporated milk

1 (10-ounce) can cream of mushroom soup

8 ounces process American cheese, cubed

1 (8-ounce) can sliced water chestnuts, drained

1 medium onion, chopped

1/2 cup chopped celery (optional)

1 (4-ounce) can mushroom stems and pieces, drained (optional)

1/2 cup butter or margarine, melted

Preheat oven to 350 degrees. Combine the broccoli, rice, evaporated milk, soup, cheese, water chestnuts, onion, celery, mushrooms and butter in a bowl and mix well. Pour into a greased 9x13-inch baking dish. Bake, covered, for 45 minutes or until hot and bubbly, stirring after 20 minutes.

Approx Per Serving: Cal 362; Prot 12 g; Carbo 25 g; T Fat 25 g; 60% Calories from Fat; Chol 57 mg; Fiber 4 g; Sod 782 mg

Caraway Cabbage   *Yield: 4 servings*

¹⁄₄ cup margarine or butter

2 tablespoons bacon drippings or olive oil

1 medium head cabbage, coarsely chopped

1 large sweet onion, chopped (optional)

1 teaspoon caraway seeds

¹⁄₄ teaspoon garlic powder

Salt and freshly ground pepper

Melt the margarine and bacon drippings in a large skillet. Stir in the cabbage, onion, caraway seeds and garlic powder. Simmer, covered, for 15 minutes or until cabbage is tender-crisp, stirring occasionally. Season with salt and pepper.

Saucy Cabbage

Stir in 1 (10-ounce) can cream of mushroom soup after cabbage has cooked; heat through.

Tomato Cabbage

Stir 1 tablespoon flour into melted margarine mixture until smooth. Add 1 (14-ounce) can diced tomatoes with cabbage.

Approx Per Serving: Cal 220; Prot 3 g; Carbo 12 g; T Fat 19 g; 73% Calories from Fat; Chol 7 mg; Fiber 5 g; Sod 212 mg

Microwave Cauliflower Supreme   *Yield: 6 servings*

1 medium head cauliflower

¹⁄₂ cup mayonnaise

1 tablespoon dried minced onion

1 teaspoon prepared mustard

³⁄₄ cup shredded sharp Cheddar cheese

Rinse the cauliflower. Place in a 1¹⁄₂-quart microwave-safe dish with a small amount of water. Microwave, covered, on High for 6 to 8 minutes or until tender; drain. Combine the mayonnaise, onion, mustard and cheese in a small bowl and mix well. Spread the cheese mixture over the cauliflower. Microwave on High for 2¹⁄₂ to 3 minutes or until cheese melts.

Approx Per Serving: Cal 217; Prot 6 g; Carbo 6 g; T Fat 19 g; 80% Calories from Fat; Chol 28 mg; Fiber 2 g; Sod 220 mg

Corn Macaroni Casserole   *Yield: 15 servings*

1 (15-ounce) can whole kernel corn

1 (15-ounce) can cream-style corn

1/2 cup margarine, softened

1/4 cup finely chopped onion

1/4 cup finely chopped green bell pepper

1 (15-ounce) can whole tomatoes

1 cup elbow macaroni

1/2 cup grated Parmesan cheese

Preheat oven to 350 degrees. Combine the kernel corn, creamed corn, margarine, onion, green pepper, tomatoes and macaroni in a large bowl and mix well, breaking up the tomatoes. Spoon into a 9x13-inch baking dish. Bake for 30 minutes. Sprinkle cheese over the top. Bake for 30 minutes longer.

Approx Per Serving: Cal 141; Prot 4 g; Carbo 17 g; T Fat 7 g; 45% Calories from Fat; Chol 3 mg; Fiber 1 g; Sod 317 mg

Hoosier growers produce some of the best sweet corn around, accounting for our national rank of 14th in sweet corn production. Boiled corn-on-the-cob and fried corn are two of the favorite local ways to serve up this summer treat.

Fresh Corn Skillet   *Yield: 4 servings*

4 ears fresh sweet corn

4 ounces fresh pea pods

1 red bell pepper, cut into strips

1/4 cup sliced green onions

2 to 3 teaspoons chopped fresh thyme or rosemary leaves

1 1/2 teaspoons reduced-sodium instant chicken bouillon

1 teaspoon sugar (optional)

2 tablespoons olive or vegetable oil

Freshly ground pepper

Hoosier sweet corn is the best! Try this colorful side dish as a tasty alternative to corn-on-the-cob.

Remove husks and silk from corn. Cut kernels from cobs. Cook the corn, pea pods, red pepper, green onions, thyme, instant bouillon and sugar in oil until tender-crisp, stirring frequently. Sprinkle with pepper.

Approx Per Serving: Cal 164; Prot 4 g; Carbo 23 g; T Fat 8 g; 40% Calories from Fat; Chol 0 mg; Fiber 4 g; Sod 18 mg

49

Native mushrooms abound in certain parts of the state, and many a mushroom hunter takes great precautions to keep his best mushroom spots a secret. Morels, with their elongated sponge-looking caps, are one of the most prevalent species and most easily recognized. If you're among the avid morel hunters who know and recognize these tasty woodland treasures, you probably don't need this recipe. But perhaps you have a very good friend (only very good friends would share their bounty) who's given you a batch of morels or you've bought some at a local produce market or farm stand. Here's a simple way to savor the earthy goodness of this springtime treat.

Mock Oyster Dressing   *Yield: 6 servings*

2 cups chopped cooked peeled
  eggplant
2 tablespoons chopped onion
6 tablespoons butter, softened
1 teaspoon salt
1/4 teaspoon pepper
1/4 teaspoon sage
1 cup cracker crumbs
1 cup cubed process
  American cheese
2 eggs, beaten
1 cup milk

Combine eggplant, onion, butter, salt, pepper, sage, cracker crumbs, cheese, eggs and milk in a bowl and mix well. Spoon into a greased 9x13-inch baking dish. Bake at 325 degrees for 40 to 45 minutes or until mixture rises and is set.

Approx Per Serving: Cal 309; Prot 10 g; Carbo 15 g; T Fat 24 g; 68% Calories from Fat; Chol 129 mg; Fiber 1 g; Sod 1063 mg

Pan-Fried Morels   *Yield: 4 servings*

1 pound morel mushrooms
1/2 to 3/4 cup flour
1 teaspoon seasoned salt
1/2 teaspoon pepper
1/4 cup butter
1/4 cup olive oil

Soak morels in cold salted water in the refrigerator for 8 to 12 hours; drain. Cut large morels in half vertically. Rinse thoroughly and trim. Soak in clear cold water for 8 to 12 hours. Drain and pat dry on paper towels. Combine the flour, salt and pepper in a shallow dish and mix well. Coat each morel with flour mixture. Melt the butter and olive oil in a skillet. Cook the morels until golden brown and crisp on both sides. Remove and drain on paper towels. Serve warm.

Approx Per Serving: Cal 680; Prot 30 g; Carbo 72 g; T Fat 31 g; 40% Calories from Fat; Chol 32 mg; Fiber 14 g; Sod 382 mg

Onion Custard Pie *Yield: 15 servings*

30 saltine crackers, crushed

½ cup melted butter

3 cups thinly sliced onions

¼ cup butter

8 ounces shredded sharp Cheddar cheese

1½ cups milk, warmed

3 eggs, beaten

½ teaspoon salt

½ teaspoon pepper

Combine the crackers and melted butter in a 9x13-inch baking dish and mix well. Pat down to form a crust. Cook the onions in the ¼ cup butter in a skillet until golden brown. Layer over the crackers. Sprinkle the cheese over the onions. May be refrigerated, covered, for several hours. Combine the milk, eggs, salt and pepper in a bowl and mix well. Pour over the layers. Bake at 350 degrees for 30 minutes or until set.

Approx Per Serving: Cal 207; Prot 7 g; Carbo 8 g; T Fat 17 g; 72% Calories from Fat; Chol 87 mg; Fiber 1 g; Sod 369 mg

Golden Parmesan Potatoes *Yield: 6 servings*

¼ cup grated Parmesan cheese

¾ teaspoon salt

⅛ teaspoon pepper

⅛ teaspoon garlic salt

¼ cup sifted flour

6 large potatoes, peeled, cut into quarters

⅓ cup butter

Preheat the oven to 375 degrees. Combine the cheese, salt, pepper, garlic salt and flour in a sealable plastic bag. Shake to mix. Add the potatoes and shake to coat. Melt the butter in a 9x13-inch baking pan in the oven. Arrange the potatoes in a single layer in the pan. Sprinkle the remaining cheese mixture in the bag over the potatoes. Bake for 1 hour or until potatoes are tender and golden, turning after 30 minutes.

Tip: The Parmesan coating mix makes a great gift. To make a quantity batch, combine 2 cups flour, 2 cups grated Parmesan cheese, 2 tablespoons salt, 1 teaspoon garlic salt and ½ teaspoon pepper in a bowl and mix well. Divide evenly among 8 small sealable plastic bags. Attach the directions for preparing the potatoes. Store in the refrigerator.

Approx Per Serving: Cal 272; Prot 6 g; Carbo 37 g; T Fat 12 g; 38% Calories from Fat; Chol 31 mg; Fiber 3 g; Sod 521 mg

All-American Twice-Baked Potatoes   *Yield: 12 servings*

6 large baking potatoes

1 tablespoon vegetable oil

1/2 (10-ounce) package light silken tofu

3/4 cup shredded light sharp Cheddar cheese, divided

1/2 cup chopped red, green and yellow bell peppers, divided

1/4 cup cooked bacon bits

1/4 cup chopped green onions

1/2 teaspoon seasoned salt

Preheat oven to 350 degrees. Rub the potatoes with oil and pierce with a fork. Bake for 1 hour or until tender. Cut potatoes in half lengthwise. Scoop out the center, leaving a 1/4-inch shell. Set shells aside. Beat the potato pulp and tofu in a mixer bowl until well blended. Stir in 1/2 cup cheese, 1/4 cup of the bell peppers, bacon, green onions and seasoned salt. Spoon into the potato shells. Refrigerate or freeze, covered, until ready to heat. Preheat oven to 350 degrees. Bake for 20 minutes or until heated through. Top with the remaining 1/4 cup cheese and 1/4 cup bell peppers.

Tip: To reheat in a microwave, place 4 stuffed potato shells in a microwave-safe dish. Cook on Medium for 2 to 3 minutes. Top with cheese. Cook on High for 45 seconds to 1 minute. Repeat with remaining shells.

Approx Per Serving: Cal 136; Prot 5 g; Carbo 24 g; T Fat 3 g; 16% Calories from Fat; Chol 4 mg; Fiber 2 g; Sod 114 mg

Gourmet Mashed Potatoes   *Yield: 6 servings*

2 pounds russet or Yukon gold potatoes, peeled, cut into quarters

Salt to taste

1/4 cup milk

2 cups shredded Cheddar cheese, divided

3/4 cup butter, melted, divided

1 1/2 cups sour cream

1/3 cup chopped onion (optional)

1 teaspoon salt

1/4 teaspoon pepper

These rich, creamy mashed potatoes are great for entertaining since they can be made ahead and refrigerated.

Preheat oven to 350 degrees. Cook the potatoes in boiling salted water in a saucepan until tender; drain. Mash the potatoes with the milk in a bowl. Stir in 1 1/2 cups of the cheese, 1/2 cup of the butter, sour cream, onion, salt and pepper. Spoon into a greased 2-quart baking dish. Drizzle remaining 1/4 cup butter over the potatoes. Sprinkle remaining 1/2 cup cheese over the potatoes. Bake for 45 minutes or until hot and bubbly.

Variation: To make ahead, prepare as directed. Refrigerate, covered, for 8 to 12 hours or longer. Let stand at room temperature for 30 minutes before baking.

Approx Per Serving: Cal 587; Prot 14 g; Carbo 27 g; T Fat 48 g; 72% Calories from Fat; Chol 129 mg; Fiber 2 g; Sod 897 mg

Cheddar Squash Puff   *Yield: 8 servings*

2 pounds zucchini, sliced,
    seeded

2 pounds yellow summer
    squash, sliced, seeded

2 onions, chopped

2 eggs

3 cups shredded Cheddar
    cheese, divided

2 cups crushed butter crackers,
    divided

Salt and freshly ground pepper

2 tablespoons butter, melted

Cook the zucchini and squash in boiling salted water in a saucepan until tender; drain. Mash in a bowl. Stir in the onions, eggs, 2 cups of the cheese and 1½ cups of the crackers. Season with salt and pepper. Spoon into a greased 9-inch square baking dish. Sprinkle with the remaining 1 cup cheese and ½ cup crackers. May be refrigerated, covered, for 2 days. Drizzle with butter. Bake at 325 degrees for 45 minutes or until puffed and light brown.

Approx Per Serving: Cal 353; Prot 16 g; Carbo 22 g; T Fat 23 g; 58% Calories from Fat; Chol 105 mg; Fiber 4 g; Sod 467 mg

Praline Sweet Potato Casserole   *Yield: 8 servings*

2 eggs

3 cups mashed cooked
    sweet potatoes

¾ cup sugar

½ cup butter, melted

⅓ cup milk

½ teaspoon salt

¼ teaspoon cinnamon

¼ teaspoon nutmeg

Praline Topping

Preheat oven to 350 degrees. Beat the eggs in a large bowl. Stir in the sweet potatoes, sugar, butter, milk, salt, cinnamon and nutmeg. Spoon into a greased 1½- to 2-quart baking dish. Sprinkle with Praline Topping. Bake for 30 minutes or until hot and bubbly.

Approx Per Serving: Cal 618; Prot 6 g; Carbo 83 g; T Fat 31 g; 44% Calories from Fat; Chol 106 mg; Fiber 3 g; Sod 388 mg

Praline Topping

1 cup packed brown sugar

⅓ cup flour

⅓ cup butter, chilled

1 cup chopped pecans

Combine brown sugar and flour in a bowl and mix well. Cut in the butter until crumbly. Stir in pecans.

Potatoes, potatoes, potatoes! Yes, they are America's favorite vegetable. And of course, you know that Idaho claims the title of biggest potato-producing state, but Indiana is on the map as the 24th largest producer. With russets for baking, golden varieties for "rich" mashed potatoes without a lot of butter, red skins for steaming and potato salad, as well as sweets, yams and the newer fingerlings and purple types, you can pick a different potato each day. And of course, the recipe repertoire is endless too—from mashed and microwaved to baked, boiled, steamed, fried, sautéed and scalloped, in salads, soups, stews and casseroles. No wonder it's our favorite!

A Herb Hint—Dill Weed

A member of the parsley family, its subtle, sweet flavor complements vegetables, fish, seafood, and egg dishes.

Fried Green Tomatoes   *Yield: 4 servings*

*4 medium to large firm
  green tomatoes*

2 cups flour

1 teaspoon salt

*1 teaspoon freshly ground
  pepper*

1/2 cup butter

1/2 cup canola oil

Slice the tomatoes thinly. Combine the flour, salt and pepper in a shallow bowl and mix well. Dredge the tomato slices in the flour mixture, shaking to remove the excess. Melt the butter and oil on medium to medium-high in a skillet until hot and bubbly. Arrange the tomatoes in a single layer in the skillet. Cook until golden brown on both sides, turning often. Remove to paper towels to drain. Serve hot.

Approx Per Serving: Cal 701; Prot 8 g;
Carbo 54 g; T Fat 51 g; 65% Calories from Fat;
Chol 62 mg; Fiber 3 g; Sod 833 mg

Batter-Fried Veggies   *Yield: 4 servings*

1 cup cauliflower florets

1 cup broccoli florets

1 cup diagonally-sliced carrots

1 cup zucchini chunks

3/4 cup cornstarch

1/2 teaspoon baking powder

1/4 teaspoon pepper

1 egg, beaten

1/4 cup flour

1/2 teaspoon salt

1/2 cup water

Wash and dry the cauliflower, broccoli, carrots and zucchini. Whisk the cornstarch, baking powder, pepper, egg, flour, salt and water together in a bowl until smooth. Dip the vegetables into the batter. Fry in a deep fryer filled with hot oil measuring 350 degrees until golden brown or they float. Remove to paper towels to drain.

Variation: May substitute vegetables of choice for the cauliflower, broccoli, carrots and zucchini.

Approx Per Serving: Cal 168; Prot 4 g;
Carbo 34 g; T Fat 2 g; 8% Calories from Fat;
Chol 53 mg; Fiber 3 g; Sod 394 mg

54

Indiana Garden Stir-Fry   *Yield: 4 servings*

1 tablespoon olive oil

2 small zucchini, cut into
    ¼-inch slices

2 small yellow summer squash,
    cut into ¼-inch slices

1 medium carrot, cut into
    thin slices

1 medium green or red
    bell pepper, cut into
    diagonal strips

2 tablespoons finely
    chopped chives

2 tablespoons finely chopped
    fresh dill

1 cup whole cherry tomatoes

2 tablespoons balsamic vinegar
    (optional)

Heat the oil in a wok or skillet until hot. Swirl to cover the bottom. Add the zucchini, squash, carrot, green pepper, chives and dill. Cook for 6 to 8 minutes or until tender-crisp, stirring frequently. Add the tomatoes. Cook until heated through. Remove to a serving plate. Sprinkle with balsamic vinegar. Garnish as desired.

Approx Per Serving: Cal 79; Prot 2 g; Carbo 11 g; T Fat 4 g; 40% Calories from Fat; Chol 0 mg; Fiber 4 g; Sod 15 mg

Savory Lemon Vegetables   *Yield: 8 servings*

1 pound carrots, peeled, cut
    into 2-inch pieces

1 medium head cauliflower,
    core removed

6 slices bacon

1 cup finely chopped onion

½ cup lemon juice

½ cup water

4 teaspoons sugar

1 teaspoon salt

1 teaspoon thyme leaves

Bring a small amount of water to a boil in a saucepan. Add the carrots and cauliflower. Cook until tender-crisp. Drain and keep warm. Cook the bacon in a skillet until crisp. Drain, leaving ¼ cup drippings in the skillet. Crumble the bacon. Cook the onion in the hot drippings in the skillet until tender. Add the lemon juice, water, sugar, salt and thyme. Bring to a boil. Arrange the carrots and cauliflower on a serving dish. Pour the onion mixture over the carrots and cauliflower. Sprinkle with crumbled bacon. Garnish with chopped parsley.

Variation: Cook the bacon, reserving ¼ cup of the drippings. Arrange the carrots and cauliflower on a large microwave-safe platter with a rim. Cover with vented plastic wrap. Microwave on High for 14 to 16 minutes. Combine the onion and ¼ cup bacon drippings in a 1-quart microwave-safe dish. Microwave on High for 1 minute. Add the lemon juice, water, sugar, salt and thyme. Microwave on High for 5½ to 6 minutes or until sauce boils. Pour the sauce over the carrots and vegetables. Sprinkle with crumbled bacon.

Approx Per Serving: Cal 152; Prot 4 g; Carbo 15 g; T Fat 9 g; 53% Calories from Fat; Chol 11 mg; Fiber 4 g; Sod 447 mg

Fried Rice   *Yield: 4 servings*

3 tablespoons vegetable oil

1 cup finely chopped cooked
  ham, chicken or pork

2 tablespoons soy sauce

1 teaspoon oyster sauce
  (optional)

4 cups cooked rice

2 eggs, beaten

1/2 cup chopped green onions

Heat the oil in a wok or skillet until hot. Add the ham. Cook quickly, stirring constantly. Add the soy sauce, oyster sauce and rice. Cook for 1 minute, stirring constantly. Add the eggs. Cook for 5 minutes or until rice is loose and dry, stirring constantly. Stir in green onions. Serve immediately.

Approx Per Serving: Cal 397; Prot 17 g; Carbo 46 g; T Fat 15 g; 35% Calories from Fat; Chol 126 mg; Fiber 1 g; Sod 1157 mg

Rice Pilaf   *Yield: 4 servings*

1/2 cup chopped onion

1/4 cup slivered almonds

1/4 cup chopped celery

1/4 cup butter or margarine

1 cup long grain rice

1 cup broken vermicelli

1 (4-ounce) can mushroom
  stems and pieces, drained

2 cups chicken broth or a
  water and broth mixture

Cook the onion, almonds and celery in butter in a saucepan until tender-crisp and almonds are lightly browned. Stir in the rice, vermicelli, mushrooms and broth. Bring to a boil. Simmer, covered, for 20 to 30 minutes. Stir, adding additional broth if needed. Cook for 5 minutes or until broth is absorbed and rice is fluffy.

Approx Per Serving: Cal 432; Prot 13 g; Carbo 56 g; T Fat 17 g; 36% Calories from Fat; Chol 31 mg; Fiber 3 g; Sod 638 mg

Savory Onion Rice

Yield: 8 servings

1 1/2 cups long grain rice

1/2 cup chopped onion

1 (4-ounce) can sliced
mushrooms

1 (10-ounce) can French
onion soup

1 (10-ounce) can beef
consommé

1 1/4 cups water

1/2 cup butter or margarine

1/2 cup chopped green bell
pepper (optional)

1/2 cup shredded carrot
(optional)

Combine the rice, onion, mushrooms,
soup, consommé, water, butter, green
pepper and carrot in a bowl and
mix well. Spoon into a 2-quart baking
dish or electric skillet. Bake, covered,
in the oven at 350 degrees or in the
skillet at 250 degrees for 1 hour. Stir
before serving.

Approx Per Serving: Cal 264; Prot 5 g;
Carbo 33 g; T Fat 13 g; 43% Calories from Fat;
Chol 32 mg; Fiber 1 g; Sod 649 mg

Mushroom Math

1 pound = 6 cups sliced =
2 cups sliced and cooked
Preparation hints: Wipe fresh
mushrooms with a clean,
damp cloth or rinse them
lightly, then dry them gently
with paper towels.

Wild Rice Casserole

Yield: 20 servings

1 cup wild rice

1 cup brown rice

1 pound mushrooms, sliced

1/3 cup chopped onions

1 cup sliced water chestnuts

1 cup butter

6 cups chicken broth

Rinse the wild rice. Cook the wild
rice, brown rice, mushrooms, onions
and water chestnuts in butter in a
skillet, stirring constantly. Stir in the
broth. Spoon into a 9x13-inch baking
dish. Bake, covered, at 325 degrees
for 1 1/2 hours.

Approx Per Serving: Cal 91; Prot 4 g;
Carbo 17 g; T Fat 1 g; 8% Calories from Fat;
Chol 0 mg; Fiber 1 g; Sod 235 mg

Pasta Vegetable Toss   *Yield: 4 servings*

8 ounces fettuccini

1/2 cup chopped onion

1 clove garlic, finely chopped

1 teaspoon Italian seasoning

1 tablespoon olive oil

1/4 cup water

2 teaspoons instant beef bouillon

2 cups broccoli florets

2 cups sliced zucchini

8 ounces mushrooms, sliced

1 red bell pepper, cut into thin strips

Cook the fettuccini using package directions. Drain and keep warm. Cook the onion, garlic and Italian seasoning in oil in a skillet until onion is tender. Stir in the water, instant bouillon, broccoli, zucchini, mushrooms and red pepper. Simmer, covered, for 5 to 7 minutes or until vegetables are tender-crisp. Combine the fettuccini and cooked vegetables in a large bowl and toss to mix. Garnish with grated Parmesan cheese.

Approx Per Serving: Cal 236; Prot 10 g; Carbo 42 g; T Fat 5 g; 18% Calories from Fat; Chol <1 mg; Fiber 5 g; Sod 546 mg

Spiced Cucumber Rings   *Yield: 6 (1-pint) jars*

1 gallon cucumbers, peeled, cut into 1/2-inch slices

1 cup lime

5 quarts water

3 cups 5% acidity cider vinegar, divided

1 1/2 teaspoons powdered alum

2 teaspoons red food coloring

7 cups sugar

4 sticks cinnamon

1 cup red hot cinnamon candies

Combine the cucumbers, lime and 4 1/2 quarts of the water in a large container; all cucumbers must be covered with water. Let stand for 24 hours, stirring occasionally; drain. Rinse the cucumbers several times in cold water or until the water runs clear. Combine the cucumbers with enough water to cover in a bowl. Let stand for 3 hours; drain. Combine the cucumbers, 1 cup of the vinegar, alum, red food coloring and enough water to cover in a large saucepan. Simmer, covered, for 2 hours; do not boil. Drain and place in a large bowl.

Combine the remaining 2 cups vinegar, remaining 2 cups of water, sugar, cinnamon and candies in a saucepan. Cook until the candies melt, stirring occasionally. Pour over the cucumbers. Let stand for 8 to 12 hours. Drain, reserving the syrup. Pack the cucumbers into hot sterilized jars. Heat the reserved syrup in a saucepan. Pour into the jars. Wipe the mouth of the jars with a clean cloth. Seal with heated 2-piece lids. Process in a boiling-water canner for 10 minutes. Remove jars and cool.

Approx Per Jar: Cal 1158; Prot 5 g; Carbo 295 g; T Fat 0 g; 0% Calories from Fat; Chol 0 mg; Fiber 5 g; Sod 11 mg

GIFT

Continued from Page 1

Michelle Plummer, who teaches classes at the Cooking School at O'Malia's in Lockerbie Marketplace, says she has found an easier way to prepare bacon with quicker cleanup. She places slices on a parchment paper-lined baking sheet and can bake a pound of bacon in 15 minutes in a 425-degree oven.

More Christmas-morning fare is available in *Across Indiana: The Best of Heartland Cooking* (Guild Press of Indiana). Published this year, it was dedicated to Ardath Burkhart, known until her death in 1983 for her skill at entertaining.

Perfect for brunch

Among the recipes her daughter, ____led was her mother's

FRENCH TOAST CASSEROLE

1 loaf Italian bread (1 pound)
1 package (8 ounces) cream cheese
½ cup sugar, divided
½ teaspoon vanilla or almond extract
½ cup pecans, chopped, optional
4 eggs
2 cups milk
1 teaspoon cinnamon
2 tablespoons butter, melted

■ Cut bread into 1-inch cubes (about 14 cups). Place half of the bread cubes in a greased 9-by-13-inch baking pan. Place the cream cheese in a microwavable bowl or measuring cup. Cover the container with plastic wrap and cook on 100 percent power for 30 seconds. Stir it with a spoon, cover again and cook another 2 minutes. It should be completely melted.

■ Stir 1/4 cup sugar and all of the extract into the cream cheese. Spoon the cream cheese mixture over the bread cubes. It will not completely cover them. Sprinkle the nuts over the cream cheese layer. Top with remaining bread cubes. In a bowl, beat the remaining sugar, eggs, milk, cinnamon and melted butter together. The egg and milk mixture will make about 3 cups for each recipe.

■ To freeze: Pour the egg-and-milk mixture over the bread cubes. Slide the pan into a labeled two-gallon freezer bag. Seal and freeze.

■ To serve: Thaw the casserole completely. Bake at 350 degrees for 35 minutes or until browned. Allow to sit at room temperature for 5 minutes or so before cutting. Serve with warm syrup or purchased or homemade fruit toppings.

Recipe comes from Web site at www.30daygourmet.com

(Makes 12 servings)

Say cheese at parties

Guests enjoy Brie dishes, and they're easy to fix. **Page 3**

Thursday, December 23, 1999

COOK IT LITE / 3
COOKING ON TV / 2
DINNERS / 2
WINE VIEW / 3

InfoLine: 624-INFO (4636)
Online: www.starnews.com

Bread & Butter Pickles   *Yield: 10 (1-pint) jars*

*1 gallon thinly sliced
  cucumbers*

8 onions, sliced

*2 medium green bell peppers,
  cut into strips*

1/2 cup salt

5 cups sugar

5 cups vinegar

1 1/2 teaspoons turmeric

2 tablespoons mustard seeds

1 tablespoon celery seeds

1/2 teaspoon cloves

Combine the cucumbers, onions, green peppers and salt in a large container. Add enough ice and cold water to cover. Let stand for 3 hours; drain. Combine the sugar, vinegar, turmeric, mustard seeds, celery seeds and cloves in a saucepan and mix well. Stir in the drained vegetables. Cook over medium heat until vegetables darken in color. Ladle into hot sterilized jars, leaving 1/4-inch headspace. Wipe the tops and outside rims of the jars with a clean cloth. Seal with new 2-piece lids. Process in a boiling-water canner for 10 minutes. Remove jars and cool.

Approx Per Jar: Cal 477; Prot 3 g;
Carbo 121 g; T Fat 1 g; 2% Calories from Fat;
Chol 0 mg; Fiber 4 g; Sod 5591 mg

Indiana ranks 9th in the production of cucumbers for processing. And many a Hoosier home gardener reaps a bountiful harvest of these green gems.

Dilly Beans   *Yield: 6 (1-quart) jars*

3 pounds tender green beans

6 cloves garlic

12 heads fresh dill

3 teaspoons cayenne

6 cups water

*6 cups 5% acidity cider
  vinegar*

1/2 cup salt

Remove stem ends of beans; leave whole. Pack lengthwise with 1 clove garlic, 2 heads dill and 1/2 teaspoon cayenne in each hot sterilized jar, leaving 1/4-inch headspace. Combine the water, vinegar and salt in a saucepan. Bring to a boil. Pour into jars, leaving 1/4-inch headspace. Wipe the tops and outside rims of the jars with a clean cloth. Seal with new 2-piece lids. Process in a boiling-water canner for 10 minutes. Remove jars and cool.

Approx Per Jar: Cal 111; Prot 4 g;
Carbo 32 g; T Fat <1 g; 3% Calories from Fat;
Chol 0 mg; Fiber 8 g; Sod 9319 mg

Want to learn more about canning that over-abundance of tomatoes from your garden or how to make strawberry freezer jam? Help is just a phone call away. The experts in the consumer affairs department of the Alltrista Consumer Products Company in Muncie, makers of Ball and Kerr home canning products, are ready to answer your food preservation questions. The Home Canners' Help Line is 1-800-240-3340, Monday-Friday, 8:30 a.m. to 4:30 p.m. Eastern Standard Time.

Classic Pesto   *Yield: 8 (¹/₄-cup) servings*

2 cups fresh basil leaves

2 tablespoons pine nuts

1 tablespoon finely chopped garlic

¹/₂ to ³/₄ cup extra virgin olive oil

¹/₂ cup freshly grated Parmesan cheese

Salt and freshly ground pepper

Fresh herbs, grown in pots on the deck or windowsill or in a small garden plot, are the good cook's secret to seasoning and garnishing a variety of foods. Basil, an annual plant with an aromatic licorice flavor, is the traditional Italian herb used to flavor pizza, spaghetti sauce and pesto.

Wash basil leaves gently. Pat dry on paper towels. Combine the basil, pine nuts and garlic in a blender container. Add the oil gradually, processing at high speed until smooth. Spoon into a bowl. Stir in the Parmesan cheese. Season with salt and pepper. Use as a topping for pizza, as a sauce for hot pasta, or as a spread on hot, crusty bread.

Tip: Pour pesto into ice cube trays; freeze. Transfer to sealable plastic freezer bags and store in freezer.

Variation: For California Pesto omit the pine nuts, reduce the basil leaves to 1 cup, add 1 to 1¹/₂ cups fresh spinach leaves, stems removed, and add 2 to 4 tablespoons walnuts.

Approx Per Serving: Cal 300; Prot 10 g; Carbo 13 g; T Fat 24 g; 71% Calories from Fat; Chol 5 mg; Fiber 10 g; Sod 127 mg

Homemade Pasta Sauce   *Yield: 7 pints*

1 gallon tomato juice

2 cups chopped onion

½ teaspoon garlic powder

½ cup sugar

2 tablespoons parsley flakes

2 tablespoons oregano leaves

2 tablespoons (or less) salt

2 teaspoons sweet basil

¾ teaspoon pepper

2 bay leaves

7 tablespoons bottled lemon
   juice, or 1¾ teaspoons citric
   acid

Combine the tomato juice, onion, garlic powder, sugar, parsley flakes, oregano leaves, salt, basil, pepper and bay leaves in a large heavy stockpot. Bring to a boil. Reduce the heat. Measure the height of the sauce using a clean metal or plastic ruler. Simmer for 2 to 2½ hours or until boiled down one-third, stirring every 10 minutes. Remove bay leaves. Pour hot sauce into hot sterilized pint jars. Add 1 tablespoon lemon juice or ¼ teaspoon citric acid to each jar. Wipe the tops and outside rims of the jars with a clean cloth. Seal with new 2-piece lids. Process in a boiling-water canner for 35 minutes. Remove jars and cool.

Approx Per Pint: Cal 172; Prot 5 g; Carbo 43 g; T Fat 1 g; 2% Calories from Fat; Chol 0 mg; Fiber 3 g; Sod 4005 mg

 ## Zesty Salsa   *Yield: 7 pints*

10 cups chopped, seeded,
   peeled tomatoes

5 cups chopped green bell
   peppers

5 cups chopped onions

2½ cups chopped seeded
   banana peppers

¾ cup lime juice

½ cup cider vinegar

3 cloves garlic, minced

2 tablespoons minced cilantro

1 tablespoon salt

1 teaspoon hot pepper sauce
   (optional)

Combine the tomatoes, green peppers, onions, banana peppers, lime juice, vinegar, garlic, cilantro, salt and hot pepper sauce in a large saucepan and mix well. Bring to a boil. Reduce the heat. Simmer for 10 minutes. Ladle hot salsa into hot sterilized jars, leaving ¼-inch headspace. Wipe the tops and outside rims of the jars with a clean cloth. Seal with new 2-piece lids. Process in a boiling-water canner for 15 minutes. Remove jars and cool.

Approx Per Pint: Cal 150; Prot 5 g; Carbo 35 g; T Fat 1 g; 8% Calories from Fat; Chol 0 mg; Fiber 8 g; Sod 1032 mg

Heads of ripened wheat against drifting summer clouds inspired this prizewinning photograph by Adams County 4-H'er Monica Manley. Wheat is but one of the grains that inspired the recipes in "Bountiful Breads & Spreads." Champion bakers share their best fruit-filled muffins, quick bread loaves, warm scones, and golden yeast breads, fragrant with herbs or spices. There are homemade jams and jellies, too.

BOUNTIFUL
BREADS
& SPREADS

CHAMPION BAKERS SHARE THEIR BEST BREADS, JAMS, AND JELLIES

Applesauce Easter Bread   *Yield: 18 servings*

¹/₂ cup water

¹/₂ cup applesauce

2 eggs

1 tablespoon lemon juice

*2¹/₂ teaspoons grated
lemon peel*

*3¹/₂ cups plus 4 teaspoons
bread flour*

¹/₂ cup sugar

1 teaspoon salt

2¹/₂ teaspoons dry yeast

Combine the water, applesauce, eggs, lemon juice, lemon peel, bread flour, sugar, salt and yeast in the bread machine pan. Set the machine for sweet bread, medium crust, rapid cycle and large loaf; do not use the delay option. Bake according to your bread machine directions.

Approx Per Serving: Cal 133; Prot 4 g; Carbo 27 g; T Fat 1 g; 7% Calories from Fat; Chol 23 mg; Fiber 1 g; Sod 137 mg

Apricot Nut Bread   *Yield: 20 servings*

2 tablespoons butter, softened

1 cup sugar

1 egg

2 cups flour

1 tablespoon baking powder

¹/₂ teaspoon baking soda

³/₄ teaspoon salt

¹/₂ cup orange juice

¹/₄ cup water

¹/₂ cup chopped dried apricots

1 cup chopped pecans

Cover the bottoms of two greased 2¹/₂x5-inch loaf pans with greased waxed paper. Beat the butter and sugar in a bowl until light and fluffy. Beat in the egg. Combine the flour, baking powder, baking soda and salt in a separate bowl and mix well. Combine the orange juice and water in a small bowl. Add to the sugar mixture alternately with the dry ingredients, mixing well after each addition. Stir in the apricots and nuts. Pour into the prepared pans. Bake at 375 degrees for 40 minutes or until loaves test done. Cool in the pan for 10 minutes; remove to a wire rack to cool completely.

Approx Per Serving: Cal 149; Prot 2 g; Carbo 24 g; T Fat 6 g; 33% Calories from Fat; Chol 14 mg; Fiber 1 g; Sod 208 mg

Confetti Banana Bread   *Yield: 10 servings*

2 eggs

1 cup mashed bananas

1/2 cup melted butter

2 cups flour

1 cup sugar

1/4 teaspoon salt

2 1/2 teaspoons baking
   powder

1/4 cup chocolate chips

1/4 cup chopped maraschino
   cherries

1/4 cup chopped pecans

Beat the eggs in a bowl until thick and pale yellow. Add the bananas and butter and mix well. Combine the flour, sugar, salt and baking powder in a large bowl and mix well. Make a well in the center. Pour in the egg mixture, chocolate chips, cherries and pecans and mix well. Spoon into a greased 5x9-inch loaf pan. Bake at 350 degrees for 1 hour or until wooden pick comes out clean. Cool in the pan for 10 minutes; remove to a wire rack to cool completely.

Approx Per Serving: Cal 330; Prot 5 g; Carbo 49 g; T Fat 14 g; 37% Calories from Fat; Chol 67 mg; Fiber 2 g; Sod 288 mg

Whole Wheat Carrot Banana Bread   *Yield: 12 servings*

1/2 cup butter or margarine

1 cup packed brown sugar

2 eggs

1 cup all-purpose flour

1 cup whole wheat flour

1 teaspoon baking soda

1/2 teaspoon baking powder

1/2 teaspoon cinnamon

1/2 teaspoon salt

1 cup mashed banana

1 cup grated carrots

1/2 cup chopped pecans or
   walnuts

Line the bottoms of 2 greased 3 1/2x7-inch loaf pans with waxed paper. Beat the butter and brown sugar in a bowl until light and fluffy. Beat in the eggs 1 at a time, mixing well after each addition. Combine the all-purpose flour, whole wheat flour, baking soda, baking powder, cinnamon and salt in a bowl and mix well. Add to the brown sugar mixture alternately with the mashed banana, mixing well after each addition. Stir in the carrots and pecans. Spoon into the prepared pans. Bake at 350 degrees for 40 to 45 minutes or until wooden pick comes out clean, covering loosely with foil after 30 minutes. Cool in the pans for 10 minutes; remove to a wire rack to cool completely.

Variation: Substitute greased muffin tins for the loaf pans and bake for 18 to 20 minutes. This will yield 12 muffins.

Approx Per Serving: Cal 275; Prot 4 g; Carbo 39 g; T Fat 12 g; 39% Calories from Fat; Chol 56 mg; Fiber 3 g; Sod 322 mg

South of the Border Bread   *Yield: 20 servings*

1 tablespoon sugar

2 eggs, beaten

1¹/₂ cups shredded
    Cheddar cheese

1 cup cream-style corn

1 hot chile pepper,
    finely chopped

³/₄ cup chopped green
    bell pepper

2 envelopes dry yeast

1 cup cornmeal

¹/₂ teaspoon baking soda

1 cup buttermilk

³/₄ cup chopped onion

¹/₂ cup butter or margarine

1 tablespoon salt

6 to 7 cups flour

2 tablespoons melted butter

Combine the sugar, eggs, cheese, corn, hot pepper and green pepper in a bowl and mix well. Combine the yeast, cornmeal and baking soda in a separate bowl and mix well. Combine the buttermilk, onion, ¹/₂ cup butter and salt in a microwave-safe bowl. Microwave on High for 2 minutes or until the mixture is 120 degrees. Stir into the cornmeal mixture and mix well. Stir in the cheese mixture. Beat for 4 minutes with a dough hook. Beat in 5 cups of the flour. Knead on a floured surface for 8 to 10 minutes or until smooth and elastic, adding the remaining flour.

Place in a greased bowl, turning to coat the surface. Let rise, covered, in a warm place for 1¹/₂ hours or until doubled in bulk. Punch the dough down. Divide the dough in half. Divide each half into 2 portions of ¹/₃ and ²/₃. Form three 14-inch long ropes from each large portion. Shape into 2 braids and place each on a greased baking sheet; seal the ends. Form three 9-inch long ropes from each smaller portion. Shape into 2 braids and place each on top of a large braid; seal the ends. Let rise, covered, for 1 hour or until doubled in bulk. Bake at 350 degrees for 35 to 45 minutes or until golden brown. Brush with melted butter. Remove to a wire rack to cool completely.

Approx Per Serving: Cal 297; Prot 9 g; Carbo 43 g; T Fat 10 g; 30% Calories from Fat; Chol 46 mg; Fiber 2 g; Sod 551 mg

Whole Wheat Honey Bread   *Yield: 20 servings*

4 to 5 cups all-purpose flour,
    divided

2 teaspoons salt

2 envelopes dry yeast

- 1 cup water

¹/₂ cup honey

¹/₄ cup butter

1 cup cottage cheese

2 eggs

1 cup whole wheat flour

¹/₂ cup oats

1 cup chopped pecans

Combine 2 cups of the all-purpose flour, salt and yeast in a large bowl and mix well. Combine the water, honey, butter and cottage cheese in a microwave-safe bowl. Microwave on High for 2 minutes or until the mixture reaches 120 degrees. Beat into the all-purpose flour mixture. Add the eggs. Beat for 3 minutes. Stir in the whole wheat flour, oats, pecans and enough of the remaining all-purpose flour to make a soft dough. Knead on a floured surface until smooth and elastic.

Place in a greased bowl, turning to coat the surface. Let rise, covered, in a warm place for 1¹/₂ hours or until doubled in bulk. Punch the dough down. Divide into 2 portions. Let rest for 15 minutes. Shape each portion into a loaf and place in greased loaf pans. Let rise, covered, for 1 hour or until doubled in bulk. Bake at 350 degrees for 35 to 40 minutes or until loaves test done, covering after 25 minutes. Cool in the pan for 10 minutes; remove to a wire rack to cool completely.

Approx Per Serving: Cal 248; Prot 7 g; Carbo 38 g; T Fat 8 g; 28% Calories from Fat; Chol 29 mg; Fiber 2 g; Sod 307 mg

Wild Rice Three-Grain Bread
Yield: 20 servings

1 envelope dry yeast

1/3 cup warm (105- to 115-degree) water

2 cups warm (105- to 115-degree) skim milk

2 tablespoons shortening, melted

1 1/2 teaspoons salt

1/2 cup honey

2 cups whole wheat flour

4 to 4 1/2 cups all-purpose flour, divided

1/2 cup rolled oats

1/2 cup rye flour

1 cup cooked wild rice

1 egg white

1 tablespoon water

1/2 cup sunflower seeds (optional)

Dissolve the yeast in the warm water in a large bowl. Add the milk, shortening, salt and honey and mix well. Stir in the whole wheat flour, 2 cups of the all-purpose flour, oats and rye flour. Stir in the rice. Let stand, covered, for 15 minutes. Stir in enough of the remaining flour to make a stiff dough. Knead on a floured surface for 10 minutes or until smooth and elastic, adding flour as needed to keep the dough from sticking.

Place in a greased bowl, turning to coat the surface. Let rise, covered, in a warm place for 2 hours or until doubled in bulk. Punch the dough down. Knead briefly on a lightly oiled surface. Divide the dough into 3 portions. Roll each portion into an 18-inch rope. Shape into a braided wreath on a greased baking sheet; seal the ends. Let rise for 45 minutes or until doubled in bulk. Preheat oven to 375 degrees. Combine the egg white and 1 tablespoon water in a small dish. Brush over the top of the wreath. Sprinkle with sunflower seeds. Bake for 45 minutes or until wreath sounds hollow when tapped. Remove to a wire rack to cool.

Approx Per Serving: Cal 216; Prot 7 g; Carbo 44 g; T Fat 2 g; 8% Calories from Fat; Chol <1 mg; Fiber 3 g; Sod 192 mg

Modern agriculture depends on honeybees to pollinate many fruits, vegetables, legumes and oilseed crops. If pollination is neglected, no amount of cultural practice will cause fruit or seed to set. The increased use of honeybees as a tool in agricultural crop production has greatly augmented the value of the beekeeping industry in Indiana. Honey is the most natural sweetener in the world, adding its golden goodness to baked products, sauces, and glazes and as an unparalleled partner for a hot, buttered biscuit or a warm dinner roll.

Four Cheeses Baking Powder Biscuits
Yield: 15 servings

2 cups flour

1 tablespoon baking powder

¹/₂ teaspoon salt

¹/₄ cup butter, chilled

¹/₄ cup shredded Wisconsin sharp Cheddar cheese

¹/₄ cup shredded Vermont white Cheddar cheese

¹/₄ cup shredded Monterey Jack natural cheese

¹/₄ cup shredded American cheese

1 cup milk

Sift the flour, baking powder and salt together in a bowl. Cut in the butter until crumbly. Stir in the sharp Cheddar cheese, white Cheddar cheese, Monterey Jack natural cheese and American cheese and mix well. Make a well in the center. Pour in the milk. Stir until the dough is soft and pulls away from the side of the bowl; do not beat. Roll ¹/₂ inch thick on a floured surface. Cut out circles with a biscuit cutter. Place on a lightly greased baking sheet. Bake at 450 degrees for 10 to 12 minutes.

Approx Per Serving: Cal 133; Prot 5 g; Carbo 14 g; T Fat 7 g; 44% Calories from Fat; Chol 19 mg; Fiber <1 g; Sod 305 mg

 ## Mile-High Herb Biscuits   *Yield: 20 servings*

3 cups flour

4¹/₂ teaspoons baking powder

2 tablespoons sugar

¹/₄ teaspoon salt

1 tablespoon oregano

1 tablespoon thyme

1 tablespoon basil

³/₄ cup butter-flavor shortening

1 egg

1 cup buttermilk

Preheat oven to 450 degrees. Combine the flour, baking powder, sugar, salt, oregano, thyme and basil and mix well. Cut in the shortening until crumbly. Stir in the egg and buttermilk until smooth. Knead on a floured surface. Roll ¹/₂ inch thick on a floured surface. Cut out circles with a biscuit cutter. Place on a lightly greased baking sheet. Bake for 12 to 15 minutes or until golden brown.

Approx Per Serving: Cal 152; Prot 3 g; Carbo 17 g; T Fat 8 g; 49% Calories from Fat; Chol 11 mg; Fiber 1 g; Sod 155 mg

Apple Streusel Muffins   *Yield: 12 servings*

1³/₄ cups flour, divided

³/₄ cup plus 3 tablespoons
    sugar, divided

1¹/₄ teaspoons cinnamon,
    divided

2 teaspoons baking powder

¹/₂ teaspoon baking soda

¹/₂ teaspoon salt

2 eggs, beaten

³/₄ cup sour cream

2 tablespoons butter, softened

1 cup chopped unpeeled apples

2 tablespoons butter, chilled

Combine 1¹/₂ cups of the flour, ³/₄ cup of the sugar, 1 teaspoon of the cinnamon, baking powder, baking soda and salt in a bowl and mix well. Combine the eggs, sour cream and softened butter in a separate bowl and mix well. Add to the dry ingredients, stirring just until moistened. Stir in the apples. Fill greased muffin cups ²/₃ full. Preheat oven to 400 degrees. Combine remaining ¹/₄ cup flour, 3 tablespoons sugar and ¹/₄ teaspoon cinnamon in a small bowl and mix well. Cut in the chilled butter until crumbly. Sprinkle the crumb mixture over the batter. Bake for 18 to 20 minutes.

Approx Per Serving: Cal 211; Prot 3 g; Carbo 32 g; T Fat 8 g; 33% Calories from Fat; Chol 52 mg; Fiber 1 g; Sod 288 mg

Orange Crunch Muffins   *Yield: 12 servings*

1¹/₂ cups sifted flour

¹/₄ cup sugar

¹/₂ cup packed brown sugar,
    divided

2 teaspoons baking powder

¹/₂ teaspoon salt

³/₄ teaspoon cinnamon,
    divided

1 egg, beaten

¹/₂ cup vegetable oil

¹/₂ cup milk

1 teaspoon freshly grated
    orange peel

¹/₄ cup chopped almonds

2 tablespoons flour

1 tablespoon butter, softened

³/₄ cup sifted powdered sugar

1 tablespoon orange juice

¹/₂ teaspoon vanilla extract

Preheat oven to 400 degrees. Combine the sifted flour, sugar, ¹/₄ cup of the brown sugar, baking powder, salt and ¹/₂ teaspoon of the cinnamon in a large bowl and mix well. Combine the egg, oil, milk and orange peel in a separate bowl and mix well. Add to the dry ingredients, stirring just until moistened. Fill greased muffin cups ²/₃ full. Combine the almonds, 2 tablespoons flour, remaining ¹/₄ teaspoon cinnamon, remaining ¹/₄ cup brown sugar and softened butter in a small bowl and mix well. Sprinkle over the batter. Bake for 20 minutes. Cool in the pan for 10 minutes; remove to a wire rack. Combine the powdered sugar, orange juice and vanilla in a small bowl and mix well. Drizzle over the warm muffins.

Approx Per Serving: Cal 250; Prot 3 g; Carbo 33 g; T Fat 12 g; 44% Calories from Fat; Chol 22 mg; Fiber 1 g; Sod 202 mg

Raspberry Lemon Muffins   *Yield: 12 servings*

1½ cups flour

¼ cup sugar

¼ cup packed brown sugar

¼ teaspoon salt

2 teaspoons baking powder

1 teaspoon cinnamon

1 egg, beaten

½ cup milk

1 teaspoon grated
  lemon peel

½ cup melted butter

1¼ cups raspberries

Pecan Topping

½ cup powdered sugar

1 tablespoon lemon juice

Preheat oven to 350 degrees. Combine the flour, sugar, brown sugar, salt, baking powder and cinnamon in a bowl and mix well. Combine the egg, milk, lemon peel and melted butter in a separate bowl and mix well. Pour into the dry ingredients, stirring just until moistened. Fold in the raspberries. Fill greased muffin cups ⅔ full. Sprinkle the Pecan Topping over the batter. Bake for 20 minutes or until muffins test done. Cool in the pan for 10 minutes; remove to a wire rack. Combine the powdered sugar and lemon juice. Drizzle over the muffins.

Approx Per Serving: Cal 291; Prot 3 g; Carbo 40 g; T Fat 14 g; 42% Calories from Fat; Chol 45 mg; Fiber 2 g; Sod 244 mg

Pecan Topping

¼ cup flour

1 teaspoon grated lemon peel

½ cup packed brown sugar

1 teaspoon cinnamon

2 tablespoons melted butter

½ cup chopped pecans

Combine the flour, lemon peel, brown sugar and cinnamon in a bowl and mix well. Add the melted butter and mix well. Stir in the pecans.

Roasted Red Pepper-Mozzarella Muffins
Yield: 12 servings

1³/₄ cups flour

3 tablespoons sugar

2 teaspoons baking powder

¹/₄ teaspoon salt

1 egg

³/₄ cup milk

¹/₄ cup vegetable oil

¹/₂ cup shredded smoked
  mozzarella cheese

²/₃ cup chopped roasted red
  bell pepper

¹/₄ teaspoon cracked pepper

Preheat oven to 400 degrees. Grease 12 muffin cups and sprinkle with cornmeal. Combine the flour, sugar, baking powder and salt in a bowl and mix well. Make a well in the center. Combine the egg, milk and oil in a separate bowl and mix well. Stir in the cheese, red pepper and cracked pepper. Pour into the dry ingredients, stirring just until moistened. Fill prepared muffin cups ²/₃ full. Sprinkle additional cracked pepper over the batter. Bake for 18 to 20 minutes or until golden. Serve warm.

Approx Per Serving: Cal 152; Prot 4 g;
Carbo 19 g; T Fat 7 g; 40% Calories from Fat;
Chol 23 mg; Fiber 1 g; Sod 218 mg

Tex-Mex Muffins   *Yield: 12 servings*

1 cup flour

2 tablespoons sugar

1 tablespoon baking powder

1 teaspoon salt

1 cup cornmeal

1³/₄ cups shredded Cheddar
  cheese, divided

1 tablespoon finely
  chopped onion

1 tablespoon chopped green
  bell pepper

1 teaspoon caraway seeds

1 cup milk

2 eggs, beaten, divided

3 tablespoons melted butter

1 tablespoon whipping cream

Sift the flour, sugar, baking powder, and salt together in a large bowl. Stir in the cornmeal, 1¹/₂ cups of the cheese, onion, green pepper and caraway seeds. Combine the milk, 1 of the beaten eggs and melted butter in a separate bowl and mix well. Pour into the dry ingredients, stirring just until moistened. Fill greased muffin cups ³/₄ full. Combine the remaining egg, cream and remaining ¹/₄ cup cheese in a bowl and mix well. Place 1 teaspoonful over each filled muffin cup. Bake for 15 to 20 minutes. Remove to a wire rack to cool.

Approx Per Serving: Cal 205; Prot 8 g;
Carbo 20 g; T Fat 11 g; 47% Calories from Fat;
Chol 65 mg; Fiber 1 g; Sod 472 mg

In the 1941 fourth division 4-H Club Baking Book, baking requirements were more numerous than today. In addition to 3 bakings of quick breads, the 4-H'er was required to make 5 bakings of yeast rolls, 4 bakings of one- or two-crust pies, 3 butter cakes with frosting and 3 sponge cakes, including angel food! Then, "Quick Breads" were defined as coffee cakes, biscuits, short cake or upside-down cake. Obviously, quick bread loaves and muffins had not yet become popular. Now many fruits and vegetables, whole wheat flour, oat bran, and nuts of all kinds are incorporated into these popular baked products.

Orange Currant Scones *Yield: 16 servings*

1/2 cup currants

13/4 cups flour

3 tablespoons sugar

21/2 teaspoons baking powder

1/4 teaspoon salt

1/3 cup butter

*1 tablespoon grated
orange peel*

1 egg, beaten

*4 to 6 tablespoons half-and-
half*

1 egg white, beaten

Preheat oven to 400 degrees. Soak the currants in warm water to cover in a bowl for 10 minutes; drain. Combine the flour, sugar, baking powder and salt in a bowl and mix well. Cut in the butter until crumbly. Stir in the orange peel, egg, currants and enough half-and-half to make a dough that is soft and free from the side of the bowl. Knead dough 10 times on a floured surface. Divide into half. Roll each half into a 1/2-inch-thick 6-inch circle. Place on a foil-lined baking sheet. Brush with the egg white. Bake for 10 to 14 minutes or until golden brown. Remove to a wire rack to cool completely. Cut each circle into 8 wedges.

Approx Per Serving: Cal 108; Prot 2 g; Carbo 14 g; T Fat 5 g; 41% Calories from Fat; Chol 26 mg; Fiber 1 g; Sod 162 mg

Golden Crescents *Yield: 24 servings*

2 envelopes dry yeast

*3/4 cup warm (110- to
115-degree) water*

1/2 cup sugar

1/4 cup butter, softened

2 tablespoons shortening

2 eggs

1 teaspoon salt

4 to 41/2 cups flour

2 tablespoons melted butter

Dissolve the yeast in the warm water in a large bowl. Add the sugar, 1/4 cup butter, shortening, eggs, salt and 2 cups of the flour. Beat until smooth. Stir in enough of the remaining flour to make a soft dough. Knead on a floured surface for 6 to 8 minutes or until smooth and elastic.

Place in a greased bowl, turning to coat the surface. Let rise, covered, in a warm place for 11/2 hours or until doubled in bulk. Punch the dough down. Divide into 2 portions. Roll each portion into a 12-inch circle. Brush each circle with the 2 tablespoons melted butter. Cut each circle into 12 wedges. Roll each wedge up from the wide end and curve to form a crescent. Place with point down 2 inches apart on greased baking sheets. Let rise, covered, for 45 minutes or until doubled in bulk. Bake at 375 degrees for 8 to 10 minutes or until golden brown. Brush with additional melted butter if desired.

Approx Per Serving: Cal 144; Prot 3 g; Carbo 22 g; T Fat 5 g; 29% Calories from Fat; Chol 25 mg; Fiber 1 g; Sod 132 mg

 **Orange Bows** *Yield: 32 servings*

1 cup milk

1/2 cup butter

1/3 cup sugar

1 teaspoon salt

Peel of 1 orange

1 envelope dry yeast

1/4 cup warm (110- to
   115-degree) water

2 eggs, beaten

1/4 cup plus 2 tablespoons
   orange juice, divided

5 1/2 to 6 cups flour

1 cup powdered sugar

2 teaspoons grated
   orange peel

Combine the milk, butter, sugar and salt in a saucepan. Heat until the butter is melted. Cool to lukewarm. Mince the orange peel in a food processor by pulsing 4 or 5 times. Dissolve the yeast in the warm water in a bowl. Combine the dissolved yeast, milk mixture, eggs, 1/4 cup of the orange juice, minced orange peel and 3 cups of the flour in a large bowl and mix well. Stir in enough of the remaining flour to make a soft dough. Knead on a floured surface for 6 to 8 minutes or until smooth and elastic.

Place in a greased bowl, turning to coat the surface. Let rise, covered, in a warm place for 1 1/2 hours or until doubled in bulk. Punch the dough down. Let stand for 15 minutes. Roll into a 10x16-inch rectangle. Cut into sixteen 1-inch wide strips. Cut each strip into half. Tie each strip into a bow. Place bows on greased baking sheets. Let rise, covered, for 1 hour or until doubled in bulk. Bake at 350 degrees for 10 minutes or until golden brown. Remove to a wire rack to cool completely. Combine the remaining 2 tablespoons orange juice, powdered sugar and the grated orange peel in a bowl and mix well. Drizzle over the bows.

Approx Per Serving: Cal 145; Prot 3 g;
Carbo 25 g; T Fat 4 g; 23% Calories from Fat;
Chol 22 mg; Fiber 1 g; Sod 110 mg

If freezing sweet yeast breads, do not frost or glaze. Thaw at room temperature, then ice, frost, or glaze according to recipe.

73

Bulk yeast is readily available in specialty shops and supermarkets. Bulk yeast is much less expensive than packaged yeast. It should be kept in the refrigerator in a sealed container. One level tablespoon of bulk yeast equals one package of yeast.

Sweetheart Cinnamon Rolls   *Yield: 24 servings*

2 (1-pound) frozen bread loaves, thawed

½ cup light soy margarine, softened, divided

¾ cup packed brown sugar

2 teaspoons cinnamon

½ cup chopped pecans

½ (10-ounce) package silken tofu

4 cups powdered sugar

1 teaspoon vanilla extract

1 tablespoon instant coffee granules

Roll each loaf into an 8x12-inch rectangle. Spread 3 tablespoons of the margarine on each rectangle. Combine the brown sugar, cinnamon and pecans in a bowl and mix well. Sprinkle evenly over the margarine. Roll each rectangle as for a jelly roll from the long side, sealing the edge and ends. Cut each into 12 slices. Place the slices cut side down in a 9x13-inch baking dish sprayed with vegetable spray. Cover and place in the refrigerator for 8 to 12 hours or let rise for 45 minutes or until doubled in bulk. Let rise for 1½ hours or until doubled in bulk after removing from the refrigerator. Preheat oven to 350 degrees. Bake for 35 to 40 minutes. Remove to a wire rack to cool completely. Process the remaining margarine, tofu, powdered sugar, vanilla and instant coffee granules in a blender. Drizzle over the rolls.

Approx Per Serving: Cal 246; Prot 5 g; Carbo 47 g; T Fat 5 g; 19% Calories from Fat; Chol 0 mg; Fiber 1 g; Sod 262 mg

Light and Tasty Whole Wheat Rolls *Yield: 18 servings*

2 envelopes dry yeast

¹/₂ cup warm (110- to 115-degree) water

1 cup warm milk

¹/₂ cup margarine, softened

1 cup instant potato flakes

¹/₂ cup packed brown sugar

1 teaspoon salt

3 eggs, divided

2 cups whole wheat flour

2 cups all-purpose flour

1 tablespoon water

Dissolve the yeast in the warm water in a bowl. Combine the milk, margarine, potato flakes, brown sugar and salt in a bowl. Beat in the yeast mixture and 2 of the eggs with a dough hook. Add the whole wheat flour. Beat for 3 minutes. Add enough of the all-purpose flour to make a soft dough. Knead with the dough hook or by hand for 7 minutes. Place in a greased bowl, turning to coat the surface. Let rise, covered, in a warm place for 1½ hours or until doubled in bulk. Divide dough into 18 pieces. Shape each into a flat ball. Place on greased baking sheets. Combine remaining egg and 1 tablespoon water in a cup and mix well. Brush the top of each roll. Let rise, covered, for 1 hour or until doubled in bulk. Bake at 350 degrees for 14 to 16 minutes or until golden brown.

Onion Buns

Add 1 envelope onion soup mix to the milk mixture and after brushing with the egg wash, sprinkle dried minced onion over the top of each roll.

Cloverleaf Rolls

After the first rising, shape the dough into 72 small balls. Grease 24 muffin cups. Place 3 balls into each muffin cup. Let rise, covered, for 1 hour or until doubled in bulk. Bake at 350 degrees for 8 to 10 minutes or until golden brown. Cool in the pan for 5 minutes. Brush tops with melted butter or margarine.

Crescent Rolls

After the first rising, divide the dough into 3 portions. Roll each portion into a 15-inch circle on a lightly floured surface. Brush with melted butter. Cut into 12 wedges. Roll wedges up from wide end. Shape into crescents 2 inches apart on foil-lined greased baking sheets. Let rise, covered, for 1 hour or until doubled in bulk. Bake at 350 degrees for 7 to 9 minutes or until golden brown. Brush with melted butter. Remove to a wire rack to cool.

Approx Per Serving: Cal 194; Prot 5 g; Carbo 29 g; T Fat 7 g; 31% Calories from Fat; Chol 37 mg; Fiber 2 g; Sod 211 mg

Yeast Bread Tips

For a nicely finished look, brush hot rolls with melted butter or margarine; or brush with egg wash made of 1 beaten egg and 1 tablespoon of water before baking.

Always remove rolls from pans to cool on racks to prevent sogginess caused by hot rolls forming steam in or against baking pan.

 Cottage Herb Breadsticks   *Yield: 12 servings*

1 envelope dry yeast

¼ cup warm (110- to 115-degree) water

2½ cups flour

¼ cup sugar

1 envelope Italian salad dressing mix

½ cup margarine, chilled

1 cup cottage cheese

1 egg, beaten

2 tablespoons melted butter

¼ cup grated Parmesan cheese

Dissolve the yeast in warm water in a bowl. Combine the flour, sugar and salad dressing mix in a bowl and mix well. Cut in the margarine until crumbly. Stir in the cottage cheese, egg and dissolved yeast and mix well. Knead on a floured surface until smooth and elastic. Place in a greased bowl, turning to coat the surface. Let rise, covered, in a warm place for 1 hour or until doubled in bulk. Punch the dough down. Roll into a ¼-inch thick rectangle. Cut into 12 strips. Place on greased baking sheets, twisting. Let rise, covered, for 1 hour or until doubled in bulk. Preheat oven to 375 degrees. Bake for 10 to 12 minutes. Brush with butter and sprinkle with Parmesan cheese while warm.

Approx Per Serving: Cal 234; Prot 7 g; Carbo ;26 g; T Fat 12 g; 45% Calories from Fat; Chol 27 mg; Fiber 1 g; Sod 437 mg

Cheesy Herb Pretzels *Yield: 12 servings*

1 cup flour

2 tablespoons grated
  Parmesan cheese

1/2 teaspoon garlic powder

1/4 teaspoon basil

1/4 teaspoon rosemary

1/4 teaspoon oregano

1/2 cup butter

1 cup finely shredded
  Cheddar cheese

2 to 3 tablespoons cold water

Combine the flour, Parmesan cheese, garlic powder, basil, rosemary and oregano in a bowl and mix well. Cut in the butter until crumbly. Stir in the Cheddar cheese. Add the water 1 tablespoon at a time, mixing with a fork until the mixture forms a ball. Divide into 12 portions. Roll each portion into an 11-inch rope on a lightly floured surface. Shape into a pretzel. Place on baking sheets. Bake at 425 degrees for 12 to 15 minutes or until light brown.

Approx Per Serving: Cal 148; Prot 4 g; Carbo 8 g; T Fat 11 g; 68% Calories from Fat; Chol 31 mg; Fiber <1 g; Sod 156 mg

Cheese Biscuit Wreath *Yield: 10 servings*

3 tablespoons margarine

1 (5-ounce) jar cheese spread
  with bacon

1 (10-count) package
  refrigerated biscuits

4 slices bacon, cooked,
  crumbled

Preheat oven to 425 degrees. Line the bottom and side of a 9-inch round baking pan with aluminum foil. Place an inverted custard cup in the center. Spray the foil and side of the custard cup with nonstick cooking spray. Combine the margarine and cheese spread in a microwave-safe bowl. Microwave on High for 1 minute or until melted. Stir to blend. Pour into the prepared pan, coating the bottom. Cut each biscuit into quarters. Arrange over the cheese mixture into a wreath shape. Bake for 12 to 14 minutes or until top is brown. Invert immediately onto a serving plate. Remove the foil and custard cup. Scrape off the cheese remaining on the foil and spread onto the wreath. Sprinkle with the bacon. Garnish with fresh parsley and pimiento.

Approx Per Serving: Cal 172; Prot 5 g; Carbo 12 g; T Fat 12 g; 62% Calories from Fat; Chol 13 mg; Fiber <1 g; Sod 632 mg

B & B Baked Oatmeal   *Yield: 15 servings*

6 cups quick-cooking or
   old-fashioned oats

1 tablespoon plus 1 teaspoon
   baking powder

1 teaspoon salt

1 teaspoon cinnamon

1 cup vegetable oil

1¹/₂ cups packed brown sugar

4 eggs

2 cups milk

1 cup chopped apple
   (optional)

1 cup raisins (optional)

¹/₂ cup flaked coconut
   (optional)

Preheat oven to 400 degrees. Combine the oats, baking powder, salt and cinnamon in a bowl and mix well. Combine the oil, brown sugar and eggs in a separate bowl and mix well. Stir in the dry ingredients. Stir in the milk, apple, raisins and coconut. Pour into a greased 9x13-inch baking dish, spreading evenly. Bake for 30 to 35 minutes. Cut into squares. Serve warm with milk or cream.

Approx Per Serving: Cal 405; Prot 9 g; Carbo 49 g; T Fat 20 g; 43% Calories from Fat; Chol 61 mg; Fiber 4 g; Sod 328 mg

 Harvest Fruit Spread   *Yield: 6 servings*

8 ounces pitted dates

1 cup raisins

1 cup dried currants

¹/₄ cup pitted prunes

1 to 1¹/₄ cups sweet red
   Passover or kosher wine

¹/₂ cup chopped walnuts or
   pecans

2 tablespoons ground
   almonds

In Jewish cooking, this rich spread made from dried fruits is called haroset.

Combine the dates, raisins, currants and prunes in a bowl. Add water to cover. Soak for 12 hours or longer. Drain the fruit, reserving the liquid. Chop the fruit coarsely. Place in a heavy nonreactive saucepan. Add 1cup of the wine and 1 cup of the reserved liquid. Bring to a boil. Reduce the heat. Simmer for 2 hours or until all the liquid has been absorbed and mixture is very thick, stirring occasionally. Remove from heat; cool. Stir in the walnuts and almonds. Add enough of the remaining wine to make of the desired consistency. Store, covered, in the refrigerator. Use as a spread on toast, plain or graham crackers or serve as a condiment with poultry or meat.

Approx Per Serving: Cal 431; Prot 5 g; Carbo 77 g; T Fat 9 g; 18% Calories from Fat; Chol 0 mg; Fiber 7 g; Sod 12 mg

Lemon Verbena Jelly   *Yield: 4 (1-cup) jars*

*2 cups (heaping) chopped
   fresh lemon verbena leaves*

2¹/₂ cups boiling water

¹/₄ cup lemon juice

4¹/₂ cups sugar

2 drops yellow food coloring

*1 (3-ounce) package liquid
   fruit pectin*

Place the leaves in a large bowl. Pour the boiling water over the leaves. Let stand, covered, for 15 minutes. Strain, reserving the liquid. Combine 2 cups of the reserved liquid, lemon juice and sugar in a saucepan. Bring to a boil over high heat, stirring frequently. Stir in the food coloring. Stir in the pectin. Bring to a boil. Boil for 1 minute, stirring constantly. Ladle the jelly into hot, sterilized jars, leaving ¹/₄-inch headspace. Wipe the tops and outside rims of the jars with a clean cloth. Seal with new 2-piece lids. Process in a boiling water bath for 5 minutes. Remove jars and cool. Serve with grilled chicken or pork, toast, biscuits or bagels.

Approx Per Jar: Cal 877; Prot <1 g;
Carbo 227 g; T Fat 0 g; 0% Calories from Fat;
Chol 0 mg; Fiber 1 g; Sod 5 mg

When choosing rhubarb, select firm and tender stalks; avoid those that are extra thick or wilted. To preserve its crisp texture, wrap raw rhubarb in plastic wrap and chill up to 1 week. One pound of rhubarb yields 3 cups sliced fruit.

 Rhubarb Spread   *Yield: 2 (2-cup) jars*

5 cups finely chopped rhubarb

3 cups sugar

*1 small package sugar-free
   strawberry gelatin*

Combine the rhubarb and sugar in a bowl and mix well. Refrigerate, covered, for 8 to 12 hours or longer. Spoon the rhubarb mixture into a saucepan. Bring to a boil, stirring constantly. Boil for 5 minutes, stirring constantly. Remove from the heat. Add the strawberry gelatin, stirring until dissolved. Spoon into 2-cup jars. Seal tightly. Store in the refrigerator for 3 weeks.

Approx Per Jar: Cal 1242; Prot 6 g;
Carbo 315 g; T Fat 1 g; 0% Calories from Fat;
Chol 0 mg; Fiber 5 g; Sod 123 mg

Calico Jam *Yield: 8 (1-cup) jars*

1½ *pounds fresh apricots,*
  finely chopped

2 *cups crushed pineapple*

1 *cup chopped maraschino*
  cherries, drained

¼ *cup lemon juice*

1 *(1¾-ounce) package*
  powdered fruit pectin

7 *cups sugar*

Place the hot water bath canner on a surface burner. Add water to half fill the canner. Cover the canner. Bring the water to a boil. Wash eight 1-cup jelly jars, lids and bands in hot sudsy water. Rinse them well and leave them in hot water until ready to be used. Combine 2 cups of the chopped apricots, pineapple, cherries, lemon juice and pectin in a Dutch oven and mix well. Bring to a boil over medium-high heat, stirring constantly. Stir in the sugar. Bring to a boil, stirring constantly. Boil for 1 minute. Remove from heat. Skim off any foam. Remove the jars from the water, one at a time and place them on a clean cloth. Ladle the jam into the jars, leaving ¼-inch headspace. Wipe the tops and outside rims of the jars with a clean cloth.

Place the lids on top and screw on the bands tightly; do not use force. Place the jars in the canner rack and lower the rack into the rapidly boiling water, adding additional boiling water to the canner if the water level is not 1 inch above jars. Cover the canner and return the water to a boil. Process for 15 minutes. Remove the jars from the canner with tongs and place them, at least 3 inches apart, on a cloth-lined surface until they are cool, for about 12 hours. Test all the jars, to be sure they are sealed, by tapping them with a spoon. A clear ringing sound means a good seal. If a jar is not properly sealed, store it in the refrigerator and use its contents within a month. Remove the bands. Wipe the jars with a clean dampened cloth.

Approx Per Jar: Cal 822; Prot 1 g; Carbo 211 g; T Fat <1 g; 0% Calories from Fat; Chol 0 mg; Fiber 3 g; Sod 3 mg

Strawberry Cranberry Fruit Spread

Yield: 14 (1-cup) jars

2 (20-ounce) packages frozen
  whole strawberries or
  2¹/₂ quarts fresh strawberries

1 pound cranberries

5 pounds sugar

2 (3-ounce) packages liquid
  fruit pectin

Grind the strawberries and cranberries in a grinder or food processor. Place in a stockpot. Stir in the sugar. Bring to a boil. Boil for 1 minute. Remove from the heat. Stir in the pectin. Cool for 5 minutes. Skim off any foam. Ladle into 14 hot, sterilized jars, leaving ¹/₄-inch headspace. Wipe the tops and outside rims of the jars with a clean cloth. Seal with new 2-piece lids. Process in a boiling water bath for 15 minutes. Remove jars and cool.

Approx Per Jar: Cal 673; Prot <1 g;
Carbo 174 g; T Fat <1 g; 0% Calories from Fat;
Chol 0 mg; Fiber 3 g; Sod 5 mg

 ## Strawberry Grape Freezer Jam

Yield: 5 (1-cup) jars

1 cup crushed strawberries

1 cup unsweetened grape juice

1 tablespoon lemon juice

4 cups sugar

1 (1³/₄-ounce) package
  powdered fruit pectin

³/₄ cup water

Combine the strawberries, grape juice, lemon juice and sugar in a bowl and mix well. Let stand for 10 minutes. Combine the pectin and water in a small saucepan. Bring to a boil. Boil for 1 minute stirring constantly. Add the pectin mixture to the fruit mixture. Stir for 4 minutes. Pour into 1-cup jars, leaving ¹/₂-inch headspace. Wipe the tops and outside rims of the jars with a clean cloth. Seal with new 2-piece lids. Let stand for 24 hours or until set. Freeze.

Approx Per Jar: Cal 726; Prot 1 g;
Carbo 183 g; T Fat <1 g; 0% Calories from Fat;
Chol 0 mg; Fiber 2 g; Sod 4 mg

What's in a Name?

JAMS are made from crushed or chopped fruit cooked to a thick, spreadable consistency.

MARMALADES are soft jellies containing suspended pieces of citrus peel and/or fruit.

PRESERVES are made with larger pieces of fruit or small whole fruits in a clear, slightly jellied syrup.

CONSERVES usually contain two or more fruits and may include raisins and nuts.

BUTTERS are fruit pulp and sugar thickened to spreadable consistency with long, slow cooking.

FRUIT SPREADS do not contain the high proportion of sugar required to be called a jam, jelly, or preserve.

In this 4-H photograph, Sylvia Eash of LaGrange County captured a rainbow arching over the farm's grain bin. Across the state, Hoosier farms produce the grain and livestock that are the heart of Indiana agriculture. In "Meats & Mainstays," here's a bonanza of family-favorite recipes with beef, pork, chicken, turkey, duckling, lamb, fish, and seafood, even venison and ostrich—satisfying main dishes for weekday suppers and special gatherings.

MEATS
& MAINSTAYS

SATISFYING MAIN DISHES FOR WEEKDAY SUPPERS AND SPECIAL GATHERINGS

Chuckwagon Roast and Vegetables   *Yield: 6 servings*

1 (3-pound) boneless beef
   chuck roast

2 tablespoons vegetable oil

3 tablespoons flour

1 cup buttermilk

1 cup water

4 teaspoons instant beef
   bouillon

½ teaspoon thyme leaves

¼ teaspoon pepper

4 medium carrots, cut into
   1-inch pieces

2 medium onions,
   cut into wedges

3 cups broccoli florets

2 cups cauliflower florets

Preheat oven to 350 degrees. Brown the roast in hot oil in a skillet. Place in a 3-quart roasting pan. Add flour to drippings. Cook until brown, stirring constantly. Add the buttermilk, water, instant bouillon, thyme and pepper. Cook for 10 minutes or until bouillon dissolves and mixture begins to thicken, stirring constantly. Arrange carrots and onions around meat. Pour sauce over the meat. Bake, covered, for 1 hour and 45 minutes or until meat is tender. Add the broccoli and cauliflower. Bake for 15 minutes longer or until broccoli and cauliflower are tender-crisp.

Approx Per Serving: Cal 456; Prot 56 g; Carbo 17 g; T Fat 17 g; 35% Calories from Fat; Chol 160 mg; Fiber 4 g; Sod 760 mg

Tex-Mex Flank Steak   *Yield: 4 servings*

1 medium onion, thinly sliced

½ cup lemon juice

½ cup vegetable oil

2 tablespoons dry sherry

2 teaspoons instant
   beef bouillon

2 teaspoons chili powder

2 teaspoons ground cumin

2 cloves garlic, minced

1 (1- to 1½-pound) flank steak,
   scored

Combine the onion, lemon juice, oil, sherry, instant bouillon, chili powder, cumin and garlic in a bowl and mix well. Pour over the steak in a shallow dish. Marinate, covered, in the refrigerator for 6 hours or longer, turning occasionally. Drain, reserving the marinade. Grill or broil for 5 to 7 minutes on each side or to desired doneness, basting frequently with reserved marinade.

Approx Per Serving: Cal 544; Prot 37 g; Carbo 7 g; T Fat 41 g; 67% Calories from Fat; Chol 88 mg; Fiber 1 g; Sod 555 mg

Beef Burgundy   *Yield: 6 servings*

1½ pounds beef stew meat

Salt and freshly ground pepper

2 tablespoons vegetable oil

1 carrot, shredded

1 clove garlic, or 1 small onion, chopped

¼ teaspoon oregano leaves

½ cup burgundy or other dry red wine

1 beef bouillon cube

1 cup boiling water

1 tablespoon flour

2 tablespoons water

Season the meat with salt and pepper. Brown the meat in hot oil on all sides in a Dutch oven. Add the carrot, garlic, oregano and wine. Cook over high heat for 2 minutes. Add the bouillon cube and boiling water. Bring to a boil. Reduce heat. Simmer, covered, for 2 hours or until meat is tender, stirring occasionally, and adding additional water as needed. Dissolve the flour in the 2 tablespoons water in a cup. Stir into the meat mixture. Cook until bubbly and thickened. Serve with noodles. Garnish with chopped parsley.

Approx Per Serving: Cal 228; Prot 22 g; Carbo 3 g; T Fat 12 g; 50% Calories from Fat; Chol 70 mg; Fiber <1 g; Sod 356 mg

Ginger Beef Stir-Fry   *Yield: 2 servings*

8 ounces beef flank steak, cut crosswise into strips

4 tablespoons soy sauce, divided

5 teaspoons cornstarch, divided

3 teaspoons sugar, divided

½ cup plus 1 teaspoon water, divided

½ teaspoon instant beef bouillon

½ teaspoon salt

2 tablespoons vegetable oil, divided

1 slice gingerroot, crushed

1 cup chopped celery

1 cup chopped green bell pepper

1 cup coarsely chopped onion

1 large tomato, chopped

This recipe was shared during a Chinese cooking class at the Honolulu YWCA in the 1960s. It's just as tasty today.

Place the steak in a sealable plastic bag. Combine 2 tablespoons of the soy sauce, 2 teaspoons of the cornstarch, 1 teaspoon of the sugar and 1 teaspoon of the water in a bowl and mix until smooth. Pour over the steak and seal the bag. Let stand for 15 minutes. Combine the remaining 2 tablespoons soy sauce, remaining 3 teaspoons cornstarch, remaining 2 teaspoons sugar, instant bouillon, salt and remaining ½ cup water in a separate bowl and mix until smooth. Drain the steak.

Heat 1 tablespoon of the oil in a wok. Add the gingerroot and steak. Cook until steak is medium rare, stirring constantly. Remove from wok. Add the remaining 1 tablespoon oil, celery, green pepper and onion. Cook until tender-crisp, stirring constantly. Stir in the soy sauce mixture. Bring to a boil. Stir in the cooked steak and gingerroot and tomato. Cook until heated through. Serve with rice.

Approx Per Serving: Cal 454; Prot 29 g; Carbo 33 g; T Fat 23 g; 45% Calories from Fat; Chol 59 mg; Fiber 5 g; Sod 3566 mg

Corned beef is a cured beef product usually made with fresh beef brisket or beef round and cured with spices added to a salt brine. Corned beef tastes slightly salty and has a deep red color. Preserving beef by "corning" was a necessity before refrigeration. Granular salt the size of wheat kernels—corn to the British—was used in the process. Today, beef is corned for flavor rather than preservation.

Corned Beef Ring with Mustard Sauce
Yield: 6 servings

1 (6-ounce) package scalloped potato mix

2½ cups boiling water

1 tablespoon margarine or butter

1½ teaspoons dry mustard

1 teaspoon prepared horseradish

2 (12-ounce) cans corned beef, chopped

2 eggs, beaten

2 cups soft bread crumbs

Mustard Sauce

Preheat oven to 350 degrees. Combine the potato mix, boiling water, margarine, mustard and horseradish in a bowl and mix well. Combine the corned beef, eggs and bread crumbs in a separate bowl and mix well. Stir in the potato mixture gently. Press into a lightly buttered 6-cup ring mold or 5x9-inch loaf pan. Bake for 45 to 50 minutes. Serve with Mustard Sauce.

Approx Per Serving: Cal 422; Prot 36 g; Carbo 27 g; T Fat 20 g; 42% Calories from Fat; Chol 174 mg; Fiber 3 g; Sod 1524 mg

Mustard Sauce   *Yield: 6 (¹/₃-cup) servings*

¹/₃ cup margarine or butter

¹/₄ cup flour

2 tablespoons prepared mustard

2 teaspoons prepared horseradish

1½ teaspoons salt

¹/₈ teaspoon cayenne

1 teaspoon dried minced onion

2 cups milk

1 tablespoon lemon juice

Melt the margarine in a saucepan. Stir in the flour, mustard, horseradish, salt, cayenne, onion and milk. Cook over medium heat until of the desired consistency, stirring constantly. Stir in the lemon juice.

Approx Per Serving: Cal 161; Prot 3 g; Carbo 8 g; T Fat 13 g; 70% Calories from Fat; Chol 11 mg; Fiber <1 g; Sod 763 mg

Hoosier Meatloaf   *Yield: 6 servings*

1¹/2 pounds lean ground beef

*1 cup tomato juice or
    vegetable juice cocktail*

1 cup quick-cooking oats

1 egg

¹/2 cup finely chopped onion

*1 tablespoon Worcestershire
    sauce*

*1¹/2 teaspoons reduced-sodium
    instant beef bouillon*

1 teaspoon garlic powder

¹/2 teaspoon pepper

¹/2 cup ketchup

3 slices bacon, cut into halves

Combine the ground beef, tomato juice, oats, egg, onion, Worcestershire sauce, instant bouillon, garlic powder and pepper in a large bowl and mix well. Shape into a loaf in a shallow pan. Spread the ketchup over the loaf. Arrange bacon on top. Bake at 350 degrees for 1 hour or until cooked through. Let stand for 5 minutes.

Cheeseburger Meatloaf
Substitute 6 slices of American cheese for the ketchup and bacon. Combine loaf ingredients as above. Shape half of the ground beef mixture into a thin loaf in a shallow pan. Cut 3 slices of American cheese into strips. Arrange the strips in the center of the loaf, leaving ¹/2 inch uncovered on each edge. Top with remaining ground beef mixture, pressing the edges together to seal. Bake at 350 degrees for 55 to 60 minutes or until cooked through. Cut 3 slices of American cheese in half diagonally. Arrange over the top of the meatloaf. Bake for 3 minutes or until cheese begins to melt.

Tex-Mex Meatloaf
Substitute 1 cup prepared salsa and 1 cup crushed corn chips for the tomato juice, oats, Worcestershire sauce, ketchup and bacon. Add 1 teaspoon chili powder and 1 teaspoon ground cumin if desired. Spread ¹/3 to ¹/2 cup salsa over the meatloaf before baking.

Approx Per Serving: Cal 379; Prot 30 g; Carbo 20 g; T Fat 19 g; 46% Calories from Fat; Chol 119 mg; Fiber 2 g; Sod 547 mg

Indiana is very diversified in cattle production. The southern half of the state has some of the best cow/calf land in the nation with farms supplying feeder calves for many other states. The northern part of Indiana, with its abundance of feed grain, is ideal for feedlot finishing. Beef continues to be one of the most popular meats with Hoosier consumers—for its versatility, great taste, and nutritional value. And the all-American hamburger reigns as an all-time favorite.

Mushroom Salisbury Steak   *Yield: 6 servings*

1 (10-ounce) can beefy
    mushroom soup, divided
1¹/₂ pounds ground beef
¹/₂ cup dry bread crumbs
1 egg, beaten
¹/₄ cup finely chopped onion
¹/₈ teaspoon pepper
¹/₄ cup water

Combine ¹/₄ cup of the soup, ground beef, bread crumbs, egg, onion and pepper in a bowl and mix well. Shape into 6 patties. Brown the patties on both sides in an ovenproof skillet; drain. Combine the remaining soup and water in a bowl and mix well. Pour over the browned patties. Bake, covered, at 350 degrees for 30 minutes or until hot and bubbly and patties are cooked through. Serve with mashed potatoes or noodles.

Approx Per Serving: Cal 328; Prot 29 g; Carbo 10 g; T Fat 18 g; 51% Calories from Fat; Chol 119 mg; Fiber <1 g; Sod 549 mg

Pecan-Breaded Lamb Chops   *Yield: 3 servings*

1 egg white
1 tablespoon honey mustard
¹/₂ cup chopped pecans
¹/₂ cup cracker crumbs
6 lamb loin chops
2 tablespoons vegetable oil

Beat the egg white in a bowl until frothy. Stir in the mustard. Combine the pecans and cracker crumbs in a shallow dish and mix well. Dip each lamb chop in the mustard mixture and roll in the pecan mixture. Cook the lamb chops in hot oil in a skillet for 10 minutes on each side or until done to taste.

Approx Per Serving: Cal 594; Prot 32 g; Carbo 16 g; T Fat 34 g; 62% Calories from Fat; Chol 87 mg; Fiber 2 g; Sod 308 mg

Lamb Stir-Fry   *Yield: 4 servings*

2 tablespoons cornstarch

1/2 cup chicken broth

1/4 cup soy sauce

1/2 teaspoon ginger

1 tablespoon minced garlic

1 pound lamb cubes or lamb,
    thinly sliced

2 tablespoons vegetable oil

1 medium onion, sliced

1 green bell pepper, sliced

Combine the cornstarch, broth, soy sauce, ginger and garlic in a bowl and mix well. Pour over the lamb cubes in a shallow dish. Let stand for 10 minutes. Drain the lamb reserving the marinade. Cook the lamb in hot oil in a wok for 3 minutes, stirring constantly. Move the lamb to the side of the wok. Add the onion and green pepper. Cook until vegetables are tender-crisp, stirring constantly. Pour in the reserved marinade. Cook until the mixture is of the desired consistency, stirring constantly. Steam, covered, for 2 to 3 minutes. Serve with rice.

Variations: May add other vegetables as desired.

Approx Per Serving: Cal 275; Prot 27 g; Carbo 11 g; T Fat 13 g; 44% Calories from Fat; Chol 77 mg; Fiber 1 g; Sod 1479 mg

Honey Mustard Pork Tenderloin   *Yield: 2 servings*

1/4 cup vegetable oil

2 tablespoons brown sugar

2 tablespoons honey

2 tablespoons lemon juice

1 tablespoon Dijon mustard

2 teaspoons instant beef or
    chicken bouillon

1 (3/4- to 1-pound) pork
    tenderloin

Combine the oil, brown sugar, honey, lemon juice, mustard and instant bouillon in a bowl and mix well. Pour over the tenderloin in a shallow dish. Marinate, covered, in the refrigerator for 6 hours or longer. Drain the tenderloin, reserving the marinade. Pour the marinade into a saucepan. Bring to a boil. Remove from heat. Grill the tenderloin over hot coals for 30 to 35 minutes or until it reaches 160 degrees on a meat thermometer, basting frequently with the marinade. Let stand for 10 minutes before slicing.

Approx Per Serving: Cal 655; Prot 49 g; Carbo 34 g; T Fat 36 g; 50% Calories from Fat; Chol 135 mg; Fiber <1 g; Sod 1155 mg

Today's pork isn't the meat that inspired phrases like "fat as a hog" and "eat like a pig." It has an average of 31% less fat, 14% fewer calories and 10% less cholesterol than the pork our parents and grandparents ate when they were young. Several cuts of pork are comparable to skinless chicken in calories and fat.

 ## Grilled Sweet & Sour Pork   *Yield: 6 servings*

6 thick pork chops or pork
   steaks
1/2 cup teriyaki sauce
1/2 cup water
1/4 cup vinegar
1/4 cup packed brown sugar
1/4 cup sugar
1/4 cup cornstarch
1/2 cup pineapple juice
1 cup chopped celery
1 medium onion, chopped
2 tablespoons vegetable oil
1 green bell pepper, chopped
1 or 2 firm tomatoes, chopped
6 cups hot cooked rice

Arrange the pork chops in a shallow dish. Pour the teriyaki sauce over the pork chops. Marinate, covered, in the refrigerator for 1 hour or longer. Combine the water, vinegar, brown sugar and sugar in a saucepan. Bring to a boil. Combine the cornstarch and juice in a bowl and mix until smooth. Pour into the sugar mixture. Cook until of the desired consistency, stirring constantly. Remove from heat and keep warm. Drain the pork chops. Grill over hot coals until cooked through, turning once. Remove from grill. Cut into small pieces and keep warm. Cook the celery and onion in hot oil in a small skillet until tender-crisp. Stir in the green pepper and tomato. Cook until heated through. Divide the rice among 6 plates. Arrange tomato mixture over the rice. Arrange the meat over the tomato mixture. Spoon the sauce over the top.

Approx Per Serving: Cal 520; Prot 27 g; Carbo 79 g; T Fat 10 g; 18% Calories from Fat; Chol 51 mg; Fiber 2 g; Sod 990 mg

Cranberry Orange Chops   *Yield: 6 servings*

1/2 to 1 teaspoon seasoned salt
6 (4-ounce) boneless pork loin
   chops
1/2 small red onion,
   thinly sliced
1 (12-ounce) container
   cranberry-orange
   crushed fruit
1 tablespoon honey
6 cups hot cooked rice

Sprinkle the salt on both sides of the pork chops. Brown with the onion in a skillet coated with nonstick cooking spray over medium-high heat. Turn the chops. Stir in the crushed fruit and honey. Bring to a boil. Simmer, covered, for 10 minutes or until chops are cooked through. Serve the pork chop mixture over the rice.

Approx Per Serving: Cal 462; Prot 27 g; Carbo 72 g; T Fat 6 g; 12% Calories from Fat; Chol 57 mg; Fiber 2 g; Sod 230 mg

Pork Medallions L'Orange   *Yield: 6 servings*

1¹/2 pounds pork tenderloin

¹/4 teaspoon salt

¹/4 teaspoon freshly ground
    pepper

¹/2 cup flour

¹/4 cup butter

¹/4 cup olive oil

¹/2 teaspoon tarragon

¹/4 cup frozen orange juice
    concentrate, thawed

¹/4 cup dry sherry

1 cup light sour cream

Cut the tenderloin into ¹/2-inch thick slices. Pound to ¹/8-inch thickness.
Sprinkle with the salt and pepper. Coat with the flour, shaking off the
excess. Heat the butter and olive oil in a skillet until bubbly. Add the
tenderloins. Cook over medium-high heat for 2 to 3 minutes on each
side or until browned. Remove and keep warm. Stir the tarragon, orange
juice concentrate and sherry into the skillet. Scrape the bottom of the
skillet to loosen the cooked particles. Cook over medium heat until liquid
is reduced by half. Reduce the heat to low. Stir in the sour cream. Cook
for 2 minutes or until heated through; do not boil. Return the tenderloins
to the skillet. Cook for 2 minutes, turning to coat both sides. Arrange
on a serving platter. Pour sauce over the tenderloins. Garnish with
orange slices.

Approx Per Serving: Cal 404; Prot 28 g; Carbo 15 g; T Fat 24 g; 55% Calories from Fat;
Chol 101 mg; Fiber <1 g; Sod 251 mg

Grilled Country Ribs   *Yield: 10 servings*

6 to 8 pounds country-style
    pork ribs

1 bay leaf

1 onion

Salt and freshly ground pepper

Thyme leaves

1 cup apricot or peach
    preserves

1 cup ketchup or
    barbecue sauce

¹/2 cup chopped onion

¹/2 cup packed brown sugar

¹/4 cup prepared mustard

3 tablespoons Worcestershire
    sauce

2 tablespoons lemon juice

1 tablespoon minced garlic

¹/8 teaspoon hot pepper sauce

Place the ribs in a large kettle. Cover with water. Add the bay leaf, onion,
salt, pepper and thyme. Bring to a boil. Reduce the heat. Simmer, covered,
for 45 to 60 minutes or until tender. Remove the ribs. Refrigerate,
covered, until ready to use. Combine the preserves, ketchup, chopped
onion, brown sugar, mustard, Worcestershire sauce, lemon juice, garlic and
hot pepper sauce in a saucepan. Simmer for 20 to 30 minutes, stirring
occasionally. Trim the fat from the ribs. Brush with the sauce. Place on a
grill rack coated with nonstick cooking spray. Grill over hot coals for 5 to
8 minutes or until heated through, turning and brushing frequently with
the sauce.

Approx Per Serving: Cal 536; Prot 43 g; Carbo 41 g; T Fat 22 g; 37% Calories from Fat;
Chol 140 mg; Fiber 1 g; Sod 484 mg

The Butcher's Ham Loaf   *Yield: 8 servings*

1¼ pounds ground pork

¾ pound ground smoked ham

¼ pound ground beef

1 cup cracker crumbs

1 (8-ounce) can tomato sauce

1 egg

½ cup finely chopped onion (optional)

Brown Sugar Glaze or Golden Glaze (optional)

Horseradish Cream (optional)

The proportions of meat in this ham loaf recipe were created by the butcher in a small grocery store in Spencer County. This ham loaf was a favorite of his sons and has since been passed on to mothers-in-law, aunts and other relatives.

Preheat oven to 350 degrees. Combine the pork, ham, beef, cracker crumbs, tomato sauce, egg and onion in a bowl and mix together. Shape into a loaf and place in a shallow baking pan. Bake for 40 minutes. Top with the Brown Sugar Glaze or half of the Golden Glaze. Bake for 30 minutes or until cooked through. Let stand for 10 minutes. Serve with remaining half of the Golden Glaze or Horseradish Cream.

Tip: Ham loaf may be served cold. Refrigerate, covered, until ready to serve.

Approx Per Serving: Cal 289; Prot 23 g; Carbo 11 g; T Fat 17 g; 52% Calories from Fat; Chol 97 mg; Fiber 1 g; Sod 748 mg

Brown Sugar Glaze

½ cup ketchup

3 tablespoons brown sugar

2 teaspoons prepared mustard

Combine the ketchup and brown sugar in a bowl and mix well. Stir in the prepared mustard.

Approx Per Serving: Cal 98; Prot <1 g; Carbo 26 g; T Fat <1 g; 1% Calories from Fat; Chol 0 mg; Fiber 1 g; Sod 23 mg

Golden Glaze

1 cup apricot, peach or pineapple preserves or orange marmalade

2 tablespoons lemon juice

1 tablespoon prepared mustard

Combine the apricot preserves and lemon juice in a bowl and mix well. Stir in the prepared mustard.

Approx Per Serving: Cal 35; Prot <1 g; Carbo 9 g; T Fat <1 g; 1% Calories from Fat; Chol 0 mg; Fiber <1 g; Sod 188 mg

Horseradish Cream

1 cup whipping cream

⅓ cup prepared horseradish

1 teaspoon salt

Whip the whipping cream in a mixer bowl until stiff peaks form. Stir in the horseradish and salt.

Approx Per Serving: Cal 103; Prot 1 g; Carbo 2 g; T Fat 11 g; 90% Calories from Fat; Chol 39 mg; Fiber <1 g; Sod 333 mg

Skillet Venison   *Yield: 4 servings*

2 pounds venison strips

1/4 cup water

1 medium onion, chopped

1 cup tomato juice

1 (4-ounce) can mushrooms

1/2 jalapeño (optional)

4 cups hot cooked rice

Combine the venison, water and onion in a Dutch oven. Cook over medium heat until venison reaches desired degree of doneness. Stir in the tomato juice, mushrooms and jalapeño. Simmer, covered, over low heat until mixture is heated through. Divide rice among 4 plates. Arrange the venison mixture over the rice. Season with salt and pepper to taste.

Approx Per Serving: Cal 502; Prot 57 g; Carbo 51 g; T Fat 6 g; 11% Calories from Fat; Chol 191 mg; Fiber 2 g; Sod 434 mg

Barbecued Chicken Breasts   *Yield: 4 servings*

1/4 cup ketchup

3 tablespoons cider vinegar

1 tablespoon prepared horseradish

2 teaspoons brown sugar

1 clove garlic, minced

1/8 teaspoon thyme

1/4 teaspoon pepper

4 boneless skinless chicken breasts

Combine the ketchup, vinegar, horseradish, brown sugar, garlic, thyme and pepper in a saucepan. Bring to a boil over medium-low heat. Cook for 5 minutes or until thickened, stirring frequently. Brush the tops of the chicken breasts with sauce. Place the chicken, sauce side down, on a grill rack. Brush chicken with sauce. Grill 3 inches from the hot coals for 5 to 7 minutes on each side or until cooked through, basting with the sauce. Let stand for 5 minutes.

Approx Per Serving: Cal 313; Prot 54 g; Carbo 8 g; T Fat 6 g; 19% Calories from Fat; Chol 146 mg; Fiber <1 g; Sod 322 mg

Poultry and egg production generates over 9.9% of the total farm income in Indiana. The state ranks seventh in the production of turkeys and third in U.S. egg production. One of the largest egg producers is Rose Acre Farms in Jackson County. Indiana leads the nation in the hatchery business as the largest producer of egg-type chicks.

Uncooked chicken should be refrigerated promptly after it is purchased and then used within 2 days. Cut-up, cooked chicken can be stored in the refrigerator for up to 2 days and a whole cooked chicken for up to 3 days.

Chicken Dijon   *Yield: 4 servings*

⅓ cup plus 1 tablespoon flour, divided

¼ teaspoon paprika

2 cups half-and-half

2 tablespoons Dijon mustard

¾ teaspoon rosemary leaves

¾ teaspoon thyme leaves

2 teaspoons instant chicken bouillon

4 boneless skinless chicken breast halves

¼ cup vegetable oil

1 cup sliced mushrooms

¾ cup chopped onion

¾ cup chopped red bell pepper

6 cups hot cooked noodles

Combine ⅓ cup flour and paprika in a shallow bowl and mix well. Mix the next 5 ingredients in a bowl. Dip the chicken in the half-and-half mixture. Coat with the flour mixture. Cook in hot oil in a skillet until cooked through. Remove from the pan and keep warm. Add the mushrooms and onion to the pan. Cook until tender. Stir in the remaining 1 tablespoon flour. Add the half-and-half mixture. Simmer for 10 minutes or until thickened, stirring constantly. Stir in the red pepper. Cook for 5 minutes. Divide the noodles among 4 plates. Place 1 chicken breast on each plate. Spoon the sauce over the chicken.

Approx Per Serving: Cal 963; Prot 71 g; Carbo 81 g; T Fat 38 g; 36% Calories from Fat; Chol 270 mg; Fiber 4 g; Sod 961 mg

Herbed Chicken   *Yield: 6 servings*

6 boneless skinless chicken breast halves

Salt and freshly ground pepper

¼ cup butter or margarine

1 (10-ounce) can cream of chicken soup

¾ cup dry white wine or water

1 (8-ounce) can water chestnuts, drained

1 (3-ounce) can mushrooms, drained

2 tablespoons chopped green bell pepper

¼ teaspoon thyme

Season the chicken with salt and pepper. Brown in butter in a skillet, turning once. Remove from the skillet. Arrange in a shallow baking pan. Add the soup to the skillet, stirring until smooth. Stir in the wine, water chestnuts, mushrooms, green pepper and thyme. Bring to a boil. Spoon over the chicken. Bake, covered, at 350 degrees for 25 minutes. Bake, uncovered, for 25 minutes longer. Serve with rice.

Approx Per Serving: Cal 442; Prot 55 g; Carbo 10 g; T Fat 17 g; 35% Calories from Fat; Chol 171 mg; Fiber 2 g; Sod 671 mg

Special Lemony Chicken   *Yield: 6 servings*

¼ cup flour

1 teaspoon instant chicken bouillon

¼ teaspoon pepper

6 boneless skinless chicken breast halves

¼ cup margarine or butter

¼ cup lemon juice

8 ounces mushrooms, sliced

6 cups hot cooked rice

Combine the flour, instant bouillon and pepper in a sealable plastic bag. Add the chicken, a few pieces at a time, and shake to coat. Brown the chicken in margarine in a skillet, turning once. Add the lemon juice and mushrooms. Reduce the heat. Simmer, covered, for 15 minutes or until the chicken is cooked through. Divide the rice among 6 plates. Place 1 cooked chicken breast over the rice. Spoon the sauce over the chicken.

Approx Per Serving: Cal 589; Prot 60 g; Carbo 51 g; T Fat 14 g; 22% Calories from Fat; Chol 146 mg; Fiber 1 g; Sod 410 mg

Buttermilk Picnic Chicken   *Yield: 8 servings*

¾ cup buttermilk

2 teaspoons reduced-sodium instant chicken bouillon

1 teaspoon poultry seasoning

3 to 4 pounds chicken pieces

1 cup flour

1 tablespoon paprika

2 teaspoons seasoned salt

¼ teaspoon pepper

¼ cup butter or margarine, melted

Try this easy oven "fried" chicken for your next pitch-in party, church gathering or tailgate picnic. The buttermilk and seasonings give the chicken coating its savory goodness. Use whatever chicken pieces your family prefers. How about all drumsticks for the next Cub Scout supper? The coating works well on boneless skinless chicken breasts, too.

Combine the buttermilk, instant bouillon and poultry seasoning in a bowl. Let stand for 10 minutes. Add the chicken, stirring to coat. Marinate, if desired, in the refrigerator for 8 to 12 hours. Preheat the oven to 350 degrees. Drain the chicken. Combine the flour, paprika, salt and pepper in a sealable plastic bag. Add the chicken, a few pieces at a time and shake to coat. Arrange in a 9x13-inch baking dish. Drizzle the butter over the chicken. Bake, uncovered, for 1 hour or until golden.

Tip: For boneless chicken breasts or tenders, increase oven temperature to 375 degrees; bake for 20 to 30 minutes or until juices run clear.

Approx Per Serving: Cal 284; Prot 27 g; Carbo 14 g; T Fat 13 g; 41% Calories from Fat; Chol 88 mg; Fiber 1 g; Sod 386 mg

Company Chicken   *Yield: 4 servings*

1/4 cup butter

1 tablespoon vegetable oil

2 1/2 to 3 pounds chicken pieces

8 ounces mushrooms, sliced

1 tablespoon flour

1 (10-ounce) can cream of
   chicken soup

1 cup dry white wine

1 cup water

1/2 cup whipping cream

1 teaspoon salt

1/4 teaspoon pepper

6 green onions, chopped

2 tablespoons chopped parsley

Preheat oven to 350 degrees. Melt the butter and oil in a large skillet. Add the chicken. Brown on all sides, turning frequently. Remove the chicken and arrange in a 9x13-inch baking pan. Add the mushrooms to the skillet. Cook for 5 minutes or until tender. Stir in the flour. Add the soup, wine and water. Cook for 10 minutes or until sauce thickens, stirring constantly. Stir in the cream, salt and pepper. Pour over the chicken. Bake for 1 hour. Stir in the green onions and parsley. Bake for an additional 5 minutes or until chicken is tender. Serve with hot cooked noodles or rice.

Approx Per Serving: Cal 612; Prot 41 g; Carbo 12 g; T Fat 40 g; 59% Calories from Fat; Chol 186 mg; Fiber 1 g; Sod 1424 mg

Oriental Glazed Duckling   *Yield: 4 servings*

1 (5-pound) frozen duckling,
   thawed

1/4 cup teriyaki sauce

1/4 cup orange marmalade

1 tablespoon prepared
   horseradish

Preheat oven to 350 degrees. Place the duckling, breast side up, on a rack in a roasting pan. Roast for 2 hours and 15 minutes. Combine the teriyaki sauce, marmalade and horseradish in a bowl and mix well. Spoon over the duckling. Roast for an additional 15 to 20 minutes or until it reaches 160 degrees on a meat thermometer, basting occasionally. Let stand for 5 minutes. Serve with hot cooked rice.

Approx Per Serving: Cal 836; Prot 45 g; Carbo 17 g; T Fat 65 g; 70% Calories from Fat; Chol 192 mg; Fiber <1 g; Sod 848 mg

Ostrich Meatballs Italian-Style   *Yield: 6 servings*

1 pound ground ostrich

1 cup grated Parmesan cheese

1/2 cup finely chopped onion

3 cloves garlic, minced, or
  1 teaspoon garlic powder

2/3 cup fresh bread crumbs

1/4 cup chopped fresh parsley

1/4 cup dry red wine or sherry

3 tablespoons olive oil

2 (28-ounce) jars pasta sauce

1 (1-pound) package thin
  spaghetti

The U.S. ostrich industry is expanding rapidly as consumers learn about the flavor which is similar to beef. This lean dark meat is versatile and very low in fat. Ostrich is often featured on the menus of more upscale restaurants and is beginning to be available at retail. In Indiana, ostrich producers can be found throughout the state and often can direct consumers to supermarkets and butchers who carry this meat. Here's an interesting way to try ostrich.

Combine the ostrich, Parmesan cheese, onion, garlic, bread crumbs, parsley and wine in a bowl and mix well. Shape into 1 1/2-inch balls. Brown on all sides in hot oil in a skillet. Add the pasta sauce. Simmer for 30 minutes or longer. Cook the spaghetti using the package directions; drain. Divide the cooked spaghetti among 6 plates. Arrange the meatballs and sauce over the spaghetti. Serve with additional Parmesan cheese.

Approx Per Serving: Cal 696; Prot 43 g;
Carbo 80 g; T Fat 21 g; 27% Calories from Fat;
Chol 59 mg; Fiber 8 g; Sod 1945 mg

Indiana produces more ducks than any other state in the nation. Headquartered in Milford, Maple Leaf Farms is the international leader in the duckling industry, producing more than 15 million ducks in 1998, primarily sold to the restaurant, hotel, and food-service markets. Culver Duck Farms in Middlebury produces 2 million ducks annually. Frozen whole duckling is the most available form at the supermarket. Continual improvements in the breeding and feeding of domestic ducks have resulted in a lean, meaty product with less fat than ever before. Duckling should be cooked to an internal temperature of 165 degrees for medium and 180 degrees for well done. Unlike chicken or turkey, properly prepared duckling will be pink inside.

Neapolitan Turkey Rolls   *Yield: 6 servings*

1 green bell pepper, cut into
    thin strips

1 red bell pepper, cut into
    thin strips

1 clove garlic, finely chopped

3 tablespoons olive oil, divided

6 (4-ounce) turkey breast slices

Salt and freshly ground pepper

3 ounces Swiss cheese, cut into
    12 strips

1 (26-ounce) jar pasta sauce

3¹/₂ cups hot cooked linguini
    or rotini

Cook the green pepper, red pepper and garlic in 2 tablespoons of the oil in a skillet until tender-crisp. Remove from the pan. Pound each turkey breast until thin. Season with salt and pepper. Place 1 strip of green pepper and red pepper and 2 strips of cheese on each turkey slice. Roll tightly and secure with a wooden pick. Heat the remaining 1 tablespoon oil in the skillet. Brown the turkey rolls over medium-high heat. Add the pasta sauce and remaining green peppers and red peppers. Reduce the heat. Simmer, covered, for 10 minutes or until heated through. Divide the pasta among 6 plates. Remove the picks from the turkey rolls. Arrange the turkey rolls and sauce over the pasta.

Approx Per Serving: Cal 484; Prot 41 g; Carbo 45 g; T Fat 15 g; 28% Calories from Fat; Chol 95 mg; Fiber 5 g; Sod 833 mg

Turkey Meatball Tetrazzini   *Yield: 4 servings*

1 slice whole wheat bread

³/₄ pound ground turkey

1 clove garlic, pressed

¹/₂ teaspoon basil leaves

¹/₂ teaspoon salt

Freshly ground pepper

1 teaspoon butter

1 medium onion, sliced

4 ounces mushrooms, sliced

2 tablespoons flour

1¹/₂ cups milk

¹/₄ cup grated Parmesan
    cheese

6 cups hot cooked angel hair
    pasta or noodles

Crumble the bread into a bowl. Add the turkey, garlic, basil, salt and pepper and mix well. Shape into 1-inch balls. Melt the butter in a large skillet. Add the meatballs. Brown on all sides. Stir in the onion and mushrooms. Cook until golden. Whisk the flour into the milk in a small bowl until smooth. Pour into the skillet. Cook until thickened, stirring constantly. Stir in the cheese. Place the pasta on a serving plate. Spoon the meatballs and sauce over the pasta. Serve with additional Parmesan cheese.

Approx Per Serving: Cal 581; Prot 35 g; Carbo 74 g; T Fat 16 g; 25% Calories from Fat; Chol 82 mg; Fiber 5 g; Sod 566 mg

Crispy Oven Fish   *Yield: 4 servings*

*2¹/₂ cups finely crushed
potato chips*

*¹/₂ cup grated Parmesan
cheese*

2 tablespoons chopped parsley

*¹/₂ cup mayonnaise or
salad dressing*

¹/₄ cup lemon juice, divided

*1 pound fish fillets, fresh
or frozen, thawed and
patted dry*

Preheat oven to 400 degrees. Combine the chips, cheese and parsley in a shallow dish and mix well. Combine the mayonnaise and 2 tablespoons of the lemon juice in a separate shallow dish and mix well. Place the remaining 2 tablespoons lemon juice in a separate shallow dish. Dip each fillet in the lemon juice, mayonnaise mixture and potato chip mixture. Arrange the coated fillets in a greased baking dish. Bake for 5 to 10 minutes or until fillets flake easily when tested with a fork.

Approx Per Serving: Cal 541; Prot 27 g; Carbo 20 g; T Fat 39 g; 65% Calories from Fat; Chol 83 mg; Fiber 2 g; Sod 674 mg

If you have questions about fish, call this toll-free Fish Hot Line of the American Seafood Institute, Wakefield, Rhode Island, from 9 a.m. to 5 p.m. Eastern Standard Time. The number is 1-800-EAT-FISH.

Fish and Vegetable Oven Dinner   *Yield: 4 servings*

*4 small baking potatoes,
thinly sliced*

3 cups thinly sliced onions

*1 teaspoon lemon-pepper
seasoning*

¹/₂ teaspoon salt

¹/₂ teaspoon dried dillweed

1 cup thinly sliced carrots

*4 (4-ounce) fish fillets, such
as halibut, cod, haddock,
grouper, snapper or tilapia*

Preheat oven to 450 degrees. Cut four 18-inch squares of heavy-duty aluminum foil. Coat 1 side of each with nonstick cooking spray. Arrange potato and onion slices evenly in centers of foil squares. Combine the lemon-pepper, salt and dillweed in a bowl and mix well. Sprinkle ¹/₃ of the mixture over the potato layers. Layer the carrot slices over the lemon-pepper mixture. Sprinkle with the remaining lemon-pepper mixture. Place a fillet over the layers. Fold the foil over the layers and crimp to seal the edges. Place the foil packets on a baking sheet. Bake for 30 to 35 minutes or until fish flakes easily when tested with a fork.

Approx Per Serving: Cal 338; Prot 18 g; Carbo 34 g; T Fat 14 g; 38% Calories from Fat; Chol 47 mg; Fiber 5 g; Sod 509 mg

Increasingly, many types of fish and seafood are being farm raised, including catfish, trout, and salmon. In Indiana, aquaculture is growing as producers supply quality fish to local and regional restaurants and supermarkets. Indiana also is home to one of the nation's finest aquaculture vocational training facilities located at South Putnam High School and state-of-the-art research facilities at Purdue University.

Salmon Potato Patties with Dill Sauce

Yield: 4 servings

1 (15-ounce) can salmon

½ cup Italian-seasoned dry bread crumbs

1 cup cold mashed cooked potatoes

1 tablespoon chopped fresh parsley

Salt and freshly ground pepper

1 tablespoon dried minced onion

2 eggs, beaten

¼ cup milk

2 tablespoons vegetable oil

Dill Sauce

Drain the salmon and remove the bones. Combine the salmon, bread crumbs, potatoes, parsley, salt, pepper, onion, eggs and milk in a bowl and mix well. Shape into 4 patties. Cook in hot oil in a skillet until brown on each side, turning once. Serve with Dill Sauce.

Approx Per Serving: Cal 368; Prot 27 g; Carbo 21 g; T Fat 20 g; 48% Calories from Fat; Chol 177 mg; Fiber 1 g; Sod 847 mg

Dill Sauce   *Yield: 4 (¼-cup) servings*

½ cup mayonnaise

½ cup sour cream

½ teaspoon lemon juice

1 teaspoon chopped fresh parsley

1 teaspoon chopped fresh dill

Combine the mayonnaise, sour cream, lemon juice, parsley and dill in a bowl and mix well. Refrigerate, covered, for 4 hours or longer.

Approx Per Serving: Cal 262; Prot 1 g; Carbo 1 g; T Fat 28 g; 97% Calories from Fat; Chol 33 mg; Fiber <1 g; Sod 166 mg

Savory Fish Roll-Ups

Yield: 4 servings

1 cup shredded carrots

1 cup shredded zucchini

2 tablespoons finely chopped
   onion

1/2 cup fresh bread crumbs

1/8 teaspoon thyme leaves

1/4 cup margarine or butter,
   melted

1/4 cup lemon juice

4 fish fillets, fresh or frozen,
   thawed

Preheat the oven to 375 degrees. Combine the carrots, zucchini, onion, bread crumbs and thyme in a bowl and mix well. Combine the margarine and lemon juice in a separate bowl and mix well. Add 1/4 cup to the carrot mixture and mix well. Place the fillets in a shallow baking dish. Top each with equal amounts of the carrot mixture. Roll up and secure with a wooden pick. Pour the remaining margarine mixture over the fish. Bake for 15 minutes or until fish flakes easily when tested with a fork.

Approx Per Serving: Cal 292; Prot 33 g; Carbo 9 g; T Fat 14 g; 42% Calories from Fat; Chol 87 mg; Fiber 2 g; Sod 307 mg

Scampi-Style Shrimp

Yield: 4 servings

2 tablespoons margarine
   or butter

2 tablespoons olive oil or
   vegetable oil

2 tablespoons sliced
   green onions

4 cloves garlic, finely chopped

1 pound medium shrimp,
   peeled, deveined

1/4 cup lemon juice

1/8 teaspoon salt

Combine the margarine and oil in a skillet. Cook over medium-high heat until margarine is melted. Add the green onions and garlic. Cook for 1 minute, stirring constantly. Add the shrimp. Cook for 3 minutes or until the shrimp turn pink, stirring constantly. Stir in the lemon juice and salt. Cook until heated through. Garnish with chopped parsley.

Approx Per Serving: Cal 188; Prot 15 g; Carbo 3 g; T Fat 13 g; 63% Calories from Fat; Chol 135 mg; Fiber <1 g; Sod 295 mg

Mediterranean Marinade   *Yield: 4 (¹/₄-cup) servings*

¹/₃ cup olive oil or vegetable oil

¹/₄ cup lemon juice

3 tablespoons dry sherry
   or water

2 teaspoons rosemary, crushed

2 cloves garlic, finely chopped

1¹/₂ teaspoons instant chicken
   bouillon

Combine the oil, lemon juice, sherry, rosemary, garlic and instant bouillon in a bowl and mix well. Pour over chicken, pork or beef in a shallow dish. Marinate, covered, in the refrigerator for 4 hours or longer, turning occasionally. Drain, reserving the marinade. Pour the marinade into a saucepan. Bring to a boil. Cook the meat as desired, basting frequently with the hot marinade.

Approx Per ¹/₄ Cup: Cal 176; Prot <1 g; Carbo 2 g; T Fat 18 g; 90% Calories from Fat; Chol <1 mg; Fiber <1 g; Sod 433 mg

Sesame Soy Marinade   *Yield: 5 (¹/₄-cup) servings*

1 cup soy sauce

2 tablespoons sesame oil

1 tablespoon peanut oil

1 to 2 tablespoons
   minced garlic

1 teaspoon minced ginger

Combine the soy sauce, sesame oil, peanut oil, garlic and ginger in a bowl and mix well. Pour over chicken, turkey or game hens in a shallow dish. Marinate, covered, in the refrigerator for 30 minutes or longer, turning occasionally. Drain, reserving the marinade. Pour the marinade into a saucepan. Bring to a boil. Cook the poultry as desired, basting frequently with the hot marinade.

Approx Per ¹/₄ Cup: Cal 117; Prot 5 g; Carbo 6 g; T Fat 8 g; 62% Calories from Fat; Chol 0 mg; Fiber <1 g; Sod 4210 mg

Teriyaki Marinade   *Yield: 13 (¹/₄-cup) servings*

2 cups low-sodium soy sauce

1 cup water

¹/₂ cup packed brown sugar

1 tablespoon dark molasses

¹/₂ teaspoon salt

1 teaspoon garlic powder

¹/₂ teaspoon crushed red pepper

Combine the soy sauce, water, brown sugar, molasses, salt, garlic powder and red pepper in a saucepan and mix well. Bring to a boil. Pour over thick-cut pork chops, pork tenderloin, chicken or turkey breasts in a shallow dish. Marinate, covered, in the refrigerator for 8 to 12 hours or longer, turning occasionally; drain. Broil or grill the meat as desired.

Approx Per ¹/₄ Cup: Cal 72; Prot 4 g; Carbo 15 g; T Fat <1 g; 1% Calories from Fat; Chol 0 mg; Fiber 0 g; Sod 1338 mg

Lamb Chop Marinade   *Yield: 3 (¹/₄-cup) servings*

¹/₄ cup vegetable oil

1 tablespoon lemon juice

*1 tablespoon chopped
   fresh parsley*

1 teaspoon minced garlic

1 teaspoon salt

¹/₂ teaspoon pepper

1 bay leaf

¹/₂ cup sliced or chopped onion

Combine the ingredients in a bowl and mix well. Pour over lamb chops in a shallow dish. Marinate, covered, in the refrigerator for 2 to 6 hours, turning occasionally; drain. Cook the lamb chops as desired.

Approx Per ¹/₄ Cup: Cal 173; Prot 1 g; Carbo 3 g; T Fat 18 g; 93% Calories from Fat; Chol 0 mg; Fiber <1 g; Sod 777 mg

Bourbon Marinade for Pork   *Yield: 2 (¹/₄-cup) servings*

¹/₄ cup bourbon

¹/₄ cup soy sauce

2 tablespoons brown sugar

Combine the ingredients in a bowl and mix well. Pour over pork chops, tenderloins or boneless roast in a shallow dish. Marinate, covered, in the refrigerator for 2 to 6 hours, turning occasionally. Drain, reserving the marinade. Pour the marinade into a saucepan. Bring to a boil. Cook the pork as desired, basting frequently with the hot marinade.

Approx Per ¹/₄ Cup: Cal 149; Prot 3 g; Carbo 16 g; T Fat <1 g; 0% Calories from Fat; Chol 0 mg; Fiber 0 g; Sod 2637 mg

Sweet & Sour Glaze for Ham
Yield: 4 (¹/₄-cup) servings

1 cup apple jelly

1 tablespoon lemon juice

1 tablespoon prepared mustard

¹/₄ teaspoon cloves

Mix the ingredients in a saucepan. Bring to a boil. Baste ham or pork chops during baking.

Approx Per ¹/₄ Cup: Cal 241; Prot <1 g; Carbo 56 g; T Fat 0 g; 0% Calories from Fat; Chol 0 mg; Fiber <1 g; Sod 54 mg

If a recipe for marinated meat, poultry or fish calls for any leftover marinade to be served with the finished food, be sure to heat the marinade to boiling before you serve it. Boiling destroys any harmful bacteria that may have been transferred from the raw meat, poultry or fish to the marinade. Never use the same unwashed plate that held raw meat to serve the cooked meat.

103

A blue ribbon assortment of entries at the State Fair—woodworking, crafts, and foods—shows just a few of the many 4-H projects offered in Indiana's 92 counties. There's something for everyone! And there's something for everyone in "Picnics & Potlucks," a collection of hearty casseroles, flavorful sandwiches, savory meat pies, and one-pot main dishes, perfect for a tailgate picnic or pitch-in supper.

PICNICS
& POTLUCKS

A COLLECTION OF CASSEROLES, SANDWICHES, AND ONE-POT MAIN DISHES

Several winners from the annual dairy recipe contest, sponsored by the American Dairy Association of Indiana, are included in this book. This Italian Cheese Rustica Pie is one.

Puffed-Up Pizza Casserole   *Yield: 10 servings*

1½ pounds lean ground beef

1 (15-ounce) can tomato sauce

1 cup chopped green bell pepper (optional)

1 cup chopped onion

½ cup water

1 envelope spaghetti sauce mix

1 teaspoon dried oregano leaves, crushed

1 clove garlic, minced, or ¼ teaspoon garlic powder

Hot pepper sauce to taste (optional)

2 cups shredded mozzarella cheese

1 cup milk

¼ cup margarine or butter, melted

2 eggs

1 tablespoon vegetable oil

1 cup flour

½ cup grated Parmesan cheese

Popular pizza flavors combine in this easy casserole. Adjust the seasonings to appeal to your family members.

Brown the ground beef in a skillet, stirring until crumbly; drain. Stir in the tomato sauce, green pepper, onion, water, spaghetti sauce mix, oregano, garlic and hot pepper sauce. Bring to a boil. Reduce heat. Simmer, covered, for 10 minutes. Spoon into a greased 9x13-inch baking dish. Preheat oven to 400 degrees. Sprinkle with the mozzarella cheese. Combine the milk, margarine, eggs and oil in a mixer bowl. Beat for 1 minute. Add the flour and beat for 2 minutes. Pour over the mozzarella layer. Sprinkle with the Parmesan cheese. Bake for 30 minutes or until puffed and golden. Let stand for 10 minutes. Cut into squares.

Approx Per Serving: Cal 394; Prot 26 g; Carbo 19 g; T Fat 24 g; 55% Calories from Fat; Chol 116 mg; Fiber 1 g; Sod 910 mg

Italian Cheese Rustica Pie *Yield: 6 servings*

4 eggs, divided

1 cup cubed cooked ham

1 cup ricotta or small curd
  cottage cheese

4 ounces shredded
  mozzarella cheese

4 ounces cubed provolone or
  Swiss cheese

4 tablespoons grated Parmesan
  cheese, divided

1 tablespoon chopped fresh
  parsley, or 1 teaspoon dried
  parsley flakes

¹/₄ teaspoon oregano

¹/₈ teaspoon pepper

1 (15-ounce) package
  refrigerated pie crusts

1 tablespoon flour

*This award-winning dairy recipe combines four kinds of cheese in a hearty main
dish pie reminiscent of northern Italian country fare.*

Place oven rack in lowest position. Preheat oven to 375 degrees.
Beat 3 eggs in a mixer bowl until pale yellow. Add the ham, ricotta,
mozzarella, provolone, 3 tablespoons of the Parmesan cheese, parsley,
oregano and pepper and mix well. Fit 1 of the pie crusts into a 9-inch pie
plate. Sprinkle with the flour. Spoon the egg mixture into the pie crust.
Top with the remaining pastry, sealing and fluting the edge and cutting
vents. Beat the remaining egg. Brush over the crust. Sprinkle with the
remaining 1 tablespoon Parmesan cheese. Bake for 50 to 60 minutes or
until crust is golden. Let stand 10 minutes.

Approx Per Serving: Cal 621; Prot 26 g; Carbo 36 g; T Fat 40 g; 59% Calories from Fat;
Chol 226 mg; Fiber <1 g; Sod 1073 mg

Cheesy Brat Supper *Yield: 8 servings*

8 bratwursts or 2 pounds link
  smoked sausage, browned

4 large potatoes, peeled,
  quartered

1 quart or 2 (16-ounce) cans
  cut green beans, drained

¹/₂ cup chopped onion

1 (16-ounce) can whole kernel
  corn, drained

1 (8-ounce) can mushroom
  stems and pieces, drained

2 (10-ounce) cans cream of
  mushroom soup

1¹/₂ cups shredded Cheddar
  cheese

Place bratwursts in a slow cooker. Add the potatoes, green beans, onion,
corn, mushrooms, soup and cheese. Cook on Low for 6 to 8 hours or
High 3 to 4 hours.

Variation: Cut the bratwursts into ¹/₂-inch slices. Brown in a skillet.
Cook the potatoes in boiling water until tender. Drain and cut into
cubes. Combine all ingredients in a greased 9x13-inch baking dish.
Cook, covered, at 350 degrees for 45 minutes or until hot and bubbly.

Approx Per Serving: Cal 567; Prot 24 g; Carbo 41 g; T Fat 36 g; 55% Calories from Fat;
Chol 74 mg; Fiber 6 g; Sod 1385 mg

Eggstra Special Spaghetti *Yield: 4 servings*

1 (7- or 8-ounce) package
  spaghetti

8 slices bacon, cut into
  1/2-inch pieces

1/2 cup chopped onion

4 eggs, slightly beaten

4 ounces process American
  cheese, chopped

Here's a 4-H demonstration award winner that proves that simple is often best. This skillet dish combines breakfast favorites with spaghetti in a casserole that's sure to please at any meal.

Cook the spaghetti using package directions; rinse and drain. Cook the bacon in a skillet until crisp. Remove with a slotted spoon to paper towel. Cook the onion in the bacon drippings in the skillet for 5 minutes or until tender. Add the cooked spaghetti and bacon. Stir in the eggs and cheese. Cook until eggs are set and cheese is melted, stirring frequently. Garnish with chopped parsley or chives.

Variation: Spoon the egg mixture into a greased 1 1/2-quart baking dish. Bake at 350 degrees for 15 minutes or until eggs are set.

Approx Per Serving: Cal 638; Prot 28 g; Carbo 42 g; T Fat 39 g; 56% Calories from Fat; Chol 262 mg; Fiber 2 g; Sod 716 mg

 4-Bean and Sausage Bake *Yield: 12 servings*

1 pound bacon

2 or 3 large onions, chopped

1 cup packed brown sugar

1/3 cup vinegar

2 tablespoons dry mustard

1 pound mild bulk country
  sausage

8 ounces hot bulk country
  sausage

1 (15-ounce) can butter beans

1 (15-ounce) can kidney beans

1 (15-ounce) can lima beans

1 (15-ounce) can pork and
  beans

To reduce the fat and cholesterol in this casserole, use turkey bacon and sausage. This hearty dish is perfect for a tailgate party. Serve with fresh vegetables and fruit, cornbread sticks or muffins.

Cook the bacon in a skillet until crisp. Remove from the skillet with a slotted spoon and crumble. Pour off all but 2 tablespoons drippings. Cook the onions in the hot drippings in the skillet until lightly browned. Add the brown sugar, vinegar and mustard and mix well. Simmer for 15 to 20 minutes. Brown the sausages in a separate skillet, stirring until crumbly; drain. Combine the crumbled bacon, onion mixture, cooked sausage, butter beans, kidney beans, lima beans and pork and beans in a Dutch oven and mix well. Bake at 325 degrees for 1 1/2 to 2 hours.

Tip: Prepare 1 day before serving and refrigerate. Bake as instructed by recipe.

Approx Per Serving: Cal 399; Prot 17 g; Carbo 44 g; T Fat 19 g; 41% Calories from Fat; Chol 39 mg; Fiber 6 g; Sod 1088 mg

Hungarian Goulash

Yield: 8 servings

2 pounds beef chuck roast

1 (15-ounce) can tomatoes

$^1/_3$ cup vegetable oil

1 cup chopped onion

1 tablespoon each flour and
  paprika

1$^1/_2$ teaspoons salt

1 (8-ounce) can tomato sauce

$^1/_4$ cup chopped celery
  with leaves

2 tablespoons chopped
  fresh parsley

1 bay leaf

1 clove garlic, minced

1 stem fresh thyme, or
  2 teaspoons dried thyme

12 cups hot cooked noodles

A Hoosier's mother brought this savory recipe from Hungary in 1900. It's been a family favorite for nearly a century.

Cut the chuck roast into 1$^1/_2$-inch cubes. Drain the tomatoes. Brown the roast in hot oil in a Dutch oven. Add the onion. Cook until onion is golden, stirring constantly. Stir in the flour, paprika and salt. Add the tomatoes, tomato sauce, celery, parsley, bay leaf, garlic and thyme and mix well. Simmer, covered, for 1$^1/_2$ to 2 hours or until the meat is tender. Remove the bay leaf and thyme stem. Divide the noodles among 8 plates. Arrange the goulash over the noodles.

Approx Per Serving: Cal 621; Prot 35 g; Carbo 67 g; T Fat 23 g; 34% Calories from Fat; Chol 155 mg; Fiber 4 g; Sod 759 mg

Fiesta Skillet Supper

Yield: 4 servings

1 pound lean ground beef

$^1/_3$ cup chopped onion

$^1/_3$ cup chopped green bell
  pepper (optional)

1 (16-ounce) can tomatoes

1 (8-ounce) can tomato sauce

$^1/_2$ cup hot water

1$^1/_4$ teaspoons chili powder

1 teaspoon salt

$^1/_8$ teaspoon cayenne

1 (12-ounce) can whole kernel
  corn with sweet peppers

1 cup elbow macaroni

4 ounces shredded Monterey
  Jack cheese

This one-pan main dish is a family favorite that even the kids (or Dad) can make in a jiffy.

Brown the ground beef with the onion and green pepper in a skillet, stirring until the ground beef is crumbly; drain. Add the next 6 ingredients, stirring to break up the tomatoes. Bring to a boil. Stir in the corn and macaroni. Simmer, covered, for 15 to 20 minutes or until macaroni is tender. Sprinkle with the cheese. Cook, covered, until cheese is melted.

Approx Per Serving: Cal 560; Prot 39 g; Carbo 46 g; T Fat 26 g; 40% Calories from Fat; Chol 106 mg; Fiber 5 g; Sod 1617 mg

Have a question about nutrition or special diets, food preparation or preservation, ingredient substitutions or food safety? Information is just a phone call away. Call the Cooperative Extension Office in your county. An Extension Educator will be happy to help you find the answers.

French Canadian Meat Pie   *Yield: 6 servings*

3 medium potatoes, peeled,
   chopped

1 large carrot, shredded

Salt to taste

1 pound lean ground beef

8 ounces bulk country sausage

1½ cups sliced mushrooms

1 medium onion, chopped

1 to 2 tablespoons
   chopped garlic

2 teaspoons flour

1 tablespoon allspice

1 teaspoon reduced-sodium
   instant beef bouillon

¼ teaspoon pepper

¼ teaspoon seasoned salt

1 (15-ounce) package
   refrigerated pie crusts

Allspice adds the unique flavor to this hearty meat pie of French Canadian origins.

Preheat oven to 350 degrees. Combine the potatoes and carrot with enough water to cover in a saucepan. Season with salt. Bring to a boil. Boil until potatoes are tender. Drain, reserving the liquid. Brown the ground beef, sausage, mushrooms, onion and garlic in a skillet, stirring until the ground beef is crumbly. Stir in the flour, allspice, instant bouillon, pepper and seasoned salt. Stir in the cooked potatoes and carrots and ⅓ cup of the reserved liquid. Fit 1 of the pie shells into a 9-inch pie plate. Spoon the ground beef mixture into the pie plate. Top with the remaining pastry, sealing and fluting the edge and cutting vents. Bake for 35 to 45 minutes or until crust is golden. Let stand for 5 minutes before serving.

Variations: May substitute ground venison or veal for the ground beef; ground pork for the bulk country sausage; and ½ teaspoon cinnamon and ½ teaspoon cloves for the allspice.

Approx Per Serving: Cal 636; Prot 24 g; Carbo 50 g; T Fat 37 g; 53% Calories from Fat; Chol 90 mg; Fiber 2 g; Sod 718 mg

Pizza Spaghetti Bake   *Yield: 12 servings*

4 eggs

1½ teaspoons garlic powder

1 teaspoon salt

¼ teaspoon pepper

½ cup grated Parmesan cheese

1 (1-pound) package spaghetti
   or vermicelli, cooked, drained

1 pound lean ground beef

1 (28-ounce) jar
   spaghetti sauce

16 ounces low-fat
   cottage cheese

2 cups shredded
   mozzarella cheese

Preheat oven to 350 degrees. Beat the eggs, garlic powder, salt, pepper and Parmesan cheese in a mixer bowl until well blended. Stir in the cooked spaghetti. Pour into a greased 9x13-inch baking dish, pressing onto the bottom of the dish. Bake for 15 minutes. Brown the ground beef in a skillet, stirring until crumbly; drain. Stir in the spaghetti sauce. Bring to a boil. Spoon half over the baked spaghetti layer. Spread cottage cheese over the spaghetti sauce layer. Spoon the remaining spaghetti sauce over the cottage cheese. Sprinkle with mozzarella cheese. Bake for 15 minutes or until heated through. Let stand for 5 minutes. Cut into squares.

Variations: May substitute bulk sausage for the ground beef. May add 1 (8-ounce) can sliced mushrooms, drained and 1 (3-ounce) package sliced pepperoni, chopped.

Approx Per Serving: Cal 421; Prot 30 g; Carbo 37 g; T Fat 17 g; 36% Calories from Fat; Chol 121 mg; Fiber 3 g; Sod 837 mg

Breakfast Casserole

Yield: 12 servings

1 pound bulk country sausage

6 to 8 slices bread,
  cubed if desired

1 to 1½ cups shredded
  Cheddar cheese

6 eggs

2 cups milk

1 teaspoon dry mustard

½ teaspoon salt

Popular all over the state, this make-ahead strata is the perfect main dish to offer at a holiday breakfast or brunch. It's equally good for a late-night supper or to share at a tailgate party or pitch-in gathering. Be creative and try alternatives to the sausage—these variations should give you lots of ideas.

Brown the sausage in a skillet, stirring until crumbly; drain. Place the bread in the bottom of a greased 9x13-inch baking dish. Arrange the sausage over the bread. Sprinkle cheese over the sausage. Beat the eggs, milk, mustard and salt in a mixer bowl until well blended. Pour over the layers. Refrigerate, tightly covered, for 8 to 12 hours or longer. Preheat oven to 350 degrees. Bake, uncovered, for 45 minutes or until a wooden pick inserted in the center comes out clean.

Variations: Ham: Substitute 1 pound cooked, chopped ham for the sausage. Add ¼ cup finely chopped onion, if desired.

Chicken: Substitute 1½ cups finely chopped cooked chicken for the sausage. Add 1 (4-ounce) jar sliced mushrooms, drained and ½ teaspoon poultry seasoning, if desired.

Approx Per Serving: Cal 252; Prot 14 g; Carbo 14 g; T Fat 15 g; 56% Calories from Fat; Chol 143 mg; Fiber 1 g; Sod 594 mg

Pork is the #1 meat around the world. The United States is the second largest pork-producing nation, after China. Indiana is the fifth largest pork producing state in the nation, producing approximately 6% of the country's pork supply.

Sausage Zucchini Skillet Casserole   *Yield: 6 servings*

1 pound bulk country sausage

1/2 cup chopped green or red bell pepper

1/2 cup chopped onion

3 cups sliced zucchini

1 cup biscuit mix

1/2 teaspoon each garlic powder, basil, oregano, seasoned salt and pepper

1/4 cup butter, melted

1/2 cup milk

3 eggs

1 1/2 cups shredded Colby cheese, divided

Somewhat like a frittata, this hearty dish is a tasty way to use garden zucchini. The casserole bakes in the skillet used to cook the sausage, so cleanup is simplified. Serve with sliced fresh tomatoes or crisp apple wedges.

Preheat oven to 350 degrees. Brown the sausage in a large ovenproof skillet, stirring until crumbly; drain. Stir in the green pepper and onion. Cook until tender. Reduce the heat. Stir in the zucchini. Cook, covered until the zucchini is tender. Combine the biscuit mix, garlic powder, basil, oregano, seasoned salt, pepper, butter and milk in a bowl and mix well. Stir in the eggs, just until blended. Stir in 1 cup of the cheese. Spoon over the sausage mixture. Sprinkle the remaining cheese over the top. Bake for 20 minutes or until a wooden pick inserted in the center comes out clean. Cut into wedges.

Approx Per Serving: Cal 475; Prot 21 g; Carbo 19 g; T Fat 35 g; 67% Calories from Fat; Chol 189 mg; Fiber 2 g; Sod 1123 mg

Baked Chicken Salad   *Yield: 6 servings*

1 pound boneless skinless chicken breasts or turkey breast tenders, cut into pieces

2 cups chopped celery

1 medium onion, chopped

2 cups water

2 teaspoons reduced-sodium instant chicken bouillon

1 (8-ounce) can sliced water chestnuts, drained

3 hard-cooked eggs, chopped

3/4 cup light mayonnaise

1 (2-ounce) jar diced pimiento, drained (optional)

1 tablespoon lemon juice

1/2 cup shredded Swiss cheese

2 slices bread, crumbled

Preheat oven to 350 degrees. Cook the chicken, celery, onion, water and instant bouillon in a saucepan until the chicken is tender. Drain, reserving the broth. Combine the chicken mixture, water chestnuts, eggs, mayonnaise, pimiento, lemon juice and 1/2 cup of the reserved broth in a bowl and mix well. Add additional broth if needed to moisten the mixture. Spoon into a greased 9-inch square or 2-quart baking dish. Combine the cheese and crumbled bread in a bowl and mix well. Sprinkle over the top. Bake for 20 minutes or until hot and bubbly.

Approx Per Serving: Cal 311; Prot 23 g; Carbo 17 g; T Fat 18 g; 50% Calories from Fat; Chol 166 mg; Fiber 3 g; Sod 397 mg

Chicken & Rice 1-2-3   *Yield: 6 servings*

1 1/2 cups instant rice

1/4 cup chopped onion

3 tablespoons butter or
   margarine

1 1/2 pounds boneless skinless
   chicken breast tenders

2 (14-ounce) cans
   chicken broth

1 teaspoon onion powder

1/2 teaspoon salt

1/2 teaspoon paprika

1/4 teaspoon pepper

Chicken breast tenders and instant rice combine in this savory main dish that's as easy as 1-2-3, ready to pop into the oven in minutes.

Preheat oven to 350 degrees. Brown the rice and onion in butter in a skillet, stirring frequently. Spoon into a buttered 9x13-inch baking dish. Arrange the chicken over the rice. Pour the broth over the chicken. Sprinkle with the onion powder, salt, paprika and pepper. Bake, covered tightly, for 45 minutes. Bake, uncovered, for 10 minutes longer or until browned.

Approx Per Serving: Cal 306; Prot 31 g; Carbo 21 g; T Fat 10 g; 30% Calories from Fat; Chol 80 mg; Fiber 1 g; Sod 1137 mg

For short-term storage, leave meat and poultry items in the store's packaging and place in the coldest section of the refrigerator. For longer storage, wrap tightly in moisture- and vapor-proof material and freeze.

Chicken Tetrazzini for a Crowd   *Yield: 18 servings*

1 pound thin spaghetti, cooked,
   drained

4 cups chopped cooked chicken
   or turkey

4 (10-ounce) cans cream of
   mushroom soup

2 cups chicken broth

1 (7-ounce) jar sliced
   mushrooms, drained

3/4 cup butter or margarine,
   melted, divided

1/2 teaspoon garlic salt

1/4 teaspoon pepper

3 cups dry bread crumbs

1 1/2 cups grated Parmesan
   cheese

Preheat oven to 325 degrees. Combine the spaghetti, chicken, soup, broth, mushrooms, 1/4 cup of the butter, garlic salt and pepper in a bowl and mix well. Spoon into one greased 9x13-inch baking dish and one 8-inch square baking dish. Combine the remaining 1/2 cup melted butter, bread crumbs and cheese and mix well. Sprinkle over the tops. Bake, covered, for 40 minutes. Bake, uncovered, for 15 minutes longer or until golden brown and bubbly.

Approx Per Serving: Cal 407; Prot 22 g; Carbo 36 g; T Fat 19 g; 43% Calories from Fat; Chol 56 mg; Fiber 2 g; Sod 1070 mg

113

Hot Chicken Rice Salad   *Yield: 12 servings*

¼ cup butter or margarine

⅓ cup flour

¼ teaspoon pepper

3 cups chicken broth

3 cups cubed cooked chicken

3 cups cooked rice

3 cups chopped celery

1 (10-ounce) package frozen green peas, thawed

½ cup chopped onion

1 to 1½ cups mayonnaise or salad dressing

2 to 3 tablespoons lemon juice (omit if using salad dressing)

½ cup sliced almonds or crushed potato chips

Melt the butter in a large saucepan. Stir in the flour and pepper until smooth. Whisk in the broth. Cook until bubbly. Stir in the chicken, rice, celery, peas, onion, mayonnaise and lemon juice. Spoon into a 9x13-inch baking dish. Sprinkle almonds over the top. Bake at 350 degrees for 45 minutes or until hot and bubbly.

Variations: Pasta—Omit the butter, flour and rice. Reduce the broth to 2 cups, mayonnaise to ½ cup and lemon juice to 1 tablespoon. Add 1 cup uncooked elbow or small shell macaroni, 1 (10-ounce) can cream of chicken soup, 1 (8-ounce) can sliced water chestnuts, drained and ½ cup shredded Cheddar cheese.

Tuna—Omit the chicken and almonds. Reduce the mayonnaise to ½ cup and lemon juice to 1 tablespoon. Add 2 (9-ounce) cans tuna, drained, 1 (10-ounce) can cream of chicken or celery soup, 1 (8-ounce) can sliced water chestnuts and 1 (2- or 4-ounce) jar diced pimientos, drained. Top with 1 (3-ounce) can French-fried onions, crushed, during last 15 minutes of baking.

Approx Per Serving: Cal 424; Prot 15 g; Carbo 20 g; T Fat 31 g; 67% Calories from Fat; Chol 62 mg; Fiber 2 g; Sod 467 mg

Layered Chicken Casserole *Yield: 10 servings*

6 slices white bread

4 cups cubed cooked chicken

8 ounces mushrooms, sliced

2 tablespoons butter

1 (8-ounce) can water
  chestnuts, drained, chopped

¼ cup mayonnaise

6 ounces Monterey Jack cheese

4 ounces American cheese

3 eggs

1½ cups milk

1 (10-ounce) can cream of
  chicken soup

1 (10-ounce) can cream of
  mushroom soup

⅔ cup dry bread crumbs

¼ cup butter, melted

Great for company or to carry to a pot-luck supper, this make-ahead dish usually brings 'em back for seconds!

Arrange bread in the bottom of a buttered 9x13-inch baking dish. Sprinkle the chicken over the bread. Cook the mushrooms in butter in a skillet until browned. Spoon over chicken. Combine the water chestnuts and mayonnaise in a bowl and mix well. Spoon evenly over the mushrooms. Cut the Monterey Jack cheese and American cheese into slices. Arrange over the mushrooms. Beat the eggs in a small bowl. Stir in the milk. Pour over the layers. Combine the chicken and mushroom soups in a bowl and mix well. Spoon over the layers. Refrigerate, covered, for 3 to 24 hours. Bake at 350 degrees for 1 hour and 15 minutes or until hot and bubbly. Combine the bread crumbs and melted butter in a bowl and mix well. Sprinkle over the top. Bake for 10 minutes longer.

Approx Per Serving: Cal 518; Prot 31 g; Carbo 25 g; T Fat 32 g; 56% Calories from Fat; Chol 171 mg; Fiber 2 g; Sod 1052 mg

Oriental Chicken Potpie *Yield: 6 servings*

1 (10-ounce) can white
  meat chicken

1 (10-ounce) can cream of
  mushroom soup

1 (8-ounce) can sliced water
  chestnuts, drained

½ cup diagonally-sliced celery

½ cup sliced green onions

¼ cup milk

3 tablespoons water

2 tablespoons soy sauce

1 cup biscuit mix

1 (6-ounce) package frozen
  pea pods, thawed, drained

1 tablespoon butter, melted

2 teaspoons sesame seeds

Preheat oven to 425 degrees. Combine the chicken, soup, water chestnuts, celery, green onions and milk in a saucepan and mix well. Bring to a boil. Reduce the heat. Cover and keep warm. Stir the water and soy sauce into the biscuit mix in a bowl until a soft dough forms. Shape into a ball. Roll into a 5x5-inch square on a lightly floured surface. Cut into 1-inch squares. Stir the pea pods into the chicken mixture. Spoon into a 1½-quart or 8-inch square baking dish. Top with the dough squares. Brush with melted butter. Sprinkle with sesame seeds. Bake for 15 minutes or until golden brown.

Variation: Add 1 (4-ounce) jar mushrooms, drained to the chicken mixture.

Approx Per Serving: Cal 284; Prot 15 g; Carbo 25 g; T Fat 14 g; 44% Calories from Fat; Chol 37 mg; Fiber 4 g; Sod 1324 mg

115

If your crackers lose their crispness, crush them and freeze in an airtight container to use as a crust for main dishes and desserts, a topping for casseroles or a coating for fried and baked foods, such as chicken and fish.

Turkey Stuffing Casserole   *Yield: 6 servings*

2 cups water

1 (8-ounce) package one-step chicken-flavor stuffing mix

1 (12-ounce) package frozen bulk turkey sausage, thawed

2 (10-ounce) packages frozen peas and carrots, thawed

1 (10-ounce) can 98% fat-free cream of chicken soup

8 ounces nonfat sour cream

1 (4-ounce) jar sliced mushrooms, drained

⅔ cup skim milk

Preheat oven to 450 degrees. Bring the water to a boil in a saucepan. Stir in the stuffing mix. Remove from heat. Let stand, covered, for 5 minutes. Brown the sausage in a large nonstick skillet coated with nonstick cooking spray, stirring until crumbly. Stir in the next 5 ingredients. Bring to a boil. Spoon ⅔ of the stuffing evenly into a 9x13-inch baking dish coated with nonstick cooking spray. Spoon the sausage mixture over the stuffing. Spoon the remaining stuffing over the sausage layer. Bake for 15 minutes or until browned and bubbly. Let stand for 5 minutes.

Approx Per Serving: Cal 325; Prot 18 g; Carbo 51 g; T Fat 6 g; 17% Calories from Fat; Chol 27 mg; Fiber 5 g; Sod 1411 mg

Succulent Scalloped Oysters   *Yield: 4 servings*

1 pint shucked fresh oysters

2 cups medium-coarse cracker crumbs

½ cup butter or margarine, melted

½ teaspoon salt

Freshly ground pepper

¾ cup light cream

½ teaspoon Worcestershire sauce

Drain the oysters, reserving ¼ cup of the liquid. Combine the crumbs, butter and salt in a bowl and mix well. Spread ⅓ of the crumbs in the bottom of a greased 9-inch square baking dish. Arrange half of the oysters over the crumbs. Sprinkle with pepper. Layer half of the remaining crumbs over the oysters. Arrange the remaining oysters over the crumb layer. Sprinkle with pepper. Combine the cream, reserved oyster liquid and Worcestershire sauce in a bowl and mix well. Pour over the layers. Top with remaining crumbs. Bake at 350 degrees for 40 minutes.

Approx Per Serving: Cal 681; Prot 24 g; Carbo 41 g; T Fat 46 g; 61% Calories from Fat; Chol 212 mg; Fiber 1 g; Sod 1307 mg

Classic Macaroni & Cheese   *Yield: 6 servings*

2 tablespoons margarine or
  butter

3 tablespoons flour

1 teaspoon dry mustard

1 teaspoon salt or
  seasoned salt

1/8 teaspoon pepper

1/8 teaspoon nutmeg

2 3/4 cups milk

2 cups shredded sharp Cheddar
  cheese, divided

1 (7- or 8-ounce) package or
  2 cups elbow, shell or rotini
  macaroni, cooked

3 tablespoons dry bread
  crumbs

Preheat oven to 375 degrees. Melt the margarine in a medium saucepan. Stir in the flour, mustard, salt, pepper and nutmeg until smooth. Stir in the milk gradually. Cook until the mixture bubbles and thickens, stirring constantly. Remove from heat. Stir in 1 1/2 cups of the cheese, stirring until melted. Add the macaroni and mix well. Spoon into a greased 8- or 9-inch square baking dish. Combine the remaining cheese and bread crumbs in a bowl and mix well. Sprinkle over the top. Bake for 20 to 25 minutes or until lightly browned and bubbly. Let stand for 5 minutes.

Tip: Eight ounces pasteurized process cheese, cut into small cubes, can be substituted for the Cheddar cheese. Combine all of the cheese cubes with the macaroni. Decrease the flour to 2 tablespoons, salt to 1/2 teaspoon and milk to 2 cups.

Tip: Freeze, covered, before baking. Bake frozen Classic Macaroni & Cheese at 375 degrees for 1 hour and 15 minutes or until bubbly and hot in center.

Variations: Add any of the following to the macaroni before baking:

1 (6-ounce) can tuna or salmon, drained, flaked
1 to 1 1/2 cups cubed cooked chicken or turkey
1 to 1 1/2 cups cubed cooked ham or luncheon meat
1 to 1 1/2 cups sliced frankfurters or smoked sausage
1 (10-ounce) package frozen chopped spinach or green peas, thawed,
    drained
1 (2-ounce) jar pimiento, drained and 1/4 cup chopped onion
1 (4-ounce) can chopped green chilies, drained, 1/2 teaspoon ground
    cumin and 1/2 teaspoon chili powder

Classic Macaroni & Cheese for a Crowd: Prepare as above using 1 pound macaroni, 1/2 cup margarine or butter, 1/3 cup flour, 2 teaspoons dry mustard, 2 teaspoons salt, 1/4 teaspoon pepper, 1/4 teaspoon nutmeg, 5 1/4 cups milk, 4 cups shredded Cheddar cheese and 1/2 cup bread crumbs. Reserve 1 cup cheese to mix with crumbs. Spoon into a greased 9x13-inch baking dish or two 1 1/2-quart baking dishes. Bake for 25 to 30 minutes. Serves 10 to 12.

Approx Per Serving: Cal 425; Prot 19 g; Carbo 40 g; T Fat 21 g; 45% Calories from Fat; Chol 55 mg; Fiber 1 g; Sod 752 mg

Creamy Egg Bake *Yield: 12 servings*

1/3 cup margarine or butter

18 eggs

8 ounces sour cream

1 cup milk

2 teaspoons salt

1/4 teaspoon pepper

Need to feed a hungry crowd for breakfast? Here's a handy baked version of scrambled eggs that's been known to appear on a Northern Indiana bed-and-breakfast menu.

Preheat oven to 350 degrees. Melt the margarine in a 9x13-inch baking dish in the oven. Beat the eggs, sour cream, milk, salt and pepper in a mixer bowl until well blended. Pour into the prepared dish. Bake for 1 hour or until set.

Approx Per Serving: Cal 210; Prot 11 g; Carbo 3 g; T Fat 17 g; 74% Calories from Fat; Chol 330 mg; Fiber 0 g; Sod 561 mg

Lazy-Day Vegetable Lasagna *Yield: 8 servings*

1 cup sliced mushrooms

1/2 cup sliced green onions

1 tablespoon soy oil or vegetable oil

1 (48-ounce) jar low-sodium, low-fat spaghetti sauce

1/2 (10-ounce) package low-fat silken tofu

1 egg

1 (10-ounce) package frozen chopped spinach, thawed, drained

1/2 teaspoon garlic powder

1/2 teaspoon oregano

1/2 teaspoon salt

1/4 teaspoon pepper

1 (8-ounce) package lasagna noodles

1 cup shredded fat-free mozzarella cheese

Preheat oven to 350 degrees. Cook the mushrooms and green onions in hot oil in a large skillet until lightly browned. Stir in spaghetti sauce. Beat the tofu and egg in a mixer bowl until well blended. Stir in spinach, garlic powder, oregano, salt and pepper. Spray a 9x13-inch baking dish with nonstick cooking spray. Layer half the spaghetti sauce mixture, half the lasagna noodles, tofu mixture, remaining lasagna noodles and remaining spaghetti sauce mixture in the prepared dish. Bake, covered, for 45 minutes. Sprinkle with mozzarella cheese. Bake for 15 minutes. Let stand for 10 minutes.

Variation: Add 1 (16-ounce) package frozen vegetable medley or 1 1/2 cups steamed chopped fresh vegetable combination such as bell peppers, broccoli, carrots, eggplant and zucchini between layers of lasagna.

Approx Per Serving: Cal 191; Prot 15 g; Carbo 26 g; T Fat 3 g; 13% Calories from Fat; Chol 32 mg; Fiber 4 g; Sod 942 mg

118

4-H Sloppy Joes   *Yield: 20 sandwiches*

5 pounds lean ground beef

¼ cup dried minced onion

½ cup flour

1 (8-ounce) can tomato sauce

1 cup ketchup

1 cup water

½ cup packed brown sugar

¼ cup prepared mustard

¼ cup cider vinegar

2 to 3 tablespoons
   Worcestershire sauce

1 to 2 tablespoons chili powder
   (optional)

⅛ teaspoon hot pepper sauce

20 hamburger buns, split

Check out the 4-H booth at the Wells County fair for this perennial favorite fare. Or make a batch for your next junior leader gathering or tailgate picnic.

Brown half the ground beef with the onion in a large kettle over high heat, stirring until crumbly; drain. Remove the meat from the kettle. Repeat with the remaining ground beef. Return the cooked ground beef to the kettle. Stir in the flour until well blended. Add the tomato sauce, ketchup, water, brown sugar, mustard, vinegar, Worcestershire sauce, chili powder and hot pepper sauce and mix well. Bring to a boil, stirring constantly. Reduce the heat. Simmer, covered, for 30 minutes or longer, stirring occasionally. Spoon about ½ cup into each bun.

Approx Per Sandwich: Cal 423; Prot 29 g;
Carbo 35 g; T Fat 18 g; 39% Calories from Fat;
Chol 81 mg; Fiber 2 g; Sod 561 mg

Hot Dog Chili Sauce   *Yield: 24 (¼-cup) servings*

2 (15-ounce) cans chili with
   beans

1 (12-ounce) can tomato paste

½ cup chopped green
   bell pepper

½ cup chopped onion

⅓ cup packed brown sugar

2 teaspoons prepared mustard

1 teaspoon chili powder

1 teaspoon salt

Combine the chili, tomato paste, green pepper, onion, brown sugar, mustard, chili powder and salt in a slow cooker and mix well. Cook on Low for 4 to 5 hours or on High for 2 to 3 hours, stirring occasionally. Serve about ¼ cup on each hot dog in a bun.

Tip: This sauce can be prepared ahead and frozen for later use.

Approx Per Serving: Cal 65; Prot 3 g;
Carbo 10 g; T Fat 2 g; 26% Calories from Fat;
Chol 6 mg; Fiber 2 g; Sod 398 mg

Health researchers continue to discover the benefits of a diet that includes soyfoods. The soybean contains phytochemicals (isoflavones) that have been identified with reduced risk of cancer and heart disease. High in protein, soyfoods are an excellent source of fiber, calcium and potassium. Soybeans have also been shown to reduce cholesterol. And for postmenopausal women, consumption of soy products that contain most or all of the bean such as tofu may provide a viable alternative to hormone replacement therapy. The health benefits of eating soyfoods are many and including soy in the diet can be as simple as using tofu in favorite family recipes like this lasagna.

Food Safety Tip

When serving hot foods, hold them for no longer than 2 hours and keep the food between 140 degrees and 165 degrees. Discard chilled food that has been at room temperature for more than 2 hours.

Corn Dogs   *Yield: 8 servings*

2/3 cup yellow cornmeal

1/3 cup flour

1 1/2 tablespoons sugar

1 teaspoon salt

1/2 cup milk

1 egg, beaten

2 tablespoons vegetable oil

8 frankfurters

8 wooden skewers

1/4 to 1/2 cup flour

Vegetable oil for deep-frying

Combine the cornmeal, 1/3 cup of flour, sugar and salt in a bowl and mix well. Add the milk, egg and oil and mix well. Insert a skewer in one end of each frankfurter. Place the 1/4 cup flour in a shallow dish. Roll the frankfurters in the flour to coat, adding additional flour as needed. Dip into the cornmeal mixture to coat. Fry, a few at a time, in deep hot oil measuring 375 degrees until golden brown. Drain on paper towels.

Approx Per Serving: Cal 324; Prot 10 g; Carbo 22 g; T Fat 22 g; 60% Calories from Fat; Chol 57 mg; Fiber 1 g; Sod 948 mg
Nutritional analysis does not include the oil for deep-frying.

The Ultimate Cheese Melt   *Yield: 4 servings*

1 (8- to 12-ounce) loaf French bread or 4 sub sandwich rolls

2 tablespoons Dijon mustard

4 ounces shredded Cheddar cheese

4 ounces shredded Swiss cheese

1/4 cup butter or margarine, softened

1 egg

4 slices bacon, cooked, crumbled

3 to 4 tablespoons chopped green onions

1/4 teaspoon Worcestershire sauce

Preheat broiler to 450 degrees. Cut the bread in half lengthwise. Cut each half into two pieces. Spread the cut side with mustard. Combine the Cheddar cheese, Swiss cheese, butter, egg, bacon, green onions and Worcestershire sauce in a mixer bowl. Beat until well mixed. Spread over the mustard. Place bread halves on a broiler pan or baking sheet. Broil for 3 to 5 minutes or until puffed and lightly browned.

Variation: May substitute Monterey Jack or provolone cheese for the Cheddar and Swiss cheese.

Approx Per Serving: Cal 522; Prot 27 g; Carbo 47 g; T Fat 36 g; 53% Calories from Fat; Chol 145 mg; Fiber 3 g; Sod 1196 mg

Slow-Simmered Barbecue   *Yield: 18 sandwiches*

*3 pounds beef or pork
  stew meat*

2 cups chopped onions

*1 cup chopped green bell
  pepper (optional)*

1 (6-ounce) can tomato paste

⅔ cup packed brown sugar

⅓ cup cider vinegar

2 to 4 tablespoons chili powder

*1 to 2 tablespoons
  Worcestershire sauce*

2 teaspoons dry mustard

2 teaspoons salt

*¼ teaspoon crushed red
  pepper (optional)*

18 hamburger buns, split

Combine the stew meat, onions, green pepper, tomato paste, brown sugar, vinegar, chili powder, Worcestershire sauce, mustard, salt and red pepper in a slow cooker and mix well. Cook on Low for 8 to 10 hours or on High for 4 to 5 hours, stirring occasionally. Shred the meat using a fork. Spoon about ⅓ cup into each bun.

Approx Per Sandwich: Cal 285; Prot 19 g; Carbo 34 g; T Fat 8 g; 25% Calories from Fat; Chol 47 mg; Fiber 2 g; Sod 492 mg

Make-Ahead Hot Ham Sandwiches   *Yield: 10 sandwiches*

1½ pounds shaved baked ham

8 ounces shredded Swiss cheese

*½ cup margarine or butter,
  softened*

¼ cup finely chopped onion

*2 tablespoons prepared
  mustard*

*1 tablespoon prepared
  horseradish (optional)*

1 tablespoon poppy seeds

10 hamburger buns, split

Who doesn't like ham and cheese sandwiches? This tasty make-ahead version is perfect for any gathering from holiday caroling parties and after-the-game suppers to church pitch-ins.

Combine the ham, cheese, margarine, onion, mustard, horseradish and poppy seeds in a bowl and mix well. Spoon equal amounts into each bun. Wrap each sandwich in aluminum foil. Refrigerate or freeze. Preheat the oven to 350 degrees. Bake the thawed sandwiches for 15 minutes or until hot.

Approx Per Sandwich: Cal 366; Prot 22 g; Carbo 24 g; T Fat 20 g; 50% Calories from Fat; Chol 53 mg; Fiber 1 g; Sod 1242 mg

Colorful canned tomatoes, sauces, and vegetables—all 4-H food preservation entries—sparkle on the windowsill of the Indiana State Fair 4-H Exhibit Hall. Such home-canned products are the foundation for many family meals and potluck favorites. In "Savory Soups & Stews," Hoosier cooks share their best recipes for chili in its infinite variety, hearty slow-simmered stews, and satisfying soups—all incomparable comfort foods!

SAVORY
SOUPS
& STEWS

HOOSIER COOKS SHARE THEIR BEST RECIPES FOR CHILI, STEWS, AND SOUPS

Chicken 'N' Rice Chili   *Yield: 8 (1-cup) servings*

2 pounds boneless skinless
   chicken breasts, chopped

1 tablespoon vegetable oil

1 medium onion, chopped

2 (14-ounce) cans stewed
   tomatoes

1 (14-ounce) can chicken broth

1 (15-ounce) can red beans

1¼ cups water

½ cup long grain rice

1 to 2 tablespoons chili powder

⅛ teaspoon salt

⅛ teaspoon pepper

⅛ teaspoon hot pepper sauce

Here's a tasty new twist on chili to add to your "comfort foods" recipe file.

Cook the chicken in hot oil in a Dutch oven for 8 minutes or until well browned, stirring frequently. Add the onion. Cook until tender, stirring constantly. Add the tomatoes, broth, beans, water, rice, chili powder, salt, pepper and hot pepper sauce and mix well. Bring to a boil. Reduce the heat. Simmer, covered, for 30 to 40 minutes or until rice is tender. Ladle into soup bowls. Serve with shredded Cheddar cheese.

Tip: This soup freezes well.

Approx Per Serving: Cal 280; Prot 30 g; Carbo 26 g; T Fat 6 g; 18% Calories from Fat; Chol 63 mg; Fiber 5 g; Sod 756 mg

Quick White Chili   *Yield: 8 (1½-cup) servings*

¾ cup chopped onion

1 teaspoon ground cumin

1 teaspoon garlic powder

½ teaspoon thyme leaves

2 tablespoons margarine

3 cups water

1 tablespoon instant chicken
   bouillon, or 3 bouillon cubes

2 cups chopped cooked turkey
   or chicken

1 (48-ounce) jar great
   northern beans

1 (4-ounce) can chopped
   green chiles

4 ounces Monterey Jack cheese,
   shredded

When time is short, the temperature is frosty and appetites are hearty, make this satisfying white bean chili. It's a great way to use leftover holiday turkey or deli turkey breast. Serve with cornbread and sliced fresh tomatoes, tortilla chips or crisp apple wedges.

Cook the onion, cumin, garlic powder and thyme in margarine in a large saucepan until the onion is tender. Stir in the water, instant bouillon, turkey, beans and chiles. Bring to a boil. Reduce the heat. Simmer, covered, for 10 minutes. Ladle into soup bowls. Serve with the cheese. Garnish with chopped parsley or cilantro.

Approx Per Serving: Cal 344; Prot 27 g; Carbo 38 g; T Fat 10 g; 25% Calories from Fat; Chol 39 mg; Fiber 9 g; Sod 739 mg

Hoosier Chili   *Yield: 11 (2-cup) servings*

2 pounds lean ground beef
  or turkey

8 ounces hot country sausage
  or turkey sausage

1 cup chopped onion

1 green bell pepper, chopped

1 teaspoon garlic powder, or
  1 clove garlic, chopped

2 tablespoons reduced-sodium
  instant beef bouillon

2 teaspoons ground cumin

2 teaspoons oregano leaves

2 teaspoons sugar

1 teaspoon seasoned salt

1 teaspoon crushed red pepper,
  or ¼ teaspoon cayenne

2 (28-ounce) cans crushed
  tomatoes, or 1 (46-ounce)
  can tomato juice

2 (28-ounce) cans tomatoes,
  cut up

1 (4-ounce) can diced
  green chiles

1 (15-ounce) can chili beans
  or kidney beans

1 (7- or 8-ounce) package
  spaghetti, broken or elbow
  macaroni, cooked

Brown the beef and sausage in a large kettle over high heat, stirring until crumbly; drain. Add the onion, green pepper, garlic powder, instant bouillon, cumin, oregano, sugar, salt and red pepper. Cook for 5 minutes, stirring constantly. Stir in the crushed tomatoes, tomatoes and chiles. Bring to a boil. Reduce the heat. Simmer, covered, for 20 minutes to 2 hours, stirring occasionally. Add the beans and spaghetti. Cook, uncovered, until heated through, stirring occasionally. Ladle into soup bowls. Garnish with shredded Colby or Monterey Jack cheese.

Tip: Spaghetti can be added to each serving rather than mixed into the chili. Add water for a thinner consistency.

Picadillo

Omit the spaghetti. Add ½ cup raisins, ½ cup sliced pimiento-stuffed green olives, ⅛ teaspoon allspice, ⅛ teaspoon cinnamon and ⅛ teaspoon cloves with the seasonings. Stir in ½ cup toasted slivered almonds before serving. Garnish with chopped parsley or cilantro. Serve with tortilla chips.

Chili Mole

Omit spaghetti. Add 1 ounce unsweetened chocolate or 1 tablespoon unsweetened cocoa, 1 tablespoon toasted sesame seeds and ½ teaspoon cinnamon with the seasonings. Serve over hot cooked rice or with warm tortillas or corn chips.

Approx Per Serving: Cal 432; Prot 31 g;
Carbo 40 g; T Fat 18 g; 37% Calories from Fat;
Chol 74 mg; Fiber 7 g; Sod 1000 mg

We're a chili state! Indiana ranks third nationally in the production of tomatoes for processing. Midwestern tomatoes are known for their great taste, so it's no wonder every gardener in the state seems to grow several varieties. And what Hoosier chili recipe doesn't include canned tomatoes of some type. So add a little Hoosier ground beef, sausage or turkey and perhaps some chili powder from Marion-Kay Spices in Brownstown and we can truly claim chili as our own! Marion-Kay is a longtime Indiana State Fair exhibitor.

Steak Chili Supreme

Yield: 8 (1-cup) servings

1 (2½- to 3-pound) beef round
  steak, partially frozen

1 large onion

1 medium green bell pepper

3 tablespoons vegetable oil

1 (28-ounce) can tomatoes

½ cup dry red wine

3 tablespoons hot chili powder

2 teaspoons salt

1 clove garlic, minced

1 teaspoon paprika

½ teaspoon cumin seeds

½ teaspoon pepper

1 (22-ounce) can hot
  chili beans

Here's a hearty Texas-style chili con carne that's thick and fairly spicy. Serve over wedges of cornbread or hot cooked rice. Sour cream and chopped onions are the perfect toppings.

Trim the fat from the steak. Cut into bite-size pieces. Chop the onion and green pepper. Brown the steak, onion and green pepper in hot oil over high heat in a Dutch oven. Stir in the tomatoes, wine, chili powder, salt, garlic, paprika, cumin seeds and pepper. Reduce the heat. Simmer, covered, for 2 hours or until meat is tender, stirring occasionally. Stir in the beans. Cook until heated through. Ladle into soup bowls.

Approx Per Serving: Cal 414; Prot 46 g; Carbo 19 g; T Fat 16 g; 35% Calories from Fat; Chol 119 mg; Fiber 6 g; Sod 1242 mg

Cajun Sausage Chowder

Yield: 9 (1½-cup) servings

3 medium onions, quartered

1 cup water

1 pound smoked sausage,
  chopped

1 (46-ounce) can tomato juice

1 (28-ounce) can diced
  tomatoes

1 bay leaf

1½ teaspoons seasoned salt

½ teaspoon garlic powder

½ teaspoon thyme leaves

¼ teaspoon pepper

4 cups chopped potatoes

1 green bell pepper, chopped

2 (15-ounce) cans kidney beans

2 teaspoons hot pepper sauce

Purée the onion and water in a blender. Brown the sausage in a large kettle; drain. Add the puréed onion, tomato juice, tomatoes, bay leaf, salt, garlic powder, thyme and pepper to the sausage and mix well. Bring to a boil. Reduce the heat. Simmer, covered, for 15 minutes. Stir in the potatoes, green pepper and beans. Cook for 15 to 20 minutes longer or until potatoes are tender. Stir in the hot pepper sauce. Remove the bay leaf. Ladle into soup bowls. Garnish with chopped parsley.

Variation: Use frozen southern-style or hash brown potatoes, thawed, instead of chopped fresh potatoes. Add 1 (14-ounce) package frozen cooked salad shrimp, thawed with the hot pepper sauce; cook until heated through.

Approx Per Serving: Cal 373; Prot 19 g; Carbo 41 g; T Fat 15 g; 37% Calories from Fat; Chol 32 mg; Fiber 7 g; Sod 1892 mg

Harvest Corn Chowder   *Yield: 12 (1½-cup) servings*

1 large onion, chopped

*1 red bell pepper, chopped, or
1 (4-ounce) jar diced
pimientos, drained
(optional)*

*1 tablespoon chopped garlic, or
1 teaspoon garlic powder*

2 teaspoons thyme leaves

1 teaspoon poultry seasoning

*2 tablespoons olive oil or
bacon drippings*

*8 ounces link smoked sausage,
sliced or chopped
smoked ham*

4 medium potatoes, cubed

*2 tablespoons reduced-sodium
instant chicken bouillon*

4 cups water, divided

*1 quart or 1 (16-ounce)
package frozen corn, thawed*

*2 cups cubed cooked chicken or
turkey*

*3 (12-ounce) cans evaporated
skim milk, or 4½ cups milk
or half-and-half*

This recipe was created to showcase our homegrown, then frozen, Indiana sweet corn—Silver Queen is our favorite variety. This hearty chowder has won raves from my husband and other family members so I often serve it at informal gatherings throughout the fall and winter. You can use a combination of evaporated milk, milk, and half-and-half.

Cook the onion, red pepper, garlic, thyme and poultry seasoning in oil in a large kettle until tender. Stir in the sausage. Cook for 5 minutes or until browned. Add the potatoes, instant bouillon and 2 cups of the water. Bring to a boil. Reduce the heat. Simmer, covered, for 10 minutes or until potatoes are tender. Stir in the corn, chicken and remaining 2 cups water. Bring to a boil. Stir in the evaporated milk. Cook until heated through. Ladle into soup bowls. Garnish with chopped parsley.

Approx Per Serving: Cal 302; Prot 20 g; Carbo 33 g; T Fat 10 g; 31% Calories from Fat; Chol 36 mg; Fiber 3 g; Sod 393 mg

A Herb Hint—Thyme

A versatile herb with a warm, pleasant flavor that combines well with pork, poultry, seafood and vegetables, especially beans.

When adding natural cheese to a hot mixture, remove the pan from the heat. You'll avoid excessive heating, which toughens the cheese.

Do not boil soups and sauces containing cheese. The protein in the cheese coagulates, or hardens and separates from the fat and water. The soup or sauce will end up watery and stringy or grainy.

Five-A-Day Broccoli Soup   *Yield: 8 (1½-cup) servings*

1 large bunch broccoli

½ small head cabbage, cut into wedges

4 medium potatoes, peeled, cut into pieces

3 medium onions, cut into halves

2 large carrots, peeled, cut into pieces

2 tablespoons chopped garlic, or 1 teaspoon garlic powder

1 quart water

3 tablespoons reduced-sodium instant chicken bouillon

6 peppercorns, or ¼ teaspoon pepper

1½ teaspoons seasoned salt

1 teaspoon poultry seasoning

1 teaspoon thyme leaves

½ teaspoon nutmeg

1 (12-ounce) can evaporated skim milk

Americans are being urged to eat five or more servings of fruits and vegetables every day. This "creamy" low-fat soup makes it easy to "eat your vegetables." A medley of fresh vegetables are cooked together then puréed to create this tasty satisfying soup.

Trim the broccoli and cut the stems into large pieces. Separate the head into small florets. Reserve 2 cups of the florets. Combine the remaining broccoli, cabbage, potatoes, onions, carrots, garlic, water, instant bouillon, peppercorns, salt, poultry seasoning, thyme and nutmeg in a large kettle. Bring to a boil. Cook, covered, for 20 minutes or until vegetables are tender. Purée, 2 cups at a time, in a blender. Return to the kettle. Steam the reserved broccoli florets until tender-crisp; drain. Stir the florets and evaporated milk into the purée. Cook until heated through. Serve with Parmesan cheese.

Red Pepper Broccoli Soup
Add 1 chopped red bell pepper to the vegetables in the kettle. Steam 1 chopped red bell pepper with the broccoli.

Broccoli Cheese Soup
Add 2 to 3 cups shredded Cheddar cheese or 2 cups cubed process American cheese along with evaporated milk.

Approx Per Serving: Cal 154; Prot 8 g; Carbo 31 g; T Fat 1 g; 5% Calories from Fat; Chol 2 mg; Fiber 5 g; Sod 262 mg

Cheeseburger Potato Soup   *Yield: 6 servings*

8 ounces lean ground beef or
    diced cooked ham

½ cup chopped onion

½ cup chopped celery

1 tablespoon vegetable oil or
    butter (optional)

4 cups peeled, chopped
    potatoes

1 teaspoon salt

¼ teaspoon pepper

1 cup water

2 tablespoons flour

3 cups milk

1 cup whipping cream

½ cup sour cream

2 cups shredded Colby or mild
    Cheddar cheese, divided

2 tablespoons chopped parsley

*Serve this hearty soup for your next Super Bowl gathering or tailgate party. It's
sure to win rave reviews, especially from the men in the crowd!*

Brown the ground beef with the onion and celery in the oil in a large
saucepan. Add the potatoes, salt, pepper and 1 cup of water. Bring to a
boil. Cook, covered, for 10 to 15 minutes or until potatoes are tender.
Dissolve the flour in a small amount of water in a cup. Stir into the
soup. Cook until thickened and bubbly, stirring constantly. Add the milk,
whipping cream, sour cream, 1 cup of the cheese and the parsley and
mix well. Cook over medium-low heat until the cheese is melted and
soup is heated through; do not boil. Ladle into soup bowls. Garnish each
serving with the remaining cheese.

Potato Cheese Soup
Omit the ground beef and increase the cheese to 3 cups, adding 2 cups
to the soup.

Approx Per Serving: Cal 579; Prot 25 g; Carbo 30 g; T Fat 40 g; 62% Calories from Fat;
Chol 142 mg; Fiber 2 g; Sod 738 mg

Instant Potato Soup Mix   *Yield: 7 servings*

1¾ cups instant potato flakes

1¾ cups nonfat dry milk

2 tablespoons reduced-sodium
    instant chicken bouillon

2 teaspoons dried minced
    onion

1½ teaspoons seasoned salt

1 teaspoon dried parsley

¼ teaspoon dried thyme leaves

¼ teaspoon white pepper

⅛ teaspoon turmeric

*Here's an easy make-ahead soup mix that's a real time saver when you want
a quick and satisfying cup of soup. Why not make a batch, divide into individual
servings and seal in small sealable plastic bags. Write the preparation directions
on a label and attach to each bag. Tuck a few soup packets into that special
college student's care package or share some with your live-alone neighbor.*

Combine the potato flakes, dry milk, instant bouillon, onion, seasoned
salt, parsley, thyme, white pepper and turmeric in a bowl and mix well. To
make the soup place ½ cup in a soup bowl. Pour in 1 cup of hot water
or milk. Stir until the bouillon is dissolved. Garnish with butter, cooked
bacon bits, shredded cheese, chives or chopped green onions.

Approx Per Serving: Cal 105; Prot ;7 g; Carbo 18 g; T Fat <1 g; 3% Calories from Fat;
Chol 3 mg; Fiber <1 g; Sod 302 mg

Old-Fashioned Vegetable Beef Soup   *Yield: 12 (1½-cup) servings*

1½ pounds beef shanks

1 tablespoon vegetable oil

4 cups tomato juice or
   vegetable juice cocktail

2 tablespoons chopped parsley

2 teaspoons salt

1 bay leaf

3 peppercorns

¼ teaspoon basil

¼ teaspoon marjoram

¼ teaspoon thyme leaves

1 cup sliced carrots

1 cup sliced celery with leaves

1 cup chopped potato

1 medium onion, chopped

3 tablespoons pearl barley

2 cups or 1 (15-ounce) can
   tomatoes

1 cup chopped cabbage

1 cup frozen corn kernels

1 cup cut green beans

1 cup frozen lima beans

½ to 1 cup frozen green peas

4 cups hot water

Adapted from an old cookbook, this traditional vegetable soup has rich flavors from long, slow simmering. If you're a from-scratch cook on the weekends, make a batch for Sunday supper and freeze the rest. When time is short, the quick version is a good choice.

Brown the beef in hot oil in a large kettle. Stir in the tomato juice, parsley, salt, bay leaf, peppercorns, basil, marjoram and thyme. Bring to a boil. Reduce the heat. Simmer, covered, 1½ to 2 hours or until beef is tender. Remove the meat from the bones and cut into small pieces. Discard the bones. Return the meat to the kettle. Add the carrots, celery, potato, onion and barley. Bring to a boil. Cook, covered, for 20 minutes. Stir in the tomatoes, cabbage, corn, green beans, lima beans, peas and water. Cook for 20 minutes or until vegetables are tender. Remove bay leaf and peppercorns. Ladle into soup bowls. This soup freezes well.

Quick Vegetable Beef Soup
Substitute 1½ pounds lean ground beef and 1 tablespoon reduced-sodium instant beef bouillon for the beef shanks, oil and barley. Brown the lean ground beef with the onion and beef bouillon. Add the tomato juice, parsley, carrots, celery, potato and seasonings. Bring to a boil. Cook, covered, for 15 minutes. Add the remaining vegetables and water. Cook for 15 minutes or until vegetables are tender.

Approx Per Serving: Cal 140; Prot 10 g; Carbo 20 g; T Fat 3 g; 17% Calories from Fat; Chol 15 mg; Fiber 4 g; Sod 788 mg

Chicken Velvet Soup

Yield: 8 (1-cup) servings

3/4 cup butter

*3/4 cup plus
   2 tablespoons flour*

1 cup milk

1 cup half-and-half

*1 (49-ounce) can
   chicken broth*

*1 1/2 to 2 cups chopped
   cooked chicken*

Salt and freshly ground pepper

Many Hoosiers have fond memories of
wonderful lunches at the L.S. Ayres tea
room in downtown Indianapolis. This rich,
creamy soup was inspired by one of their
favorite menu offerings.

Melt the butter in a large saucepan.
Stir in the flour until smooth and
bubbly. Add the milk, half-and-half
and broth, whisking constantly. Bring
to a boil over medium heat, stirring
constantly. Reduce the heat. Stir in the
chicken. Cook until heated through.
Season with salt and pepper.

Tip: This soup freezes well.

Variations: Add 1 (7-ounce) can sliced
mushrooms, drained, or 8 ounces fresh
mushrooms, sliced and browned in
2 tablespoons butter, with the chicken.

Cook 1/2 cup chopped onion in the
butter. Add 1 (2-ounce) jar diced
pimiento, drained with the chicken.
Garnish with toasted sliced almonds.

Add 1 cup chopped steamed
asparagus or small broccoli florets
and 1/4 teaspoon ground nutmeg with
the chicken.

Cook 1 cup peeled, chopped tart
apple, 1/2 cup chopped onion,
1/2 teaspoon curry powder and 1/4
teaspoon ground nutmeg in the
butter. Garnish with sliced green
onions or chopped peanuts.

Approx Per Serving: Cal 381; Prot 21 g;
Carbo 14 g; T Fat 26 g; 62% Calories from Fat;
Chol 95 mg; Fiber <1 g; Sod 1320 mg

Special French Onion Soup   *Yield: 4 servings*

3 cups thinly sliced onions

3 tablespoons butter or
   margarine

2 tablespoons flour

2 (14-ounce) cans beef broth

1/4 cup half-and-half, at room
   temperature

Salt to taste

4 slices French bread, toasted

4 ounces Swiss cheese,
   shredded

The touch of half-and-half in this recipe is what makes this classic soup special—better than what you'll find at any restaurant.

Cook the onions in butter in a large heavy skillet until lightly browned. Sprinkle with flour. Cook until golden, stirring constantly. Add the broth, whisking constantly. Bring to a boil. Reduce the heat. Simmer for 20 minutes. Stir in the half-and-half slowly. Cook until heated through. Season with salt. Ladle into 4 ovenproof bowls. Place a toast slice over the soup in each bowl. Sprinkle with the cheese. Broil in a preheated broiler until brown. Serve immediately.

Approx Per Serving: Cal 342; Prot 17 g; Carbo 27 g; T Fat 19 g; 50% Calories from Fat; Chol 63 mg; Fiber 2 g; Sod 1763 mg

White Gazpacho   *Yield: 6 (1-cup) servings*

4 teaspoons reduced-sodium
   instant chicken bouillon

2 cups boiling water

3 medium cucumbers, peeled,
   seeded, chopped

2 cups sour cream

2 tablespoons lemon juice

1/4 teaspoon garlic powder

1/4 teaspoon pepper

Looking for a cool, refreshing accompaniment for a chicken or tuna salad? Look no further. This chilled gazpacho features the bounty of the summer garden— cucumbers, tomatoes, bell peppers (or in Hoosier lingo, "mangos").

Dissolve the bouillon in boiling water in a bowl; cool. Purée the cucumbers and 1/2 cup of the bouillon liquid in a blender. Combine the cucumber purée, remaining bouillon liquid, sour cream, lemon juice, garlic powder and pepper in a bowl and mix well. Refrigerate until completely chilled. Ladle into soup bowls. Serve with chopped fresh tomatoes, sliced green onions, chopped green or red bell peppers, toasted slivered almonds and/or croutons.

Approx Per Serving: Cal 183; Prot 3 g; Carbo 8 g; T Fat 16 g; 77% Calories from Fat; Chol 34 mg; Fiber 1 g; Sod 46 mg

Sweet Potato Apple Soup   *Yield: 10 (1-cup) servings*

1 medium onion, sliced

3 all-purpose apples, peeled, sliced

2¹/₂ teaspoons curry powder

1 teaspoon cinnamon

1 teaspoon ginger

3 tablespoons butter or margarine

3 sweet potatoes, peeled, cut into chunks

2 tablespoons reduced-sodium instant chicken bouillon

2 tablespoons chopped fresh parsley

6 cups hot water

1 teaspoon salt

Freshly ground pepper

Here's a light soup that combines two fall favorites—sweet potatoes and apples. Serve as a holiday meal starter or as a soup-and-sandwich supper along with turkey or ham sandwiches.

Cook the onion, apples, curry powder, cinnamon and ginger in butter in a large kettle over low heat until onion is tender. Add the sweet potatoes, instant bouillon, parsley, water, salt and pepper and mix well. Bring to a boil. Reduce the heat. Simmer, covered, for 40 minutes or until potatoes are very tender. Purée the soup in batches in a blender. Return to kettle. Heat through. Ladle into soup bowls. Garnish with chopped nuts, parsley or nutmeg.

Approx Per Serving: Cal 112; Prot 1 g; Carbo 19 g; T Fat 4 g; 30% Calories from Fat; Chol 9 mg; Fiber 2 g; Sod 277 mg

The sweet potato, sometimes incorrectly called a "yam," is a large edible root belonging to the morning glory family. Native to the tropical areas of the Americas, the many varieties of sweet potatoes can generally be divided into the pale, not-sweet, yellow-flesh types that have a dry, mealy texture after cooking, and the darker orange, thicker skin varieties that are sweet and moist. Sweet potatoes are high in vitamins A and C.

Traditional Oyster Stew   *Yield: 4 (2-cup) servings*

1 pint shucked fresh oysters

¼ teaspoon celery salt

¼ teaspoon pepper

¼ teaspoon seasoned salt

¼ teaspoon paprika

2 tablespoons butter or
   margarine

4 cups half-and-half

2 cups milk

Hot pepper sauce to taste
   (optional)

This wintertime family favorite is so easy—perfect for a fireside supper that's ready in minutes. Serve this rich, warming classic with crusty bread and fresh fruit.

Drain the oysters, reserving the liquid. Cut the large oysters into thirds. Combine the reserved liquid, celery salt, pepper, seasoned salt, paprika, butter, half-and-half and milk in a saucepan. Cook until heated through; do not boil. Stir in the oysters and hot pepper sauce. Cook for 3 to 5 minutes or until edges of oysters begin to curl. Ladle into soup bowls.

Approx Per Serving: Cal 605; Prot 30 g; Carbo 26 g; T Fat 42 g; 63% Calories from Fat; Chol 222 mg; Fiber <1 g; Sod 580 mg

Herbed Lamb Stew   *Yield: 6 (1-cup) servings*

1½ pounds boneless lamb
   roast, cut into 1-inch cubes

1 clove garlic, minced

1 bay leaf

½ teaspoon marjoram

½ teaspoon oregano leaves

½ teaspoon thyme leaves

2 tablespoons vegetable oil

2 cups hot water

2 beef bouillon cubes

½ teaspoon salt

¼ teaspoon pepper

4 carrots, cut into ½-inch slices

4 ribs celery, cut into
   1-inch slices

1 cup frozen green peas

2 medium onions, chopped

½ cup sour cream

¼ cup flour

3 tablespoons water

Brown the lamb with the garlic, bay leaf, marjoram, oregano and thyme in hot oil in a Dutch oven. Add 2 cups hot water, bouillon cubes, salt and pepper. Bring to a boil. Reduce the heat. Simmer, covered, for 30 minutes. Add the carrots, celery, peas and onions. Simmer for 25 minutes or until meat and vegetables are tender. Remove the bay leaf. Combine the sour cream, flour and 3 tablespoons water in a bowl and stir until smooth. Stir ½ cup of the hot broth into the sour cream mixture and mix well. Stir into the stew. Cook until thickened and bubbly, stirring constantly. Serve with rice.

Approx Per Serving: Cal 318; Prot 23 g; Carbo 17 g; T Fat 17 g; 49% Calories from Fat; Chol 76 mg; Fiber 4 g; Sod 613 mg

Classic Beef Stew   *Yield: 8 (1-cup) servings*

1/2 cup flour

1 teaspoon salt

1/4 teaspoon pepper

2 pounds beef stew meat, cut
    into 1-inch cubes

2 tablespoons vegetable oil or
    shortening

4 cups hot water, divided

2 tablespoons reduced-sodium
    instant beef bouillon

1 bay leaf

1 tablespoon Worcestershire
    sauce

1 teaspoon thyme leaves

4 large carrots, peeled, cut into
    1-inch pieces

4 medium potatoes,
    peeled, cubed

4 small onions, cut into halves

2 ribs celery, cut into
    1-inch pieces

1 green bell pepper, cut into
    1-inch pieces (optional)

When it comes to comfort food, nothing beats a flavorful, satisfying beef stew. Add some crusty bread or warm rolls and coleslaw and enjoy!

Combine the flour, salt and pepper in a plastic bag. Add the meat, a few pieces at a time. Shake to coat well. Brown the meat in hot oil in a Dutch oven. Add 2 cups of the water, instant bouillon, bay leaf, Worcestershire sauce and thyme. Bring to a boil. Reduce the heat. Simmer, covered, 1 1/2 to 2 hours or until meat is tender, stirring occasionally. Add the carrots, potatoes, onions, celery, green pepper and remaining 2 cups water and mix well. Simmer 30 minutes or until vegetables are tender. Remove bay leaf. Garnish with chopped parsley.

Rosy Beef Stew
Reduce water to 2 cups and add 1 (15-ounce) can tomato sauce and 2 whole allspice before simmering beef.

Baked Beef Stew
Reduce water to 1 cup. Brown the meat. Combine meat, vegetables, seasonings, 1 cup water, 1 (15-ounce) can stewed tomatoes and 3 table-spoons tapioca; mix well. Bake, tightly covered, at 250 degrees for 6 hours; do not uncover during baking.

Slow-Cooker Beef Stew
Reduce water to 1/4 cup. Combine all ingredients in slow cooker. Cook on Low for 10 to 12 hours. Stir occasionally.

Approx Per Serving: Cal 314; Prot 25 g;
Carbo 27 g; T Fat 12 g; 33% Calories from Fat;
Chol 70 mg; Fiber 3 g; Sod 551 mg

With 2,700 sheep operations across the state, Indiana is the 28th largest producer of sheep and lambs in the U.S. Today's lamb is lower in calories and leaner than ever before. Nutritionists call lamb a "high nutrient density" food product and recommend its consumption by health conscious consumers.

A huge Indiana sunflower, photographed by 4-H'er Katie Shannon of Wells County, beams a back-door welcome to family and friends. And the spicy, sweet aroma of freshly baked cookies beckons them into the kitchen. This collection of prizewinner "Cookies, Confections & Candies"—chocolate bars, raisin-studded oatmeal cookies, creamy fudge, and crunchy caramel corn—promises the baker plenty of blue ribbon praise.

COOKIES
CONFECTIONS
& CANDIES

A COLLECTION OF PRIZEWINNING COOKIE, CONFECTION, AND CANDY RECIPES

Using a Cookie Scoop

Blue ribbon winners know they must enter a plate of drop cookies that are uniform in size. Many use a cookie scoop, which holds a level measuring tablespoon of dough. A squeeze of the spring-action handle releases the dough and works well for a soft or slightly stiff dough.

 Pecan Frosties *Yield: 36 cookies*

2 cups flour

½ teaspoon baking soda

¼ teaspoon salt

½ cup butter, softened

1¼ cups packed brown sugar, divided

1 egg

1 teaspoon vanilla extract

½ cup chopped pecans

2 tablespoons sour cream

Preheat oven to 350 degrees. Combine the flour, baking soda and salt in a bowl and mix well. Beat the butter and 1 cup of the brown sugar in a mixer bowl until light and fluffy. Beat in the egg and vanilla. Add the dry ingredients gradually, mixing well after each addition. Shape into 1-inch balls. Place 2 inches apart on cookie sheets. Combine the pecans, sour cream and remaining ¼ cup brown sugar in a bowl and mix well. Make a shallow depression in center of each ball. Fill with ½ teaspoon of pecan mixture. Bake for 10 to 12 minutes or until browned.

Approx Per Cookie: Cal 91; Prot 1 g; Carbo 13 g; T Fat 4 g; 39% Calories from Fat; Chol 13 mg; Fiber <1 g; Sod 65 mg

Persimmon Spice Cookies *Yield: 24 cookies*

2 cups flour

2 teaspoons baking powder

1 teaspoon salt

1 teaspoon cinnamon

½ teaspoon cloves

¼ teaspoon ginger

½ cup shortening

1 cup sugar

1 cup persimmon pulp

2 eggs, beaten

1 cup chopped hickory nuts

1 cup raisins

Preheat oven to 350 degrees. Combine the flour, baking powder, salt, cinnamon, cloves and ginger in a bowl and mix well. Beat the shortening and sugar in a mixer bowl until light and fluffy. Beat in the persimmon pulp and eggs. Add the dry ingredients and mix well. Stir in the nuts and raisins. Drop by teaspoonfuls onto a cookie sheet sprayed with nonstick cooking spray. Bake for 14 to 15 minutes or until set and lightly browned.

Variation: May substitute pumpkin for the persimmon pulp.

Approx Per Cookie: Cal 179; Prot 3 g; Carbo 26 g; T Fat 8 g; 39% Calories from Fat; Chol 18 mg; Fiber 1 g; Sod 144 mg

 **Brickle Bars**   *Yield: 24 bars*

1¹/₂ cups sifted flour

1 teaspoon baking powder

¹/₂ teaspoon salt

¹/₂ cup packed brown sugar

1 cup sugar

¹/₂ cup margarine, softened

2 eggs

1 teaspoon vanilla extract

*1 (7-ounce) package
    brickle bits*

Preheat oven to 350 degrees. Sift the flour, baking powder and salt together. Beat the brown sugar, sugar and margarine in a mixer bowl until light and fluffy. Beat in the eggs and vanilla. Add the dry ingredients and mix well. Stir in the brickle bits. Spread evenly in a greased 9x13-inch baking pan. Bake for 30 minutes. Cut into bars.

Approx Per Bar: Cal 160; Prot 1 g; Carbo 23 g; T Fat 7 g; 39% Calories from Fat; Chol 20 mg; Fiber <1 g; Sod 167 mg

 German Chocolate Brownies   *Yield: 24 brownies*

*1 (2-layer) package German
    chocolate cake mix*

¹/₂ cup margarine, melted

1 cup chopped pecans

*²/₃ cup evaporated milk,
    divided*

*1 (14-ounce) package light
    caramels*

*1 (6-ounce) package milk
    chocolate chips*

Preheat oven to 350 degrees. Combine the cake mix, margarine, pecans and ¹/₃ cup of the evaporated milk in a bowl and mix well. Spread half the mixture into a greased 9x13-inch baking pan. Bake for 6 minutes. Melt the caramels with the remaining ¹/₃ cup evaporated milk in a saucepan, stirring frequently. Pour over the baked cake layer. Sprinkle the milk chocolate chips over the caramel layer. Spoon the remaining cake mixture over the top. Bake for 15 to 18 minutes. Cool completely. Cut into bars.

Approx Per Brownie: Cal 269; Prot 4 g; Carbo 34 g; T Fat 14 g; 45% Calories from Fat; Chol 10 mg; Fiber 1 g; Sod 253 mg

Rockie Road Brownies   *Yield: 12 brownies*

1 (6-ounce) package semisweet
  chocolate chips

½ cup margarine

1½ cups flour

1 cup sugar

½ teaspoon baking powder

¼ teaspoon salt

½ teaspoon vanilla extract

2 eggs

⅓ (7-ounce) package brickle
  bits (optional)

2 cups miniature
  marshmallows

1 cup chopped pecans

Preheat oven to 375 degrees. Melt ½ cup of the chocolate chips and margarine in a saucepan over low heat; cool. Combine the flour, sugar, baking powder, salt, vanilla, eggs and chocolate mixture in a bowl and mix well. Spread in a 9-inch square baking dish. Bake for 15 minutes. Sprinkle with the remaining chocolate chips, brickle bits, marshmallows and pecans. Bake until the marshmallows are golden brown. Cut into squares.

Approx Per Brownie: Cal 360; Prot 4 g; Carbo 46 g; T Fat 20 g; 47% Calories from Fat; Chol 35 mg; Fiber 2 g; Sod 174 mg

 ## Sugar-Free Pineapple Nut Brownies   *Yield: 32 brownies*

1 cup flour

½ teaspoon baking powder

¼ teaspoon baking soda

¼ teaspoon salt

½ cup margarine

1 square baking chocolate

Sugar substitute equivalent to
  ½ cup sugar

1 egg

1 egg white

1 (8-ounce) can crushed
  pineapple, drained

1 teaspoon almond extract

⅓ cup chopped walnuts

Preheat oven to 350 degrees. Sift the flour, baking powder, baking soda and salt together. Melt the margarine and chocolate in a large saucepan. Stir in the sugar substitute. Remove from heat. Beat in the egg, egg white, pineapple and almond extract. Add the dry ingredients and mix well. Fold in the walnuts. Pour into a greased 8-inch square baking pan. Bake for 30 to 35 minutes or until brownies begin to pull from sides of pan. Cool on a wire rack. Cut into 1x2-inch bars.

Approx Per Brownie: Cal 58; Prot 1 g; Carbo 5 g; T Fat 4 g; 61% Calories from Fat; Chol 7 mg; Fiber <1 g; Sod 73 mg

Chocolate Chip Tofu Bars   *Yield: 24 bars*

2 (16-ounce) packages
    refrigerated chocolate chip or
    oatmeal chocolate chip slice
    and bake cookie dough,
    softened
1 (10-ounce) package firm
    silken tofu
2 eggs
1 cup sugar
1 teaspoon vanilla extract

Preheat oven to 350 degrees. Spread 1 package of the cookie dough over the bottom and up the sides of a 9x13-inch baking pan sprayed with nonstick cooking spray. Combine the tofu, eggs, sugar and vanilla in a food processor container. Process until smooth. Spread over the cookie dough layer. Drop the remaining package of cookie dough by teaspoonfuls over the tofu mixture layer. Bake for 40 to 45 minutes. Cut into bars.

Approx Per Bar: Cal 213; Prot 3 g;
Carbo 32 g; T Fat 8 g; 35% Calories from Fat;
Chol 27 mg; Fiber 1 g; Sod 89 mg

 ## Date Casserole Cookies   *Yield: 42 cookies*

2 eggs
1 1/2 cups sugar, divided
1 teaspoon vanilla extract
1/2 teaspoon almond extract
1/4 teaspoon salt
1 cup flaked coconut
1 cup chopped pecans
1 cup finely chopped dates

Preheat oven to 350 degrees. Beat the eggs and 1 cup of the sugar in a mixer bowl until well mixed. Add the vanilla, almond extract and salt and mix well. Stir in the coconut, pecans and dates. Spoon into a 2-quart baking dish. Bake for 15 minutes. Stir with a wooden spoon. Bake for 15 to 20 minutes. Remove from oven and stir with a wooden spoon. Cool. Shape into balls. Roll in the remaining 1/2 cup sugar. Let stand until partially dried.

Approx Per Cookie: Cal 65; Prot 1 g;
Carbo 11 g; T Fat 3 g; 34% Calories from Fat;
Chol 10 mg; Fiber 1 g; Sod 17 mg

What is Tofu?

Tofu is a solid cake made of curdled soymilk with a cheese-like consistency and a bland flavor that blends well with many other ingredients. Tofu is available in both soft and hard varieties, packed in aseptic brick packages, water- or vacuum-packed tubs, sold in the produce or dairy section of most larger supermarkets. Silken tofu has a smooth, creamy texture. Use for dips, dressings, desserts. Soft tofu is moist and somewhat firmer than the silken variety. Use for dressings and dips. Firm/Extra firm tofu will hold its texture in salads, stir-frys and soups.

Low-Fat Spread Not the Best Choice for Baking

Low-fat "spreads" definitely have a place in the diet of anyone who wants to cut down on fat. But don't use them to replace full-fat margarine or butter in a cookie recipe. Besides having a lower amount of fat, these spreads contain more water. Cookies made with them will have a different texture and appearance and won't stay fresh as long.

Lemon-Glazed Persimmon Bars   *Yield: 36 bars*

1 cup persimmon pulp
1 teaspoon baking soda
1 egg
$\frac{1}{2}$ cup vegetable oil
1 cup sugar
1 cup raisins
$1\frac{1}{2}$ cups flour
1 teaspoon cinnamon
1 teaspoon nutmeg
$\frac{1}{2}$ teaspoon salt
$\frac{1}{4}$ teaspoon cloves
1 cup chopped pecans
1 cup powdered sugar
2 teaspoons lemon juice

Preheat oven to 350 degrees. Combine the persimmon pulp and baking soda in a medium bowl and mix well. Beat the egg in a small bowl. Add the oil and sugar and beat until well mixed. Stir in the raisins. Add the raisin mixture to the persimmon pulp mixture.

Combine the flour, cinnamon, nutmeg, salt and cloves in a separate bowl and mix well. Add the flour mixture to the persimmon pulp mixture. Stir in the pecans. Spoon the batter into a greased 10x15-inch baking pan. Bake for 20 minutes. Cool for 5 minutes. Combine the powdered sugar and lemon juice in a small bowl and mix well. Spread over the top of the baked layer. Cool completely. Cut into bars.

Approx Per Bar: Cal 125; Prot 1 g; Carbo 19 g; T Fat 6 g; 38% Calories from Fat; Chol 6 mg; Fiber 1 g; Sod 70 mg

Toffee Cookie Bars   *Yield: 24 bars*

½ cup butter

1½ cups graham cracker crumbs

1 (14-ounce) can sweetened condensed milk

1 (7-ounce) package almond brickle chips

1 (7-ounce) package milk chocolate-covered English toffee bits

1 (6-ounce) package semisweet chocolate chips

1 cup chopped pecans

½ to ⅔ cup sliced natural almonds

These rich, buttery one-pan cookie bars couldn't be easier—just layer the ingredients in the baking pan. If you line the pan with aluminum foil, you won't even have one pan to wash.

Preheat oven to 325 degrees. Spray the sides of a 9x13-inch baking pan with nonstick cooking spray. Melt the butter in the prepared pan in the oven. Sprinkle the graham cracker crumbs evenly over the butter. Pour the condensed milk over the crumbs. Sprinkle the brickle chips, toffee bits, chocolate chips, pecans and almonds over the layers in the order listed. Press down firmly. Bake for 25 minutes or until edges are golden brown. Cool. Cut into bars. Store tightly covered.

Toffee Fruit Bars
Omit the toffee bits and chocolate chips; add 1 (10-ounce) package chocolate-covered raisins or use the 6 ounces chocolate chips and add ¾ cup raisins, and add 1 cup chopped dried apricots combined with 2 tablespoons apricot brandy or amaretto.

Tropical Toffee Bars
Omit the toffee bits, pecans and almonds; add 1 cup chopped dried pineapple combined with 2 tablespoons rum or amaretto, ¾ cup flaked coconut and 1 (3-ounce) jar macadamia nuts, chopped.

Peanut Cookie Bars
Omit the almond brickle chips, toffee bits, pecans and almonds; add 1 (10-ounce) package peanut butter chips and 1½ cups coarsely chopped dry-roasted or Spanish peanuts.

Approx Per Bar: Cal 292; Prot 3 g; Carbo 30 g; T Fat 18 g; 55% Calories from Fat; Chol 23 mg; Fiber 1 g; Sod 176 mg

143

Sugar-Free Apple Walnut Drop Cookies   *Yield: 48 cookies*

3 cups flour

1½ teaspoons baking soda

¾ cup margarine, softened

Brown sugar substitute
    equivalent to 2 cups
    brown sugar

¾ teaspoon salt

1½ teaspoons allspice

1½ teaspoons cinnamon

¾ teaspoon nutmeg

2 eggs

⅓ cup milk

1½ cups chopped walnuts

1½ cups chopped raisins

1½ cups finely chopped apples

Preheat oven to 400 degrees. Sift the flour and baking soda together. Combine the margarine, brown sugar substitute, salt, allspice, cinnamon, nutmeg and eggs in a bowl and mix well. Add the milk and sifted dry ingredients and mix well. Stir in the walnuts, raisins and apples. Drop by rounded teaspoonfuls onto lightly greased cookie sheets. Bake for 10 to 15 minutes or until lightly browned.

Approx Per Cookie: Cal 109; Prot 2 g; Carbo 15 g; T Fat 5 g; 41% Calories from Fat; Chol 9 mg; Fiber 1 g; Sod 114 mg

 ## No-Sugar Applesauce Prune Cookies   *Yield: 18 cookies*

1 cup chopped prunes

1 cup flour

½ teaspoon salt

1 teaspoon baking powder

1 teaspoon cinnamon

½ teaspoon nutmeg

1 teaspoon baking soda

¼ cup margarine

1 egg

⅓ cup vegetable oil

Brown sugar substitute
    equivalent to ¾ cup
    brown sugar

1 cup unsweetened applesauce

1 cup rolled oats

Preheat oven to 350 degrees. Cook the prunes in enough water to cover in a saucepan until plump; drain. Sift the flour, salt, baking powder, cinnamon, nutmeg and baking soda together. Combine the margarine, egg, oil and brown sugar substitute in a bowl and mix well. Add the applesauce, oats and cooked prunes and mix well. Stir in the dry ingredients. Add additional flour if batter is too moist. Drop by teaspoonfuls onto greased cookie sheets. Bake for 12 minutes. Remove to a wire rack to cool completely. Store in the refrigerator or freezer.

Approx Per Cookie: Cal 153; Prot 2 g; Carbo 21 g; T Fat 7 g; 41% Calories from Fat; Chol 12 mg; Fiber 2 g; Sod 196 mg

Breakfast Cookies

Yield: 48 cookies

3 cups flour
1 teaspoon baking powder
1 teaspoon baking soda
1/2 teaspoon salt
1 cup butter-flavor shortening
1 cup sugar
1 cup packed brown sugar
2 tablespoons orange juice
1 teaspoon vanilla extract
2 eggs
1 cup quick-cooking oats
1/2 cup crushed cornflakes
1 cup white chocolate chips
1 cup pecan pieces

Preheat oven to 350 degrees. Combine the flour, baking powder, baking soda and salt in a bowl and mix well. Beat the shortening, sugar and brown sugar in a mixer bowl until light and fluffy. Beat in the orange juice, vanilla and eggs. Beat in the flour mixture gradually. Stir in the oats, cornflakes, chocolate chips and pecans. Drop by heaping teaspoonfuls 3 inches apart onto greased cookie sheets. Bake for 10 to 12 minutes. Cool on cookie sheets for 3 minutes. Remove to a wire rack to cool completely.

Approx Per Cookie: Cal 150; Prot 2 g; Carbo 19 g; T Fat 8 g; 44% Calories from Fat; Chol 10 mg; Fiber 1 g; Sod 78 mg

 ## Butterscotch Almond Cookies

Yield: 24 cookies

1 cup packed brown sugar
1 cup sugar
1 1/2 cups margarine, softened
2 eggs
1 teaspoon baking soda
2 teaspoons baking powder
1/4 teaspoon salt
1 teaspoon almond extract
1 teaspoon vanilla extract
2 tablespoons vinegar
4 cups flour

Preheat oven to 350 degrees. Beat the brown sugar, sugar and margarine in a mixer bowl until light and fluffy. Beat in the eggs, baking soda, baking powder, salt, almond extract, vanilla and vinegar. Add the flour gradually, mixing well after each addition. Drop by tablespoonfuls onto cookie sheets. Bake for 12 to 15 minutes or until edges are light brown and center is soft. Cool. Store in a covered container.

Approx Per Cookie: Cal 251; Prot 3 g; Carbo 34 g; T Fat 12 g; 43% Calories from Fat; Chol 18 mg; Fiber 1 g; Sod 260 mg

Cookie Sheets

Flat baking sheets with just one side allow better heat circulation, so cookies bake more evenly. If you only have a jellyroll pan, invert it and bake the cookies on the back. Shiny aluminum cookie sheets are best. Avoid dark metal pans. Cookies baked on them will brown unevenly and are more likely to burn on the bottom.

145

Best Chocolate Chip Cookies *Yield: 100 cookies*

5 cups rolled oats

4 cups flour

2 teaspoons baking powder

2 teaspoons baking soda

1 teaspoon salt

2 cups butter, softened

2 cups packed brown sugar

2 cups sugar

4 eggs

2 teaspoons vanilla extract

24 ounces milk chocolate or
semisweet chocolate chips

3 cups chopped pecans or
walnuts

Preheat oven to 350 degrees. Process the oats in a food processor to a fine powder. Combine the processed oats, flour, baking powder, baking soda and salt in a bowl and mix well. Beat the butter, brown sugar and sugar in a mixer bowl until light and fluffy. Beat in the eggs and vanilla. Add the dry ingredients gradually, mixing well after each addition. Stir in the chocolate chips and pecans. Drop by large scoopfuls 2 inches apart onto greased cookie sheets. Bake for 10 minutes; do not overbake.

Approx Per Cookie: Cal 160; Prot 2 g; Carbo 20 g; T Fat 9 g; 47% Calories from Fat; Chol 20 mg; Fiber 1 g; Sod 106 mg

Low-Sugar Oatmeal Chocolate Chip Cookies *Yield: 24 cookies*

1/4 cup margarine, softened

1/3 cup sugar

9 packets saccharin

2 egg whites

2 teaspoons vanilla extract

1/2 cup flour

1 teaspoon baking soda

1/4 teaspoon salt

1 1/2 cups rolled oats or
quick-cooking oats

1/4 cup miniature chocolate
chips

Preheat oven to 350 degrees. Beat the margarine, sugar and sugar substitute in a mixer bowl at medium speed until well blended. Beat in egg whites and vanilla. Beat in the flour, baking soda and salt. Stir in the oats and chocolate chips. Drop by rounded tablespoonfuls onto cookie sheets, pressing down slightly with the back of a spoon. Bake for 6 to 8 minutes or until golden brown around the edges. Cool on the cookie sheets for 1 minute. Remove to a wire rack to cool completely.

Approx Per Cookie: Cal 73; Prot 2 g; Carbo 10 g; T Fat 3 g; 36% Calories from Fat; Chol 0 mg; Fiber 1 g; Sod 105 mg

146

Peanut Butter Chocolate Chip Snaps

Yield: 48 cookies

1⅓ cups flour

½ teaspoon baking powder

¾ teaspoon baking soda

¼ teaspoon salt

½ cup butter

1 ounce unsweetened chocolate

½ cup packed brown sugar

⅔ cup peanut butter

⅔ cup honey

1 teaspoon vanilla extract

1 egg

1 cup chopped walnuts

2 cups semisweet
  chocolate chips

½ cup sugar

Sift the flour, baking powder, baking soda and salt together. Melt the butter and chocolate in a large saucepan, stirring constantly. Remove from heat. Stir in the brown sugar, peanut butter, honey, vanilla and egg until smooth; cool. Stir in the sifted dry ingredients. Stir in the walnuts and chocolate chips. Cover with plastic wrap. Refrigerate for 2 hours. Preheat oven to 350 degrees. Shape dough into 1-inch balls and roll in sugar or drop by tablespoonfuls and sprinkle with sugar. Place 2 inches apart on cookie sheets. Bake for 10 to 15 minutes or until set. Cool on cookie sheets for 2 minutes. Remove to a wire rack to cool completely.

Approx Per Cookie: Cal 136; Prot 2 g; Carbo 17 g; T Fat 8 g; 49% Calories from Fat; Chol 10 mg; Fiber 1 g; Sod 77 mg

The only difference between old-fashioned and quick oats is that quick oats have been cut into two or three pieces to shorten cooking time.

Kitchen Parchment Paper

More blue ribbon bakers are discovering the convenience of using kitchen parchment paper to line baking sheets. Cookies bake evenly on it, and most can be baked without greasing the paper.

Chocolate-Covered Cherry Cookies
Yield: 36 cookies

1½ cups flour

¼ teaspoon salt

¼ teaspoon baking powder

¼ teaspoon baking soda

½ cup unsweetened cocoa

½ cup butter or margarine, softened

1 cup sugar

1 egg

1½ teaspoons vanilla extract

1 (10-ounce) jar maraschino cherries

1 cup semisweet chocolate chips

½ cup sweetened condensed milk

Preheat oven to 350 degrees. Combine the flour, salt, baking powder, baking soda and cocoa in a bowl and mix well. Beat the butter and sugar in a mixer bowl until light and fluffy. Beat in the egg and vanilla until well blended. Add the dry ingredients gradually, mixing well after each addition. Shape into 1-inch balls. Place on cookie sheets. Press down the center of each ball with thumb. Drain the maraschino cherries, reserving 4 teaspoons of the juice. Place a cherry in the center of each cookie.

Combine the chocolate chips and condensed milk in a saucepan. Heat until the chocolate chips are melted, stirring constantly. Stir in the reserved cherry juice. Spoon 1 teaspoon of the chocolate mixture over each cherry, spreading to cover the cherry. Bake for 10 minutes or until cookies test done. Remove to a wire rack to cool.

Approx Per Cookie: Cal 113; Prot 2 g; Carbo 18 g; T Fat 5 g; 35% Calories from Fat; Chol 14 mg; Fiber 1 g; Sod 62 mg

Chocolate-Covered Raisin Snickerdoodles *Yield: 36 cookies*

1 cup shortening

1½ cups plus 2 tablespoons
  sugar

2 eggs

2¾ cups flour

2 teaspoons cream of tartar

1 teaspoon baking soda

½ teaspoon salt

1 (10-ounce) package
  chocolate-covered raisins

2 teaspoons cinnamon

Beat the shortening and 1½ cups of the sugar in a mixer bowl until light
and fluffy. Beat in the eggs. Add the flour, cream of tartar, baking soda and
salt and mix well. Stir in chocolate-covered raisins. Refrigerate dough,
covered, until chilled. Preheat oven to 400 degrees. Shape the dough into
1-inch balls. Combine the cinnamon and remaining 2 tablespoons sugar
in a bowl and mix well. Roll the balls in the cinnamon-sugar. Place 2
inches apart on cookie sheets. Bake for 8 to 10 minutes. Cool on cookie
sheets for 2 minutes. Remove to a wire rack to cool completely.

Approx Per Cookie: Cal 155; Prot 2 g; Carbo 22 g; T Fat 7 g; 41% Calories from Fat;
Chol 12 mg; Fiber 1 g; Sod 74 mg

Coconut Cookies *Yield: 36 cookies*

3 cups flour

¾ teaspoon baking powder

½ teaspoon baking soda

½ teaspoon salt

1¼ cups sugar

1 cup shortening

2 eggs

¼ cup corn syrup

1 teaspoon vanilla extract

1½ cups flaked coconut,
  divided

1 egg, beaten

Preheat oven to 375 degrees. Combine the flour, baking powder, baking
soda and salt in a bowl and mix well. Beat the sugar and shortening in a
mixer bowl until light and fluffy. Add the eggs, corn syrup and vanilla
and beat until well blended. Add the flour mixture gradually, mixing
well after each addition. Stir in 1 cup of the coconut. Drop by rounded
tablespoonfuls 2 inches apart onto cookie sheets. Brush the cookie
dough with the beaten egg. Sprinkle with the remaining ½ cup coconut.
Bake for 7 to 9 minutes.

Approx Per Cookie: Cal 142; Prot 2 g; Carbo 18 g; T Fat 7 g; 45% Calories from Fat;
Chol 18 mg; Fiber <1 g; Sod 69 mg

Date Nut Pinwheels *Yield: 44 cookies*

1¾ cups flour

½ teaspoon baking soda

½ teaspoon cream of tartar

⅛ teaspoon salt

½ cup shortening

1 cup packed light
 brown sugar

1 egg

1 tablespoon milk

½ teaspoon vanilla extract

12 ounces chopped dates

⅓ cup sugar

⅓ cup water

½ cup finely chopped walnuts

Sift the flour, baking soda, cream of tartar and salt together. Beat the shortening and brown sugar in a mixer bowl until light and fluffy. Beat in the egg. Add the milk and vanilla and mix well. Add the sifted dry ingredients gradually, mixing well after each addition. Divide the dough into 2 equal portions. Place each portion on waxed paper over a pastry board or cloth. Roll each portion into a 7x11-inch rectangle.

Combine the dates, sugar, water and walnuts in a bowl and mix well. Spread half the date mixture over each rectangle. Roll from the long end to enclose the filling. Seal the edges and sides. Place on a cookie sheet and cover with plastic wrap. Refrigerate for 8 to 12 hours or until firm. Preheat oven to 400 degrees. Cut cookie rolls into ¼-inch slices. Place slices on greased and floured cookie sheets. Bake for 10 minutes.

Approx Per Cookie: Cal 95; Prot 1 g; Carbo 16 g; T Fat 3 g; 31% Calories from Fat; Chol 5 mg; Fiber 1 g; Sod 25 mg

Fudge Puddles *Yield: 18 cookies*

1¼ cups flour

¾ teaspoon baking soda

½ teaspoon salt

½ cup butter or margarine,
 softened

½ cup sugar

½ cup packed light
 brown sugar

1 egg

½ cup creamy peanut butter

1½ teaspoons vanilla extract,
 divided

1 cup milk chocolate chips

1 cup semisweet
 chocolate chips

1 (14-ounce) can sweetened
 condensed milk

Combine the flour, baking soda and salt in a bowl and mix well. Beat the butter, sugar and brown sugar in a mixer bowl until light and fluffy. Beat in the egg. Add the peanut butter and ½ teaspoon of the vanilla and mix well. Add the flour mixture gradually, mixing well. Refrigerate, covered, for 1 hour. Preheat oven to 325 degrees. Spray miniature muffin cups with nonstick cooking spray. Shape dough into 1-inch balls. Place in prepared pans. Bake for 10 to 14 minutes or until lightly browned. Remove from oven and immediately make an indentation in the center of each by pressing lightly with a melon baller. Cool in pans for 5 minutes. Remove to a wire rack to cool completely.

Combine the milk chocolate chips and semisweet chocolate chips in a 1½-quart microwave-safe dish. Microwave on High for 2 minutes, stirring after 1 minute. Stir until completely melted. Stir in the condensed milk vigourously. Stir in the remaining 1 teaspoon vanilla until smooth. Spoon a portion into the center of each cookie.

Approx Per Cookie: Cal 331; Prot 6 g; Carbo 43 g; T Fat 17 g; 43% Calories from Fat; Chol 35 mg; Fiber 2 g; Sod 245 mg

150

Cookie Jar Gingersnaps   *Yield: 48 cookies*

2 cups sifted flour

1 tablespoon ginger

2 teaspoons baking soda

1 teaspoon cinnamon

1/2 teaspoon salt

3/4 cup shortening

1 1/2 to 1 3/4 cups sugar

1 egg

1/4 cup molasses

Preheat oven to 350 degrees. Sift the flour, ginger, baking soda, cinnamon and salt together. Beat the shortening and 1 cup of the sugar in a mixer bowl until light and fluffy. Beat in the egg and molasses. Beat in the sifted dry ingredients, mixing well. Shape, by teaspoonfuls into balls. Roll in the remaining sugar. Place 2 inches apart on cookie sheets. Bake for 12 to 15 minutes or until tops are slightly rounded, crackly and lightly browned. Remove to a wire rack to cool completely. Store in an airtight container.

Approx Per Cookie: Cal 80; Prot 1 g; Carbo 12 g; T Fat 3 g; 37% Calories from Fat; Chol 4 mg; Fiber <1 g; Sod 79 mg

Gingerbread Cookies   *Yield: 72 cookies*

4 1/2 cups sifted flour

1 teaspoon baking soda

1 teaspoon salt

1 teaspoon cinnamon

3/4 teaspoon ginger

1 cup butter, softened

1/2 cup packed brown sugar

1/2 cup sugar

1/3 cup dark molasses

2/3 cup light corn syrup

Sift the flour, baking soda, salt, cinnamon and ginger together. Beat the butter, brown sugar and sugar in a mixer bowl until light and fluffy. Beat in the molasses and corn syrup. Add the dry ingredients and mix well. Knead on a lightly floured surface until smooth. Wrap in plastic wrap. Refrigerate for up to 10 hours or until firm. Preheat oven to 350 degrees. Roll 1/8 inch thick on a floured surface. Cut with floured cookie cutters. Place on cookie sheets. Bake for 8 minutes. Remove to a wire rack to cool.

Approx Per Cookie: Cal 72; Prot 1 g; Carbo 12 g; T Fat 3 g; 32% Calories from Fat; Chol 7 mg; Fiber <1 g; Sod 81 mg

About Refrigerator Cookies

Most refrigerator cookies contain a high proportion of fat and are crisp rather than chewy. For blue ribbon results, use butter. For the best-shaped cookies, keep the dough refrigerated until you start slicing it. Use your sharpest knife. A dull knife will push the dough out of shape. Rotating the roll a quarter turn each time you cut it also will give you a better shape. If your hands are warm, slip a plastic bag over the one that holds the roll to insulate it. Heat from your hand can soften the dough.

Honey Pecan Snaps   *Yield: 48 cookies*

4 cups flour

2¹/₂ teaspoons baking soda

1 teaspoon cloves

1 teaspoon cinnamon

¹/₂ teaspoon ginger

¹/₂ teaspoon salt

¹/₂ cup butter or margarine,
  softened

¹/₂ cup shortening

2 to 2¹/₄ cups sugar, divided

¹/₂ cup honey

2 eggs

2 tablespoons lemon juice

1 cup chopped pecans

Preheat oven to 350 degrees. Combine the flour, baking soda, cloves, cinnamon, ginger and salt in a bowl and mix well. Beat the butter, shortening and 1¹/₂ cups of the sugar in a mixer bowl until light and fluffy. Beat in the honey, eggs and lemon juice. Add the dry ingredients gradually and mix well after each addition. Fold in the pecans. Shape into 1-inch balls. Roll in the remaining sugar. Place on cookie sheets. Bake for 12 to 13 minutes or until golden brown. Cool on cookie sheets for 2 minutes. Remove to a wire rack to cool completely.

Approx Per Cookie: Cal 141; Prot 2 g; Carbo 21 g; T Fat 6 g; 38% Calories from Fat; Chol 14 mg; Fiber <1 g; Sod 112 mg

 ## Oatmeal Crunchies   *Yield: 42 cookies*

1 cup sifted flour

³/₄ cup sugar, divided

¹/₂ teaspoon baking powder

¹/₂ teaspoon baking soda

¹/₄ teaspoon salt

¹/₂ cup packed brown sugar

¹/₂ cup shortening

1 egg

¹/₄ teaspoon vanilla extract

³/₄ cup quick-cooking oats

¹/₄ cup chopped walnuts

Preheat oven to 375 degrees. Sift the flour, ¹/₂ cup of the sugar, baking powder, baking soda and salt in a bowl. Beat in the brown sugar, shortening, egg and vanilla. Stir in the oats and walnuts. Shape into small balls. Dip tops in the remaining ¹/₄ cup sugar. Place on cookie sheets. Bake for 10 to 12 minutes. Remove to a wire rack to cool completely.

Approx Per Cookie: Cal 68; Prot 1 g; Carbo 10 g; T Fat 3 g; 41% Calories from Fat; Chol 5 mg; Fiber <1 g; Sod 37 mg

Oatmeal Peanut Cookies   *Yield: 36 cookies*

1 1/2 cups flour

3 cups quick-cooking oats

1 teaspoon baking soda

1 cup shortening, or
   1/2 cup margarine and
   1/2 cup shortening

1 cup sugar

1 cup packed brown sugar

2 eggs

2 teaspoons vanilla extract

8 ounces salted peanuts

Preheat oven to 375 degrees. Combine the flour, oats and baking soda in a bowl and mix well. Beat the shortening, sugar and brown sugar in a mixer bowl until light and fluffy. Add the eggs 1 at a time, mixing well after each addition. Beat in the vanilla. Add the dry ingredients and mix well. Stir in the peanuts. Drop by heaping teaspoonfuls onto cookie sheets. Bake for 10 to 12 minutes; do not overbake.

Approx Per Cookie: Cal 186; Prot 4 g; Carbo 22 g; T Fat 10 g; 46% Calories from Fat; Chol 12 mg; Fiber 2 g; Sod 69 mg

Pawpaw Cookies   *Yield: 36 cookies*

2 cups flour

1/4 teaspoon allspice

1 teaspoon baking soda

1/4 teaspoon salt

1 cup sugar

1 cup margarine

1 cup pawpaw pulp or
   persimmon pulp

1 egg, beaten

1/3 cup raisins (optional)

1/3 cup chopped pecans

1 cup powdered sugar

1/4 teaspoon vanilla extract

1 teaspoon melted margarine

1 tablespoon water

Preheat oven to 350 degrees. Sift the flour, allspice, baking soda and salt together. Beat the sugar and margarine in a mixer bowl until light and fluffy. Beat in the pawpaw pulp and egg. Add the sifted dry ingredients and mix well. Stir in the raisins and pecans. Drop by teaspoonfuls onto greased cookie sheets. Bake for 10 to 12 minutes. Remove to a wire rack to cool completely. Combine the powdered sugar, vanilla, melted margarine and water in a bowl and mix well. Drizzle over cookies.

Approx Per Cookie: Cal 121; Prot 1 g; Carbo 16 g; T Fat 6 g; 45% Calories from Fat; Chol 6 mg; Fiber <1 g; Sod 113 mg
Nutritional analysis was derived by substituting banana for the pawpaw.

Here's a trivia tidbit that might stump even the best Jeopardy contestant: Name the "tropical" fruit that grows in Indiana. It's the pawpaw! Sometimes called the Hoosier banana, the pawpaw fruit has a white flesh that's smooth and custardy similar to a banana but with vanilla, pineapple and mango flavor notes. Pawpaws can be harvested when fully ripe on the tree, when their yellow-green skin turns blackish brown, or they can be picked while still green and allowed to finish ripening indoors.

Traditional Peanut Butter Cookies   *Yield: 36 cookies*

½ cup butter, softened

½ cup peanut butter

½ cup sugar

½ cup packed brown sugar

1 egg

¾ teaspoon baking soda

½ teaspoon baking powder

¼ teaspoon salt

1¼ cups unbleached flour

Preheat oven to 350 degrees. Beat the butter, peanut butter, sugar, brown sugar and egg in a bowl until fluffy. Add the baking soda, baking powder and salt and mix well. Add the flour and mix well. Shape into 1-inch balls. Place 3 inches apart on cookie sheets greased with butter. Flatten to a 2-inch thickness in a crisscross pattern with a fork dipped in flour. Bake for 10 to 12 minutes; do not overbake. Remove to a wire rack to cool completely. Store in an airtight container.

Approx Per Cookie: Cal 84; Prot 2 g; Carbo 10 g; T Fat 5 g; 47% Calories from Fat; Chol 13 mg; Fiber <1 g; Sod 95 mg

Giant Peanut Butter Oatmeal Cookies   *Yield: 96 cookies*

12 eggs

5 cups packed brown sugar

4 cups sugar

1 tablespoon vanilla extract

1 tablespoon vegetable oil

8 teaspoons baking soda

1 pound butter, softened

3 pounds peanut butter

18 cups rolled oats

1 (12-ounce) package chocolate chips

1 (1-pound) package candy-coated milk chocolate pieces

Preheat oven to 350 degrees. Combine the eggs, brown sugar and sugar in a large container, such as a dishpan, and mix well. Add the vanilla and oil and mix well. Add the baking soda, butter and peanut butter and mix well. Stir in the oats and chocolate chips. Drop by ¼-cup scoops 2 inches apart onto cookie sheets. Press 7 or 8 milk chocolate pieces on top of each scoop. Bake for 10 to 12 minutes; do not overbake.

Approx Per Cookie: Cal 316; Prot 8 g; Carbo 40 g; T Fat 15 g; 42% Calories from Fat; Chol 38 mg; Fiber 3 g; Sod 226 mg

Peanut Blossoms   *Yield: 36 cookies*

1¾ cups flour

1 teaspoon baking soda

½ teaspoon salt

½ cup shortening

½ cup peanut butter

¾ to 1 cup sugar, divided

½ cup packed brown sugar

1 egg

2 tablespoons milk

1 teaspoon vanilla extract

36 solid milk chocolate candy
    stars or kisses

Preheat oven to 375 degrees. Sift the flour, baking soda and salt together. Beat the shortening and peanut butter in a mixer bowl until well blended. Beat in ½ cup of the sugar and brown sugar. Add the egg, milk and vanilla and mix well. Add the dry ingredients gradually, mixing well after each addition. Shape by rounded teaspoonfuls into balls. Roll in the remaining sugar. Place on cookie sheets. Bake for 8 minutes. Remove from oven. Place a chocolate star on top of each cookie. Bake for 2 to 5 minutes or until cookies test done. Remove to a wire rack to cool.

Approx Per Cookie: Cal 116; Prot 2 g; Carbo 15 g; T Fat 6 g; 42% Calories from Fat; Chol 6 mg; Fiber <1 g; Sod 90 mg

Spicy Pecan Drops   *Yield: 48 cookies*

4 to 5 cups flour

1 teaspoon cinnamon

1 teaspoon nutmeg

1 teaspoon cloves

1 teaspoon allspice

1½ cups butter, softened

3 eggs, beaten

3 cups packed light
    brown sugar

1 teaspoon baking soda

1 teaspoon water

2 tablespoons vinegar

2 cups chopped pecans

Preheat oven to 350 degrees. Sift 4 cups of the flour, cinnamon, nutmeg, cloves and allspice together. Mix the butter, eggs and brown sugar in a bowl. Dissolve the baking soda in the water in a cup. Add to the butter mixture and mix well. Add the dry ingredients alternately with the vinegar, mixing well after each addition. Add the remaining 1 cup flour if dough is too moist. Stir in the pecans. Drop by rounded teaspoonfuls onto cookie sheets. Bake for 7 to 9 minutes. Remove to a wire rack to cool.

Approx Per Cookie: Cal 188; Prot 2 g; Carbo 24 g; T Fat 10 g; 45% Calories from Fat; Chol 29 mg; Fiber 1 g; Sod 94 mg

Freezing Cookies

Almost all cookies freeze well. They will keep their oven-fresh quality for several months as long as they are packaged airtight and kept at 0 degrees. Cool the cookies to room temperature before packaging. Freezer-weight plastic bags and tightly sealed cookie tins make excellent containers. Label the container with the date and the name of the cookie. You can freeze cookie dough or even unbaked shaped dough for a week or two, as long as they are tightly wrapped.

155

Corn is the major feed grain grown by U.S. farmers, leading all other crops in value and volume of production. Indiana ranks fourth in corn-for-grain cash receipts in the nation. Corn is also a major component in many food items like cereals, peanut butter and snack foods. There are more than 3,500 different uses for corn products, and more are being discovered every day. Corn sweetener captures more than 50% of the non-diet sweetener market, making it America's favorite sweetener. Lafayette is home to a large A.E. Staley corn syrup processing plant.

Bourbon Balls *Yield: 40 balls*

3½ to 4 cups powdered sugar
6 tablespoons unsweetened cocoa
3 cups vanilla wafers, crushed
3 cups chopped walnuts
¾ cup whiskey
4½ tablespoons corn syrup

Combine 3 cups of the powdered sugar and cocoa in a bowl and mix well. Add the wafer crumbs and walnuts and mix well. Combine the whiskey and corn syrup in a bowl and mix well. Pour into the powdered sugar mixture and mix well. Shape by teaspoonfuls into balls. Place the remaining powdered sugar in a sealable plastic bag. Drop the balls into the bag and shake to coat. Place on waxed paper to dry. Refrigerate for up to 3 months.

Approx Per Ball: Cal 143; Prot 2 g; Carbo 19 g; T Fat 6 g; 38% Calories from Fat; Chol <1 mg; Fiber 1 g; Sod 18 mg

 ## Caramel Pecan Puddles *Yield: 30 pieces*

2 cups chopped pecans
1 (14-ounce) package caramels
2 tablespoons whipping cream
1 pound chocolate candy coating

Toast the pecans in a skillet over medium heat for 5 to 7 minutes. Combine the caramels and whipping cream in a microwave-safe dish. Microwave on High for 3½ to 4 minutes, stirring every minute; do not overcook. Stir in the toasted pecans. Drop by teaspoonfuls onto waxed or parchment paper. Cool for 1 hour or until no longer sticky. Melt candy coating using package directions in a double boiler. Lift each puddle gently off the paper and dip into the melted chocolate, covering completely. Place on waxed paper. Let stand until coating sets. Store in an airtight container in a cool place or freeze.

Approx Per Piece: Cal 186; Prot 1 g; Carbo 22 g; T Fat 11 g; 52% Calories from Fat; Chol 2 mg; Fiber 1 g; Sod 33 mg

Microwave Chocolate Peanut Butter Candy   *Yield: 117 squares*

*1 (12-ounce) package
  chocolate chips*
1 (18-ounce) jar peanut butter
24 ounces white almond bark
Nuts (optional)

Combine the chocolate chips, peanut butter and almond bark in a microwave-safe dish. Microwave on High for 4 to 5 minutes; stir. Microwave for 1 minute longer. Add the nuts and mix well. Pour into a buttered 9x13-inch dish. Refrigerate, covered, until cool. Cut into 1-inch squares.

Approx Per Square: Cal 71; Prot 1 g; Carbo 6 g; T Fat 5 g; 59% Calories from Fat; Chol 0 mg; Fiber <1 g; Sod 27 mg

 ## English Toffee   *Yield: 81 pieces*

1 cup sugar
3 tablespoons water
1 cup butter
1 teaspoon vanilla extract
3 (1½-ounce) chocolate bars
¼ cup chopped pecans

Combine the sugar, water and butter in a heavy saucepan. Cook over medium heat to 300 degrees on a candy thermometer, stirring constantly. Remove from heat. Stir in the vanilla. Pour into a buttered 9-inch square pan. Lay the chocolate bars over the layer. Spread as chocolate melts. Sprinkle with the pecans. Let cool completely. Turn the pan upside down and remove toffee. Break into pieces.

Approx Per Piece: Cal 40; Prot <1 g; Carbo 3 g; T Fat 3 g; 65% Calories from Fat; Chol 6 mg; Fiber <1 g; Sod 24 mg

Classic Caramels   *Yield: 64 pieces*

2 cups sugar
2 cups light corn syrup
½ cup butter
2 cups evaporated milk
1 teaspoon vanilla extract
⅛ teaspoon salt

Combine the sugar and corn syrup in a heavy saucepan and mix well. Cook to 245 degrees on a candy thermometer, stirring occasionally with a wooden spoon. Add the butter and evaporated milk gradually, maintaining a boil. Cook to 242 degrees on a candy thermometer. Stir in the vanilla and salt. Pour into a buttered 8-inch square pan. Do not scrape the bottom or side of the pan. Cool until firm. Cut into squares. Wrap squares in plastic wrap.

Approx Per Piece: Cal 76; Prot 1 g; Carbo 15 g; T Fat 2 g; 22% Calories from Fat; Chol 5 mg; Fiber 0 g; Sod 39 mg

Butter Math

4 sticks = 1 pound = 2 cups

2 sticks = ½ pound = 1 cup

1 stick = ¼ pound = ½ cup

⅔ stick = 2⅔ ounces = ⅓ cup

½ stick = 2 ounces = ¼ cup

¼ stick = 1 ounce = 2 tablespoons

1 pat = 1 teaspoon

 # Festive Fudge   *Yield: 30 servings*

2¼ cups sugar

¾ cup evaporated skim milk

16 large marshmallows

¼ cup margarine

1 teaspoon salt

1 (6-ounce) package semisweet chocolate chips

1 cup chopped pecans or black walnuts

1 teaspoon vanilla extract

Combine the sugar, evaporated milk, marshmallows, margarine and salt in a heavy 2-quart saucepan. Bring to a boil over medium heat, stirring constantly. Cook for 5 minutes, stirring constantly. Remove from heat. Stir in chocolate chips until melted. Stir in the pecans and vanilla. Spread in a buttered 9-inch square pan. Cool completely. Cut into 30 pieces.

Approx Per Serving: Cal 142; Prot 1 g; Carbo 23 g; T Fat 6 g; 35% Calories from Fat; Chol <1 mg; Fiber 1 g; Sod 105 mg

 # Sweet Potato Fudge   *Yield: 36 pieces*

3 cups sugar

¾ cup butter

1½ teaspoons pumpkin pie spice

1 cup mashed cooked sweet potato

1 (5-ounce) can evaporated milk

3 cups butterscotch chips

1 (7-ounce) jar marshmallow creme

1 cup chopped pecans

2 teaspoons vanilla extract

Combine the sugar, butter, pumpkin pie spice, sweet potato and evaporated milk in a heavy saucepan. Bring to a boil, stirring constantly. Boil for 10 minutes or until mixture reaches 228 degrees on a candy thermometer, stirring constantly. Remove from heat. Stir in butterscotch chips until melted. Add the marshmallow creme, pecans and vanilla and mix well. Pour into a buttered 9x13-inch pan quickly, spreading until even. Let cool completely. Cut into 36 squares. Store, tightly wrapped, in the refrigerator.

Approx Per Piece: Cal 230; Prot 1 g; Carbo 34 g; T Fat 10 g; 40% Calories from Fat; Chol 11 mg; Fiber <1 g; Sod 62 mg

White Chocolate Swirled Fudge   *Yield: 81 pieces*

½ cup butter

¾ cup evaporated milk

1½ cups sugar

¼ teaspoon salt

12 ounces white chocolate, coarsely chopped

2 cups miniature marshmallows

1 teaspoon vanilla extract

1 cup milk chocolate chips, melted

Combine the butter and evaporated milk in a heavy 3-quart saucepan. Cook over medium heat until butter is melted, stirring occasionally. Stir in the sugar and salt. Bring to a boil, stirring constantly. Boil for 6 minutes, stirring constantly. Remove from heat. Stir in the white chocolate until melted. Add the marshmallows and vanilla. Beat with a wire whisk until smooth. Pour into a buttered 9-inch square pan. Spoon the melted milk chocolate onto the fudge. Pull a knife or spatula through the mixture, creating a marbled effect. Refrigerate, covered, for 2 hours or longer. Cut into 1-inch squares.

Approx Per Piece: Cal 66; Prot 1 g; Carbo 9 g; T Fat 3 g; 44% Calories from Fat; Chol 5 mg; Fiber <1 g; Sod 27 mg

Microwave Peanut Brittle   *Yield: 80 pieces*

1 cup sugar

¼ teaspoon salt

½ cup light corn syrup

1 cup dry roasted peanuts

1 teaspoon butter

1 teaspoon vanilla extract

1 teaspoon baking soda

Combine the sugar, salt and corn syrup in a microwave-safe 1½-quart dish. Microwave on High for 3 minutes. Stir in the peanuts. Microwave for 5 to 7 minutes longer or until peanuts are light brown, stirring every 2 minutes. Add the butter and vanilla and mix well. Add the baking soda and stir gently until light and foamy. Pour onto a greased baking sheet. Let cool for 30 minutes to 1 hour. Break into small pieces.

Approx Per Piece: Cal 27; Prot <1 g; Carbo 4 g; T Fat 1 g; 31% Calories from Fat; Chol <1 mg; Fiber <1 g; Sod 26 mg

Old-Fashioned Peanut Brittle   *Yield: 8 (2-ounce) pieces*

2 cups sugar

½ cup water

½ cup light corn syrup

2 cups raw Spanish peanuts

2 teaspoons baking soda

Combine the sugar, water and corn syrup in a saucepan. Bring to a boil over high heat. Stir in the peanuts. Reduce heat to medium-high. Cook to 290 to 295 degrees on a candy thermometer or until candy is brittle when dropped into cold water. Remove from heat. Stir in the baking soda rapidly. Pour onto a greased 13x17-inch baking sheet. Let candy spread naturally and harden or when candy is set but still soft turn over and spread as thin as possible using 2 spoons.

Approx Per Piece: Cal 459; Prot 10 g; Carbo 71 g; T Fat 18 g; 33% Calories from Fat; Chol 0 mg; Fiber 3 g; Sod 348 mg

Chunky Candy Crunch   *Yield: 40 (½-cup) servings*

1½ pounds almond-, maple-, butterscotch- or chocolate-flavor confectioners' coating (bark)

¼ cup vegetable oil

3 cups corn chips

3 cups dry roasted peanuts

3 cups pretzels

3 cups round oat cereal

3 cups crunchy peanut butter-flavor cereal

This sweet and salty crunchy snack makes a great gift.

Combine the confectioners' coating and vegetable oil in a microwave-safe bowl. Microwave on Low until melted, stirring frequently. Add the corn chips, peanuts, pretzels, oat cereal and peanut butter-flavor cereal, stirring lightly to coat evenly. Spread onto baking sheets lined with aluminum foil; cool. Break into chunks. Store in an airtight container.

Approx Per Serving: Cal 208; Prot 4 g; Carbo 20 g; T Fat 13 g; 56% Calories from Fat; Chol 0 mg; Fiber 1 g; Sod 114 mg

Microwave Caramel Corn   *Yield: 16 (2-cup) servings*

8 quarts air-popped popcorn

1 turkey-size microwave-safe cooking bag

1 cup packed brown sugar

1/2 cup butter or margarine

1/4 cup light corn syrup

1/2 teaspoon salt

1/2 teaspoon baking soda

Place popped popcorn in cooking bag. Combine the brown sugar, butter, corn syrup and salt in a 1-quart glass measuring cup. Microwave for 2 minutes. Stir until well blended. Microwave for 2 minutes. Stir in the baking soda. Pour the syrup mixture over the popcorn in the bag. Shake well, coating all of the popcorn. Microwave on High for 1 1/2 minutes, leaving the bag open; shake well. Repeat. Microwave on High for 45 seconds, leaving the bag open; shake well. Repeat. Microwave on High for 30 seconds, leaving the bag open; shake well. Repeat. Pour on 4 baking sheets to cool.

Approx Per Serving: Cal 178; Prot 2 g; Carbo 30 g; T Fat 6 g; 31% Calories from Fat; Chol 16 mg; Fiber 2 g; Sod 183 mg

Almost all the popcorn consumed throughout the world is grown in the midwestern United States, with Indiana being the #1 producing state! The largest popcorn producer is Weaver Farms.

Homemade "Tootsie" Rolls   *Yield: 24 pieces*

2 tablespoons butter, softened

1/2 cup light corn syrup

2 (1-ounce) squares chocolate, melted

1 teaspoon vanilla extract

3/4 cup nonfat dry milk

1/4 teaspoon salt

2 1/4 to 3 cups powdered sugar

Combine the butter, corn syrup, chocolate, vanilla, powdered milk and salt in a bowl and mix well. Add the powdered sugar gradually, mixing and kneading after each addition. Divide into 3 or 4 portions. Shape each portion into a rope. Cut into 2-inch-long pieces. Let stand for 1 hour. Wrap in plastic wrap.

Approx Per Piece: Cal 106; Prot 1 g; Carbo 22 g; T Fat 2 g; 18% Calories from Fat; Chol 3 mg; Fiber <1 g; Sod 54 mg

This restored Hoosier cabinet, blue ribbon project of a Carroll County 4-H'er, pays tribute to the homemaker whose kitchen was the heart of the home. There scrumptious peach pies, rich chocolate cakes, and spicy persimmon pudding filled the air with tempting aromas, promise of a sweet treat to come. In "Delightful & Delicious Desserts," award-winning recipes for luscious pies, cakes, and desserts carry on this proud Indiana tradition.

DELIGHTFUL
& DELICIOUS
DESSERTS

AWARD-WINNING RECIPES FOR LUSCIOUS PIES, CAKES, AND DESSERTS

Native persimmon trees are found throughout southern and central Indiana, producing their flavorful fruits in the fall. When ripe, usually after the first frost, these soft, pale yellow-orange fruits fall from the tree, ready to bring their sweet, honey-like flavor to puddings, cookies and breads. One bite will tell you if the persimmons are ready for use—you'll pucker up if they're not ripe yet!

Hoosier Persimmon Pudding *Yield: 12 servings*

2 cups sifted flour

1 1/2 cups sugar

1 teaspoon salt

1/2 teaspoon baking soda

1/2 teaspoon cinnamon

1/2 teaspoon cloves (optional)

1/2 teaspoon nutmeg

2 cups persimmon pulp

3 eggs

1 3/4 cups milk

3 tablespoons butter or margarine, melted

1 teaspoon vanilla extract (optional)

Recipes for this traditional fall dessert have been handed down in Indiana families for generations. Most are rich custard mixtures spiced with cinnamon, nutmeg and cloves.

Preheat oven to 325 degrees. Sift the flour, sugar, salt, baking soda, cinnamon, cloves and nutmeg together. Combine the persimmon pulp, eggs and milk in a bowl and mix well. Add the dry ingredients and mix well. Stir in the butter and vanilla. Pour into a greased 9x13-inch baking pan. Bake for 1 hour or until lightly browned and a wooden pick inserted in the center comes out clean. Cool. Cut into squares. Serve with whipped cream.

Approx Per Serving: Cal 285; Prot 5 g; Carbo 55 g; T Fat 6 g; 17% Calories from Fat; Chol 66 mg; Fiber 1 g; Sod 310 mg

Saucy Persimmon Pudding *Yield: 12 servings*

1 cup packed brown sugar

1 cup water

2 tablespoons margarine or butter

1 cup persimmon pulp

1/2 cup milk

1 1/3 cups flour

1 cup sugar

2 tablespoons baking powder

1 teaspoon vanilla extract

1/2 teaspoon cinnamon

1/4 teaspoon salt

Preheat oven to 350 degrees. Mix the brown sugar, water and margarine in a saucepan. Bring to a boil. Boil until brown sugar is dissolved. Pour into a 9x13-inch baking dish. Combine the persimmon pulp, milk, flour, sugar, baking powder, vanilla, cinnamon and salt in a large bowl and mix well. Drop by spoonfuls over the hot sugar mixture. Bake for 30 to 40 minutes or until hot and bubbly. Cool. Serve with whipped cream.

Approx Per Serving: Cal 235; Prot 2 g; Carbo 53 g; T Fat 2 g; 9% Calories from Fat; Chol 1 mg; Fiber 1 g; Sod 327 mg

Baklava   *Yield: 20 servings*

1 (16-ounce) package phyllo
  dough, thawed

1¹/₂ cups butter

3 cups walnuts, finely chopped

1¹/₂ cups sugar, divided

¹/₂ teaspoon cinnamon

4 teaspoons rose water,
  divided

1¹/₂ cups water

3 to 4 drops lemon juice

Let phyllo package stand at room temperature for 2 hours. Do not open package until ready to use dough. Cut phyllo dough in half with a sharp knife. Cover with waxed paper topped with a damp towel to prevent drying out, removing phyllo sheets as needed. Melt the butter in a saucepan; cool. Brush the bottom of a 9x13-inch baking pan with melted butter. Place one sheet of the phyllo dough gently in the prepared pan. Brush with the melted butter. Repeat until half of the phyllo sheets are used.

Combine the walnuts, ¹/₂ cup of the sugar, cinnamon and 1 teaspoon of the rose water in a bowl and mix well. Sprinkle over the layered phyllo sheets. Place one sheet of the remaining phyllo dough over the walnut mixture. Brush with melted butter. Repeat until all the sheets are used. Cut decorative pattern in the top layers of dough using a sharp knife. Bake at 325 degrees for 1 hour. Combine the remaining 1 cup sugar, water and remaining 3 teaspoons rose water in a saucepan. Bring to a boil. Boil for 15 minutes. Stir in the lemon juice; cool. Pour over the hot baklava.

Approx Per Serving: Cal 344; Prot 4 g; Carbo 30 g; T Fat 24 g; 62% Calories from Fat; Chol 37 mg; Fiber 1 g; Sod 252 mg

Pinwheel Apple Cobbler   *Yield: 8 servings*

¹/₂ cup butter or margarine

1 cup sugar

1 cup water

¹/₂ cup shortening

1¹/₂ cups sifted self-rising flour

¹/₃ cup milk

2 cups finely chopped
  peeled apples

1 teaspoon cinnamon

Preheat oven to 350 degrees. Melt the butter in a 9x13-inch baking pan in the oven. Combine the sugar and water in a saucepan. Cook until sugar dissolves, stirring occasionally. Cut the shortening into the flour in a bowl until crumbly. Add the milk, mixing with a fork until the mixture leaves the side of the bowl. Place on a lightly floured surface. Knead gently just until smooth. Roll into a ¹/₄-inch thick 10x12-inch rectangle. Combine the apples and cinnamon in a bowl and mix well. Sprinkle over the dough. Roll as for a jelly roll from the long side, sealing the edge and ends. Cut into sixteen ¹/₂-inch thick slices. Arrange the slices in the prepared pan. Pour the sugar syrup over the slices. Bake for 40 to 45 minutes or until golden brown. Let stand for 15 minutes.

If self-rising flour is unavailable, substitute 1¹/₂ cups of all-purpose flour sifted with 2 teaspoons baking powder and ¹/₂ teaspoon salt.

Approx Per Serving: Cal 413; Prot 3 g; Carbo 46 g; T Fat 25 g; 53% Calories from Fat; Chol 32 mg; Fiber 1 g; Sod 396 mg

Chocolate Marble Cheesecake   *Yield: 12 servings*

2 cups chocolate wafer cookie
  crumbs

5 tablespoons butter, melted

24 ounces cream cheese,
  softened

1 cup sugar

5 eggs

2 (1-ounce) squares semisweet
  chocolate, melted, cooled

6 (1-ounce) squares semisweet
  chocolate, melted

1/2 cup sour cream

Preheat oven to 300 degrees. Combine the cookie crumbs and melted butter in a bowl and mix well. Press over the bottom of a 9-inch springform pan. Beat the cream cheese, sugar and eggs in a mixer bowl at medium speed until light and fluffy. Pour half of the cream cheese mixture into the prepared pan. Stir the melted cooled chocolate into the remaining cream cheese mixture until well blended. Drizzle over the prepared layer in the pan, making swirls. Bake for 50 minutes or until set. Cool completely on a wire rack. Refrigerate, covered, for 2 hours or longer. Combine the melted chocolate and sour cream in a bowl and mix well. Spread over the cheesecake. Place on a serving plate and remove the side of the pan.

Approx Per Serving: Cal 542; Prot 10 g; Carbo 44 g; T Fat 39 g; 62% Calories from Fat; Chol 169 mg; Fiber 1 g; Sod 376 mg

Frozen Peppermint Cheesecake   *Yield: 12 servings*

1 1/4 cups chocolate wafer
  cookie crumbs

1/4 cup sugar

1/4 cup margarine or butter,
  melted

8 ounces cream cheese,
  softened

1 (14-ounce) can sweetened
  condensed milk

1 cup crushed hard
  peppermint candy

Red food coloring (optional)

2 cups whipping cream,
  whipped

Combine the cookie crumbs, sugar and margarine in a bowl and mix well. Press firmly over the bottom and halfway up the side of a 9-inch springform pan. Beat the cream cheese in a mixer bowl until light and fluffy. Beat in the condensed milk gradually until smooth. Stir in the crushed candy and red food coloring. Fold in the whipped cream. Pour into the prepared pan. Freeze, covered, for 6 hours or until firm. Place on a serving plate and remove the side of the pan.

Approx Per Serving: Cal 485; Prot 6 g; Carbo 51 g; T Fat 30 g; 54% Calories from Fat; Chol 87 mg; Fiber <1 g; Sod 244 mg

166

Sour Cream-Topped Silken Cheesecake

Yield: 10 servings

1 (9-ounce) package chocolate wafer cookies, crushed

6 tablespoons margarine, melted

1/4 cup sliced almonds, crushed or finely chopped

16 ounces light cream cheese, softened

1 (10-ounce) package firm silken tofu

1 1/4 cups plus 1/3 cup sugar, divided

4 eggs

3 tablespoons lemon juice

2 cups light sour cream

1 teaspoon vanilla extract

2 tablespoons chocolate-flavored syrup, chilled

Preheat oven to 350 degrees. Mix the cookie crumbs, margarine and almonds in a bowl. Press over the bottom and up the side of a 10-inch springform pan. Beat the cream cheese, tofu and 1 1/4 cups of the sugar in a mixer bowl until smooth. Beat in the eggs and lemon juice. Pour into the prepared pan. Bake for 50 minutes. Remove from the oven. Reduce oven temperature to 300 degrees. Combine the sour cream, remaining 1/3 cup sugar and vanilla in a bowl and mix well. Spread over the cheesecake. Drizzle the chocolate-flavored syrup over the top. Draw a knife through the syrup to create a marble effect. Bake for 20 to 25 minutes or until center is firm. Cool on a wire rack for 1 hour. Refrigerate, covered, for 8 to 10 hours or longer. Place on a serving plate. Remove the side of the pan. Serve with fresh fruit.

Approx Per Serving: Cal 484; Prot 15 g; Carbo 58 g; T Fat 22 g; 41% Calories from Fat; Chol 116 mg; Fiber 1 g; Sod 466 mg

Cheesecake Basics

For best distribution of added ingredients or for even marbling, do not oversoften or overbeat cream cheese.

Cool the baked cheesecake to room temperature before chilling thoroughly.

The dairy industry contributes significantly to the state's economy. Indiana ranks 5th in ice cream production (1996 figures) and 17th in milk production. Indiana's dairy farmers, like those across the nation, actively promote consumption of dairy products and their nutritional benefits. Today lowfat and fat-free products offer the consumer many choices from the dairy case.

Easy Homemade Vanilla Ice Cream   *Yield: 6 servings*

1 (14-ounce) can sweetened
  condensed milk
4 cups half-and-half
1 tablespoon vanilla extract

Combine the condensed milk, half-and-half and vanilla in an ice cream freezer container and mix well. Freeze according to manufacturer's instructions.

Fresh Fruit Ice Cream
Decrease half-and-half to 3 cups. Add 1 cup puréed fresh fruit such as peaches, strawberries, bananas or raspberries.

Fudgy Chocolate Ice Cream
Decrease half-and-half to 2 cups. Add 5 (1-ounce) squares unsweetened baking chocolate, melted, 2 cups whipping cream and ½ cup chopped nuts.

Mint Chocolate Chip Ice Cream
Decrease half-and-half to 2 cups and omit the vanilla. Add 2 teaspoons peppermint extract, green food coloring (optional), 2 cups whipping cream and ¾ cup miniature semi-sweet chocolate chips.

Approx Per Serving: Cal 428; Prot 10 g; Carbo 43 g; T Fat 24 g; 50% Calories from Fat; Chol 82 mg; Fiber 0 g; Sod 150 mg

Hot Fudge Sauce   *Yield: 16 servings*

1 cup semisweet chocolate chips, or 4 (1-ounce) squares semisweet baking chocolate

2 tablespoons butter or margarine

1 (14-ounce) can sweetened condensed milk

2 tablespoons water

1 teaspoon vanilla extract

Combine the chocolate, butter, condensed milk and water in a heavy saucepan. Cook over medium heat until butter and chocolate are melted and the mixture thickens, stirring frequently. Stir in the vanilla. Serve warm over ice cream or as a fruit dipping sauce. Store, covered, in the refrigerator. To reheat, place in a saucepan with a small amount of water. Cook over low heat, stirring constantly.

Variation: Spirited—Add $1/3$ cup almond-, coffee-, mint- or orange-flavored liqueur with the vanilla.

Approx Per Serving: Cal 143; Prot 2 g; Carbo 20 g; T Fat 7 g; 40% Calories from Fat; Chol 12 mg; Fiber 1 g; Sod 47 mg

Easy Eggnog Cream   *Yield: 7 (1/2-cup) servings*

1 1/2 cups prepared dairy eggnog

1 (4-ounce) package vanilla instant pudding mix

1 cup whipping cream, whipped

Combine the eggnog and pudding mix in a bowl and mix well. Fold in the whipped cream. Refrigerate, covered, for 30 minutes. Spoon into 7 dessert bowls.

Eggnog Cream Cake
Slice a prepared angel food cake in half crosswise. Spoon 1 1/2 cups Easy Eggnog Cream between the layers. Spoon remainder over the top of the cake. Garnish with fresh or canned fruit.

Approx Per Serving: Cal 243; Prot 3 g; Carbo 21 g; T Fat 17 g; 61% Calories from Fat; Chol 79 mg; Fiber 0 g; Sod 246 mg

Almond-Crusted Torte   *Yield: 8 servings*

1²/₃ cups flour

1¹/₂ cups sugar

1 cup butter, melted

¹/₈ teaspoon salt

2 to 3 teaspoons almond extract

2 eggs, beaten

¹/₂ to ²/₃ cup sliced almonds

Combine the flour, sugar, butter, salt, almond extract and eggs in a bowl and mix well. Pour into a 9-inch torte pan that has been sprayed with nonstick cooking spray. Sprinkle the almonds over the top. Bake at 325 degrees for 35 to 40 minutes or until lightly browned.

Approx Per Serving: Cal 513; Prot 6 g; Carbo 59 g; T Fat 29 g; 49% Calories from Fat; Chol 115 mg; Fiber 2 g; Sod 288 mg

Walnut Cream Torte   *Yield: 8 servings*

¹/₂ cup butter, softened

1¹/₂ cups plus 3 tablespoons sugar, divided

4 eggs, separated, at room temperature

¹/₄ cup milk

³/₄ cup flour

1 teaspoon baking powder

1 teaspoon vanilla extract

¹/₂ to 1 cup chopped walnuts

1 cup whipping cream

Beat the butter and ¹/₂ cup of the sugar in a mixer bowl until light and fluffy. Add the egg yolks, milk, flour, baking powder and vanilla and mix well. Spread into two greased 8- or 9-inch round cake pans. Beat the egg whites in a separate bowl until soft peaks form. Add 1 cup of the sugar gradually, beating until stiff peaks form. Spread evenly over the batter. Sprinkle the walnuts over the top.

Place the pans in a cold oven. Bake at 325 degrees for 20 to 25 minutes or until set and golden. Cool on a wire rack. Beat the whipping cream in a bowl until soft peaks form. Add the remaining 3 tablespoons sugar gradually, beating until stiff peaks form. Remove the layers from the pans. Spread the whipped cream between the layers and over the top.

Approx Per Serving: Cal 549; Prot 7 g; Carbo 55 g; T Fat 35 g; 55% Calories from Fat; Chol 179 mg; Fiber 1 g; Sod 227 mg

Frozen Fruit Cups   *Yield: 12 servings*

8 ounces fat-free cream cheese

1 cup fat-free sour cream

1½ teaspoons aspartame
  sweetener for recipes or
  8 packets aspartame
  sweetener

¾ teaspoon lemon juice

1 cup coarsely chopped
  peaches

1 cup blueberries

1 cup raspberries or
  strawberries, cut into halves

1 cup chopped pineapple

1 (11-ounce) can mandarin
  orange segments, drained

6 pecans, cut into halves

Beat the cream cheese, sour cream, aspartame sweetener and lemon juice in a mixer bowl until smooth. Fold in the peaches, blueberries, raspberries, pineapple and mandarin orange segments. Spoon into 12 paper-lined muffin cups or an 8-inch square dish. Arrange pecan halves over the top. Freeze, covered, for 6 to 8 hours or until firm. Let stand at room temperature for 10 to 15 minutes or until slightly softened before serving. Garnish with fresh fruit, mint leaves or sauce of puréed raspberries or strawberries.

Approx Per Serving: Cal 86; Prot 5 g; Carbo 17 g; T Fat <1 g; 2% Calories from Fat; Chol 1 mg; Fiber 2 g; Sod 109 mg

Layered Raspberry Dessert   *Yield: 18 servings*

1 cup butter, softened

1½ cups flour

2 tablespoons sugar

8 ounces cream cheese,
  softened

1 cup plus 3 tablespoons
  powdered sugar, divided

1 (12-ounce) container
  nondairy whipped topping,
  divided

1 cup chopped pecans

1 (3-ounce) package
  raspberry gelatin

1 cup boiling water

1 (10-ounce) package frozen
  raspberries, thawed

Preheat oven to 350 degrees. Mix the butter, flour and sugar in a bowl. Press over the bottom of a 9x13-inch baking pan. Bake for 20 minutes. Cool completely. Beat the cream cheese, 1 cup of the powdered sugar and 1 cup of the whipped topping in a mixer bowl until smooth. Spread over the cooled crust. Sprinkle with the pecans. Dissolve the gelatin in boiling water in a bowl. Stir in the raspberries; cool slightly. Pour over the layers. Refrigerate, covered, until set. Mix the remaining whipped topping and remaining 3 tablespoons powdered sugar in a bowl. Spread over the top. Refrigerate, covered, until firm.

Approx Per Serving: Cal 345; Prot 3 g; Carbo 32 g; T Fat 23 g; 60% Calories from Fat; Chol 41 mg; Fiber 1 g; Sod 153 mg

Grandma's Apple Cake *Yield: 8 servings*

1 cup flour

1 teaspoon baking soda

1 teaspoon cinnamon

1 teaspoon nutmeg

½ teaspoon salt

½ cup butter or shortening

1 cup sugar

2 eggs

2 cups chopped, peeled all-purpose apples

½ cup chopped walnuts or pecans

Butter Cream Sauce

Fresh apples make this easy spice cake especially moist. The distinctive flavor of black walnuts complements the apples. This cake is equally good made with pecans, almonds, walnuts, black walnuts or hickory nuts.

Preheat oven to 350 degrees. Sift the flour, baking soda, cinnamon, nutmeg and salt together. Beat the butter and sugar in a mixer bowl until light and fluffy. Add the eggs 1 at a time, mixing well after each addition. Add the dry ingredients, mixing well. Stir in the apples and walnuts. Spoon into a greased and floured 8- or 9-inch square baking pan. Bake for 30 to 40 minutes or until the center springs back when lightly touched. Serve warm with Butter Cream Sauce, whipped cream or vanilla ice cream.

Approx Per Serving: Cal 593; Prot 5 g; Carbo 69 g; T Fat 35 g; 51% Calories from Fat; Chol 136 mg; Fiber 1 g; Sod 565 mg

Butter Cream Sauce

½ cup butter

½ cup whipping cream

½ cup packed brown sugar

½ cup sugar

Combine the butter, whipping cream, brown sugar and sugar in a saucepan. Bring to a boil over medium heat, stirring frequently. Cook until of the desired consistency. Serve warm.

Sugarless Applesauce Cake   *Yield: 16 servings*

1 cup raisins

*1 cup chopped dried
   mixed fruit*

2 cups water

2 cups flour

1 teaspoon baking soda

¹/₂ teaspoon salt

¹/₂ teaspoon nutmeg

1¹/₂ teaspoons cinnamon

*Egg substitute equivalent to
   2 eggs*

1 cup unsweetened applesauce

*2 tablespoons liquid artificial
   sweetener*

³/₄ cup vegetable oil

1 teaspoon vanilla extract

*¹/₂ cup chopped walnuts,
   toasted*

Preheat oven to 350 degrees.
Combine the raisins, dried fruit and
water in a saucepan. Cook until water
has evaporated and fruit is soft; cool.
Combine the flour, baking soda, salt,
nutmeg and cinnamon in a bowl and
mix well. Combine the egg substitute,
applesauce, sweetener, oil and vanilla
in a separate bowl and mix well. Stir
in the fruit mixture and walnuts.
Add to the dry ingredients and mix
well. Pour into a 10-inch fluted tube
pan sprayed with nonstick cooking
spray. Bake for 35 minutes or until a
wooden pick inserted in the center
comes out clean. Cool in the pan
for 10 minutes. Invert onto a
serving plate.

Variation: Decrease the flour to
1³/₄ cups and add ¹/₄ cup unsweetened cocoa.

Approx Per Serving: Cal 235; Prot 4 g;
Carbo 29 g; T Fat 13 g; 48% Calories from Fat;
Chol <1 mg; Fiber 2 g; Sod 168 mg

Indiana ranks 15th in the
nation for cash receipts
received for apples. Golden
and Red Delicious, Jonathan
and Fuji are just a few of the
commercial apple varieties
grown in Indiana. Many
orchards sell direct, giving
Hoosiers a wonderful
"excuse" for a leisurely
autumn drive in the country.

Banana Picnic Cake   *Yield: 12 servings*

2 cups flour

1 teaspoon baking powder

1 teaspoon baking soda

¼ teaspoon salt

½ cup butter or margarine,
   softened

1½ cups sugar

2 eggs

1 cup sour cream or
   buttermilk

1 cup mashed ripe bananas

½ cup chopped nuts
   (optional)

1 teaspoon vanilla extract

Caramel Icing

This moist cake is delicious with or without frosting. Or top with vanilla pudding and sliced bananas.

Preheat oven to 350 degrees. Sift the flour, baking powder, baking soda and salt together. Beat the butter and sugar in a mixer bowl until light and fluffy. Add the eggs 1 at a time, mixing well after each addition. Add the dry ingredients and sour cream alternately, mixing well after each addition. Stir in the bananas, nuts and vanilla. Pour into a greased and floured 9x13-inch baking pan. Bake for 40 minutes or until a wooden pick inserted in the center comes out clean. Cool in the pan. Spread the Caramel Icing on the cooled cake.

Approx Per Serving: Cal 522; Prot 4 g; Carbo 89 g; T Fat 18 g; 30% Calories from Fat; Chol 78 mg; Fiber 1 g; Sod 352 mg

Caramel Icing

5 tablespoons butter

1 cup packed brown sugar

¼ cup milk

2½ cups powdered sugar

Combine the butter, brown sugar and milk in a saucepan. Cook over low heat for 3 minutes, stirring constantly. Cool. Beat in powdered sugar until smooth.

Brombeerkuchen (Blackberry Cake)

Yield: 12 servings

3 cups flour

2 cups sugar

1 teaspoon salt

1 teaspoon nutmeg

1 teaspoon cinnamon

1 teaspoon cloves

3 eggs, beaten

1 cup butter, melted

1 cup buttermilk

1½ cups fresh blackberries

1 tablespoon baking soda

½ cup chopped pecans

½ cup raisins

Nutmeg Glaze

Preheat oven to 350 degrees. Combine the flour, sugar, salt, nutmeg, cinnamon and cloves in a large bowl and mix well. Add the eggs, butter, buttermilk and blackberries. Beat for 1 minute at medium speed. Stir in the baking soda, pecans and raisins. Spoon batter into a greased and floured 10-inch tube pan. Bake for 55 to 60 minutes or until cake tests done. Cool in the pan for 10 minutes. Invert onto a serving plate. Let cool completely. Drizzle Nutmeg Glaze over cooled cake.

Approx Per Serving: Cal 482; Prot 6 g; Carbo 71 g; T Fat 21 g; 38% Calories from Fat; Chol 95 mg; Fiber 2 g; Sod 704 mg

Nutmeg Glaze

½ cup sifted powdered sugar

2 teaspoons orange juice

¼ teaspoon nutmeg

Combine the powdered sugar, orange juice and nutmeg in a bowl and mix until smooth. Add additional orange juice to make of the desired consistency.

If you don't happen to have buttermilk on hand when you need it for baking or if you run across a recipe that calls for sour milk, here's an easy substitute. For each cup of buttermilk or sour milk, place 1 tablespoon lemon juice or vinegar in a glass measuring cup. Add enough milk to make 1 cup total liquid: stir. Let stand 5 minutes before using.

Indiana's blueberry industry ranks 7th in U.S. production with more than 60% going to the fresh market, the remainder into processed products. Most growers are in the northern part of the state.

Brownie Pudding Cake   *Yield: 8 servings*

1 cup flour

3/4 cup sugar

6 tablespoons unsweetened cocoa, divided

2 teaspoons baking powder

1/2 teaspoon salt

1/2 cup milk

2 tablespoons butter or shortening, melted

1 teaspoon vanilla extract

3/4 cup chopped pecans or walnuts

3/4 cup packed brown sugar

1 3/4 cups hot water

Preheat oven to 350 degrees. Sift the flour, sugar, 2 tablespoons of the cocoa, baking powder and salt together in a bowl. Add the milk, butter and vanilla, mixing until smooth. Stir in the pecans. Spread into a greased 8- or 9-inch square baking dish. Combine the brown sugar and remaining 4 tablespoons cocoa in a bowl and mix well. Sprinkle over the batter. Pour hot water over the top. Bake for 35 to 40 minutes or until top springs back when lightly touched. Let stand for 5 minutes.

Approx Per Serving: Cal 326; Prot 4 g; Carbo 56 g; T Fat 12 g; 30% Calories from Fat; Chol 10 mg; Fiber 3 g; Sod 314 mg

Berry Batter Cake   *Yield: 6 servings*

2 cups fresh or frozen blueberries or fresh blackberries, raspberries or strawberries

1/4 cup lemon juice

1 3/4 cups sugar, divided

1 cup flour

1 teaspoon baking powder

1/4 teaspoon salt

1/4 teaspoon nutmeg (optional)

1/2 cup milk

1/4 teaspoon almond extract

1/4 teaspoon vanilla extract

1 tablespoon cornstarch

1 cup boiling water

Preheat oven to 350 degrees. Butter an 8- or 9-inch square or 7x11-inch baking dish. Arrange the berries over the bottom of the dish. Drizzle with lemon juice. Combine 3/4 cup of the sugar, flour, baking powder, salt and nutmeg in a large bowl and mix well. Add the milk, almond extract and vanilla, stirring just until blended. Spread evenly over the berries. Combine the remaining 1 cup sugar and cornstarch and mix well. Sprinkle over the batter. Pour boiling water over the top. Bake for 45 minutes or until golden and bubbly. Serve warm with whipped cream or vanilla ice cream.

Approx Per Serving: Cal 349; Prot 3 g; Carbo 84 g; T Fat 1 g; 3% Calories from Fat; Chol 3 mg; Fiber 2 g; Sod 192 mg

Moist Carrot Cake *Yield: 12 servings*

2 cups flour

2 cups sugar

2 teaspoons baking soda

1¹/₂ teaspoons cinnamon

1 teaspoon baking powder

¹/₄ teaspoon salt

2 cups finely shredded carrots

¹/₄ cup buttermilk

¹/₄ cup vegetable oil

1 (8-ounce) can crushed
   pineapple, drained

¹/₂ cup raisins

3 eggs

¹/₂ cup flaked coconut

¹/₂ cup chopped nuts
   (optional)

1 teaspoon vanilla extract

Cream Cheese Frosting

Preheat oven to 350 degrees. Combine the flour, sugar, baking soda, cinnamon, baking powder and salt in a large bowl and mix well. Add the carrots, buttermilk, oil, pineapple, raisins, eggs, coconut, nuts and vanilla. Mix for 3 minutes. Spoon into a greased and floured 9x13-inch baking pan. Bake for 40 to 50 minutes or until center springs back when lightly touched. Cool on a wire rack. Spread the Cream Cheese Frosting on the cooled cake.

Approx Per Serving: Cal 597; Prot 6 g; Carbo 98 g; T Fat 21 g; 32% Calories from Fat; Chol 95 mg; Fiber 2 g; Sod 463 mg

Cream Cheese Frosting

¹/₂ cup butter or margarine,
   softened

8 ounces cream cheese,
   softened

1 pound powdered sugar, sifted

1 teaspoon vanilla extract

Beat the butter and cream cheese in a mixer bowl until light and fluffy. Beat in the powdered sugar and vanilla until smooth.

Chocolate Zucchini Cake   *Yield: 12 servings*

3 cups flour

1½ teaspoons baking powder

1 teaspoon baking soda

1 teaspoon cinnamon

½ teaspoon salt

1 cup chopped nuts (optional)

4 eggs

1½ cups vegetable oil

3 cups sugar

3 cups finely shredded
zucchini, drained

2 (1-ounce) squares
unsweetened chocolate,
melted, cooled

White Glaze or Chocolate
Glaze

Preheat oven to 350 degrees. Combine the flour, baking powder, baking soda, cinnamon and salt in a bowl and mix well. Combine ¼ cup of the flour mixture with the nuts in a bowl and stir to coat the nuts. Beat the eggs, oil and sugar in a mixer bowl until light. Stir in the zucchini and chocolate and mix well. Beat in the dry ingredients, just until blended. Stir in the nut mixture. Spoon into a greased 12-cup fluted tube pan or two 5x9-inch loaf pans. Bake for 1 hour or until a wooden pick inserted in the center comes out clean. Cool in the pan for 5 minutes. Invert onto a wire rack to cool completely. Place on a serving plate. Drizzle with White Glaze or Chocolate Glaze.

Approx Per Serving: Cal 666; Prot 7 g; Carbo 92 g; T Fat 32 g; 42% Calories from Fat; Chol 71 mg; Fiber 2 g; Sod 288 mg

White Glaze

1½ cups powdered sugar

2 to 3 teaspoons milk

Combine the powdered sugar and enough milk to make of the desired consistency in a bowl and mix well.

Chocolate Glaze

2 (1-ounce) squares semisweet
chocolate

2 tablespoons butter

½ teaspoon vanilla extract

Combine the chocolate and butter in a saucepan. Melt over low heat, stirring frequently. Stir in the vanilla. Cool slightly.

What is "White Chocolate?"

White chocolate contains milk or milk solids, sugar, fat (vegetable fat or cocoa butter), and vanilla flavoring.

White chocolate that contains cocoa butter has a chocolate like aroma. But white chocolate is not a true chocolate because it lacks chocolate liquor (the thick, rich brown paste that comes from ground cocoa beans).

Lemon and White Chocolate Celebration Cake   *Yield: 24 servings*

8 ounces white chocolate

1 cup whipping cream

4 cups flour

2 teaspoons baking soda

¼ teaspoon salt

1 cup butter, softened

2⅓ cups sugar, divided

6 eggs

2 teaspoons lemon extract

Grated peel of 1 lemon

1¼ cups buttermilk

⅓ cup water

2 tablespoons lemon juice

Lemon Curd, chilled

Butter Creme Icing

Preheat oven to 350 degrees. Grease three 9-inch round cake pans. Line with parchment or waxed paper. Melt the chocolate with the cream in a heavy saucepan over low heat, stirring until smooth; cool. Sift the flour, baking soda and salt in a bowl. Beat the butter and 2 cups of the sugar in a mixer bowl until light and fluffy. Add the eggs 1 at a time, mixing well after each addition. Beat in the chocolate mixture, lemon extract and lemon peel. Add the sifted dry ingredients and the buttermilk alternately, mixing well after each addition. Pour equally into the prepared pans.

Bake for 30 to 35 minutes or until a wooden pick inserted in the center comes out clean. Cool in the pans on a wire rack for 10 minutes. Remove from pans to a wire rack to cool completely. Combine remaining ⅓ cup sugar and water in a saucepan. Cook until sugar dissolves and mixture come to a boil, stirring constantly. Pour into a bowl. Stir in the lemon juice. Refrigerate, covered, until cooled to room temperature. Drizzle lemon syrup over the cake layers and let soak in. Repeat. Place cake layers on a serving plate, spreading the Lemon Curd between the layers. Frost the top and side with Butter Creme Icing. Store in the refrigerator.

Approx Per Serving: Cal 622; Prot 6 g; Carbo 89 g; T Fat 28 g; 40% Calories from Fat; Chol 124 mg; Fiber 1 g; Sod 335 mg

Lemon Curd

1 cup sugar

6 tablespoons butter

⅓ cup lemon juice

3 eggs

Combine the sugar, butter and lemon juice in a saucepan. Cook over low heat until sugar dissolves and butter melts, stirring constantly. Beat the eggs in a mixer bowl until pale yellow. Stir a small amount of the hot mixture into the beaten eggs. Stir the eggs into the hot mixture. Cook over medium heat for 5 to 12 minutes or until thick and creamy, stirring constantly. Refrigerate, covered, until chilled.

Butter Creme Icing

1 cup shortening

½ cup water

1 teaspoon butter flavoring

1 teaspoon clear vanilla extract

½ teaspoon popcorn salt

2 pounds powdered sugar

Beat the shortening, water, butter flavoring, vanilla, popcorn salt and powdered sugar in a mixer bowl until smooth.

179

Sweepstakes Cocoa Cake   *Yield: 12 servings*

1³/₄ cups flour

³/₄ cup unsweetened cocoa

1¹/₂ teaspoons baking soda

1¹/₂ teaspoons baking powder

¹/₂ teaspoon salt

2 cups sugar

1 egg

¹/₂ cup vegetable oil

2 teaspoons vanilla extract

1 cup milk

1 cup boiling water

Cocoa Frosting

Preheat oven to 350 degrees. Sift the flour, cocoa, baking soda, baking powder and salt together. Beat the sugar, egg, oil and vanilla in a mixer bowl until smooth. Add the dry ingredients and milk alternately, mixing well after each addition. Beat for 2 minutes on medium speed. Stir in the boiling water. Pour into 2 greased and floured 9-inch round cake pans or a 9x13-inch baking pan. Bake for 30 to 40 minutes or until a wooden pick inserted in the center comes out clean. Cool in the pan for 10 minutes. Remove to a wire rack to cool completely. Spread Cocoa Frosting between the layers and over the top and side of the cooled cake.

Approx Per Serving: Cal 478; Prot 5 g; Carbo 81 g; T Fat 18 g; 32% Calories from Fat; Chol 37 mg; Fiber 4 g; Sod 396 mg

Cocoa Frosting

³/₄ cup unsweetened cocoa

2²/₃ cups powdered sugar

6 tablespoons butter

¹/₃ cup milk

1 teaspoon vanilla extract

Combine the cocoa and sugar in a bowl and mix well. Beat the butter in a mixer bowl until light and fluffy. Add the cocoa mixture and milk alternately, mixing well after each addition. Add enough milk to make of the desired consistency. Stir in the vanilla.

Coffee Spice Cake with Mocha Frosting

Yield: 12 servings

2 eggs, separated

2 cups flour

1 tablespoon baking powder

$1/8$ teaspoon salt

1 teaspoon cinnamon

$1/4$ teaspoon cloves

$1/4$ teaspoon allspice

$1/3$ cup shortening

1 cup sugar

$2/3$ cup strong cold coffee

Mocha Frosting

Preheat oven to 375 degrees. Beat the egg whites in a mixer bowl until stiff peaks form. Sift the flour, baking powder, salt, cinnamon, cloves and allspice together. Beat the shortening and sugar in a separate mixer bowl until light and fluffy. Beat in the egg yolks. Beat in the coffee. Add the dry ingredients and mix well. Fold in the beaten egg whites. Pour into 2 greased 8- or 9-inch round cake pans. Bake for 25 minutes or until a wooden pick inserted in the center comes out clean. Cool in the pans for 10 minutes. Remove to a wire rack to cool completely. Spread Mocha Frosting between the layers and over the top and side of cooled cake.

Approx Per Serving: Cal 359; Prot 4 g; Carbo 54 g; T Fat 15 g; 37% Calories from Fat; Chol 74 mg; Fiber 1 g; Sod 241 mg

Mocha Frosting

$1/2$ cup butter, melted

3 tablespoons unsweetened cocoa

3 tablespoons strong cold coffee

1 egg, beaten

$1/2$ teaspoon vanilla extract

2 cups powdered sugar

Melt the butter in a medium saucepan. Stir in the cocoa and coffee until smooth. Whisk a small amount of the butter mixture into the egg. Whisk the egg into the butter mixture. Cook over medium-low heat until smooth and glossy, stirring constantly. Add the vanilla. Beat in powdered sugar until smooth.

Softening in the Microwave

$1/2$ cup margarine or butter

Medium-Low

30 to 50 seconds

3 ounces cream cheese

Medium

30 to 60 seconds

8 ounces cream cheese

Medium

1 to $1 1/2$ minutes

Holiday Fruit & Nut Cake   *Yield: 72 slices*

1 pound candied red cherries

1 pound pitted dates, chopped

1 pound chopped candied pineapple

1 cup chopped dried apricots

1 cup golden raisins

1 cup peach or apricot brandy

3 cups pecan halves

1 cup whole natural almonds

2 cups flour

1 teaspoon baking powder

1/2 teaspoon cinnamon

1/2 teaspoon mace or nutmeg

1/2 cup butter, softened

1 cup sugar

3 eggs

1 tablespoon vanilla extract

1/4 cup light corn syrup

2 to 3 tablespoons brandy

Combine the cherries, dates, pineapple, apricots and raisins in a sealable plastic bag. Pour the peach brandy over the fruit. Marinate for 24 hours or longer. Grease two 5x9-inch loaf pans and line with parchment or waxed paper. Preheat oven to 275 degrees. Combine the marinated fruit, pecans, almonds and 1 cup of the flour in a bowl and mix well. Combine the remaining 1 cup flour, baking powder, cinnamon and mace in a bowl and mix well. Beat the butter in a mixer bowl until smooth. Add the sugar, eggs and vanilla and beat until fluffy. Stir in the flour mixture. Add to the fruit mixture and mix well. Spoon into the prepared pans, pressing with floured hands or a spoon.

Bake for 2 hours. Brush the tops of the cakes with corn syrup. Garnish with additional cherries and nuts pressed into the tops of the cakes. Bake for 30 minutes or until a wooden pick inserted in the center comes out clean. Cool in the pans for 10 minutes. Remove to a wire rack to cool completely. Wrap in cheesecloth. Place in large sealable plastic bags. Pour brandy over cakes until the cheesecloth is well moistened. Store, tightly covered, in the refrigerator or at room temperature for 2 weeks or longer, keeping the cheesecloth moistened.

Approx Per Slice: Cal 161; Prot 2 g; Carbo 26 g; T Fat 6 g; 30% Calories from Fat; Chol 12 mg; Fiber 1 g; Sod 25 mg

Peaches & Cream Cake   *Yield: 16 servings*

1 (2-layer) package yellow cake mix

1 (6-ounce) package vanilla instant pudding mix

4 eggs

1 cup vegetable oil

1 cup water

1 (15-ounce) can peach slices

8 ounces cream cheese, softened

1 cup sugar

Preheat oven to 350 degrees. Beat the cake mix, pudding mix, eggs, oil and water in a mixer bowl on low speed until well blended. Beat on medium speed for 3 minutes. Pour into a greased and floured 9x13-inch baking pan. Drain the peaches, reserving the liquid. Cut the peach slices into thin slices. Arrange over the batter. Beat the cream cheese, sugar and reserved peach liquid in a mixer bowl until smooth. Pour evenly over the peaches. Bake for 45 minutes or until top springs back when lightly touched. Cool. Store, covered, in the refrigerator.

Approx Per Serving: Cal 431; Prot 4 g; Carbo 52 g; T Fat 24 g; 49% Calories from Fat; Chol 69 mg; Fiber 1 g; Sod 402 mg

Peanut Butter Lover's Cake *Yield: 16 servings*

2 cups flour

1 teaspoon baking soda

¹/₂ teaspoon salt

³/₄ cup butter or margarine,
softened

2 cups sugar

5 eggs, separated

1 cup creamy peanut butter

1 cup buttermilk

1 teaspoon vanilla extract

Peanut Butter Frosting

¹/₂ cup chopped peanuts

Combine the flour, baking soda and salt in a bowl and mix well. Beat the butter in a mixer bowl at medium speed until light and fluffy. Add the sugar gradually, beating constantly until blended. Add the egg yolks 1 at a time, mixing well after each addition. Beat in the peanut butter. Add the dry ingredients and buttermilk alternately, mixing well after each addition. Stir in the vanilla. Beat the egg whites in a small mixer bowl at high speed until stiff peaks form. Fold into the batter. Pour into 3 greased and floured 9-inch round cake pans. Bake at 350 degrees for 25 to 30 minutes or until a wooden pick inserted in the center comes out clean. Cool in the pans for 10 minutes. Remove to a wire rack to cool completely. Frost with Peanut Butter Frosting. Sprinkle the peanuts over the top.

Approx Per Serving: Cal 684; Prot 14 g; Carbo 79 g; T Fat 38 g; 48% Calories from Fat; Chol 114 mg; Fiber 3 g; Sod 516 mg

Peanut Butter Frosting

³/₄ cup butter or margarine,
softened

1 cup creamy peanut butter

4¹/₂ cups powdered sugar

¹/₃ cup milk

1 teaspoon vanilla extract

Beat the butter in a mixer bowl at medium speed until light and fluffy. Beat in the peanut butter. Add the powdered sugar gradually, beating constantly until well blended. Add the milk and vanilla and mix well. Add additional milk, 1 tablespoon at a time, until of the desired consistency.

Easy Cran-Apple Cobbler

An easy 3-ingredient recipe that yields a wonderful baked dessert.

1 (15-ounce) can apple pie filling

1 (14-ounce) can whole cranberry sauce

1 (16-ounce) roll refrigerated sugar cookie dough

Preheat oven to 350 degrees. Pour apple pie filling into a round 8- or 9-inch baking dish. Spread cranberry sauce on top. Slice cookie dough about ¹/₄ inch thick and place over apples and cranberry sauce. Bake for 20 minutes or until lightly browned. Serve warm or cold with vanilla ice cream or whipped topping. Serves 6.

183

Marshmallows have long been a favorite cocoa topper, sweet treat at campfires and recipe ingredient of Hoosier cooks. Originally made from the extracted root of the marshmallow plant, today's confections are a blend of corn syrup, gelatin and flavorings. Indiana is home to Favorite Brands International, maker of Kidd Marshmallows.

Pineapple Upside-Down Cake

Yield: 10 servings

1¹⁄₃ cups butter, divided

1 cup packed brown sugar

1 (20-ounce) can pineapple slices, drained

8 red candied cherries

Pecans, cut into halves (optional)

2 cups flour

2 teaspoons baking powder

1 teaspoon baking soda

¹⁄₂ teaspoon salt

1¹⁄₂ cups sugar

2 eggs

1 teaspoon vanilla extract

1 cup buttermilk

Upside-down cakes are seeing a resurgence in popularity. And no wonder, who doesn't enjoy a slice of warm, buttery cake glistening with caramelized fruit. Serve with a tall glass of cold milk or a steaming cup of coffee or tea.

Preheat oven to 350 degrees. Melt ²⁄₃ cup of the butter in a saucepan. Stir in the brown sugar. Spread on the bottom of a 9x13-inch baking pan. Arrange the pineapple slices over the brown sugar mixture, placing 4 slices on each side of the pan and 2 slices, cut into halves, in the center. Place a cherry in the center of each pineapple slice. Arrange the pecan halves around the pineapple slices.

Combine the flour, baking powder, baking soda and salt in a bowl and mix well. Beat the remaining ²⁄₃ cup butter and the sugar in a mixer bowl until light and fluffy. Beat in the eggs and vanilla. Add the dry ingredients alternately with the buttermilk, mixing well after each addition. Pour carefully over the pineapple. Bake for 40 to 50 minutes or until a wooden pick inserted in the center comes out clean. Invert immediately onto a serving tray. Let stand for 5 minutes.

Variation: Add ¹⁄₂ teaspoon cinnamon and ¹⁄₂ teaspoon nutmeg to the flour mixture for a spiced variation.

Approx Per Serving: Cal 571; Prot 5 g; Carbo 82 g; T Fat 26 g; 40% Calories from Fat; Chol 110 mg; Fiber 1 g; Sod 638 mg

Topsy-Turvy Rhubarb Cake *Yield: 12 servings*

3 to 4 cups chopped fresh
  rhubarb, or 1 (16-ounce)
  package frozen cut rhubarb,
  thawed

1 cup sugar

1 cup water

1 (3-ounce) package
  strawberry gelatin

2 cups miniature
  marshmallows

1 (2-layer) white cake mix

2 eggs

½ cup vegetable oil

Preheat oven to 350 degrees. Combine the rhubarb, sugar and water in a saucepan. Bring to a boil. Stir in the gelatin until dissolved. Arrange the marshmallows over the bottom of a greased 9x13-inch baking pan. Prepare the cake mix using the eggs and oil and following the package directions. Pour over the marshmallows. Spoon the rhubarb mixture over the cake batter. Bake for 30 to 35 minutes or until a wooden pick inserted in the center comes out clean. Cool on a wire rack. Serve with vanilla ice cream.

Approx Per Serving: Cal 402; Prot 4 g; Carbo 65 g; T Fat 15 g; 32% Calories from Fat; Chol 35 mg; Fiber 1 g; Sod 322 mg

Shoofly Cake *Yield: 20 servings*

1 cup sorghum molasses

1 teaspoon cinnamon

2 teaspoons baking soda

2 cups boiling water

4 cups flour

2 cups packed brown sugar

⅔ cup shortening

⅓ cup applesauce

¼ cup chopped pecans

½ cup powdered sugar

2 teaspoons warm milk

¼ teaspoon vanilla extract

Preheat oven to 350 degrees. Combine the molasses, cinnamon and baking soda in a bowl and mix well. Pour the boiling water over the mixture. Combine the flour and brown sugar in a bowl and mix well. Cut in the shortening until crumbly. Stir in the applesauce. Set aside 1 cup of the crumb mixture. Stir the remaining crumb mixture into the molasses mixture. Pour into a greased and floured 9x13-inch baking pan. Sprinkle the reserved crumb mixture over the top. Sprinkle with pecans. Bake for 40 to 45 minutes or until cake begins to pull away from the sides of the pan and a wooden pick inserted in the center comes out clean. Combine the powdered sugar, milk and vanilla in a bowl and mix until smooth. Drizzle over the warm cake. Garnish with pecans.

Approx Per Serving: Cal 303; Prot 3 g; Carbo 56 g; T Fat 8 g; 24% Calories from Fat; Chol <1 mg; Fiber 1 g; Sod 142 mg

An Apple Almanac

VARIETY (FLAVOR) USES

CORTLAND
(slightly tart, rich)
eating, baking

EMPIRE
(mildly tart)
eating, salads

FUJI
(tangy-sweet)
eating, salads

GALA
(sweet, tart accent)
all-purpose

GOLDEN DELICIOUS
(sweet, rich)
all-purpose

GRANNY SMITH
(tart)
all-purpose

MCINTOSH
(tart)
eating, salads, sauces

RED DELICIOUS
(rich, sweet)
eating, salads

ROME BEAUTY
(slightly tart)
baking, cooking

WINESAP
(spicy-tart, winelike)
all-purpose

Amish Pat-in-the-Pan Crust

Yield: 1 (9-inch) pastry shell

1½ cups plus 3 tablespoons
  flour
1½ *teaspoons sugar*
½ *teaspoon salt*
½ *cup vegetable oil*
3 *tablespoons cold milk*

Combine the flour, sugar and salt
in a 9-inch pie plate and mix well.
Combine the oil and milk in a 1-cup
measure and beat with a fork until
creamy. Pour over the flour mixture
and mix well. Pat the dough with
fingers over the side and bottom of
the pie plate.

Approx Per Piecrust: Cal 1784; Prot 23 g;
Carbo 169 g; T Fat 113 g; 57% Calories from Fat;
Chol 6 mg; Fiber 6 g; Sod 1189 mg

Hot Water Piecrust

Yield: 2 (8- or 9-inch) piecrusts

2 *cups flour*
½ *teaspoon salt*
3 *tablespoons sugar*
¼ *cup hot water*
⅔ *cup vegetable oil*

Combine the flour, salt and sugar in a
mixer bowl and mix well. Beat in the
water and oil. Refrigerate, wrapped
in plastic wrap, for 10 to 15 minutes.
Divide dough into 2 portions. Roll
each into a 12-inch circle between
2 sheets of waxed paper. Fit into the
pie plates. Line with pieces of waxed
paper and fill to a depth of ½-inch
with dried beans or rice. Bake at 400
degrees for 20 minutes or until lightly
browned. Remove beans and waxed
paper. Cool.

Approx Per Piecrust: Cal 1170; Prot 13 g;
Carbo 114 g; T Fat 74 g; 57% Calories from Fat;
Chol 0 mg; Fiber 3 g; Sod 584 mg

Butterscotch Meringue Pie   *Yield: 8 servings*

2 eggs, separated, at room
   temperature

3 tablespoons cornstarch

1 cup milk

¼ cup butter

1 cup packed brown sugar

1 cup hot water

1½ teaspoons vanilla extract,
   divided

1 (9-inch) baked piecrust

¼ teaspoon cream of tartar

¼ cup sugar

Preheat oven to 350 degrees. Beat the egg yolks in a mixer bowl. Beat in the cornstarch and milk. Melt the butter in an iron skillet over medium heat. Stir in the brown sugar. Pour in the water slowly. Stir in the egg yolk mixture. Cook until thickened, stirring constantly. Remove from heat. Stir in 1 teaspoon of the vanilla. Pour into the piecrust. Beat the egg whites, remaining ½ teaspoon vanilla and cream of tartar in a separate mixer bowl on medium speed for 1 minute or until soft peaks form. Add the sugar gradually, beating until stiff peaks form. Spread over the warm filling, sealing to the edge. Bake for 10 to 15 minutes or until golden. Cool on a wire rack for 3 to 4 hours.

Approx Per Serving: Cal 346; Prot 4 g; Carbo 48 g; T Fat 16 g; 41% Calories from Fat; Chol 73 mg; Fiber <1 g; Sod 222 mg

No-Sugar Apple Pie   *Yield: 6 servings*

4½ cups peeled chopped
   apples

1 cup apple cider

Artificial sweetener equivalent
   to ½ cup sugar

1 teaspoon cinnamon

¼ cup cornstarch

1 tablespoon lemon juice

2 tablespoons margarine

1 recipe (2-crust) pie pastry

1 tablespoon milk

Preheat oven to 400 degrees. Combine the apples, cider, sweetener, cinnamon, cornstarch, lemon juice and margarine in a microwave-safe bowl and mix well. Microwave until mixture thickens, stirring occasionally. Roll half of the pie pastry into a 12-inch circle on a lightly floured surface. Fit into 9-inch pie plate. Spoon the apple mixture into the pastry shell. Roll the remaining half of the pie pastry into a 12-inch circle on a lightly floured surface. Place over the hot apple filling sealing the edge and cutting vents. Brush with milk. Bake for 10 minutes. Reduce the temperature to 350 degrees. Bake for 20 to 25 minutes longer.

Approx Per Serving: Cal 438; Prot 4 g; Carbo 54 g; T Fat 24 g; 48% Calories from Fat; Chol <1 mg; Fiber 4 g; Sod 359 mg

Cornstarch

A white, powdery thickening agent that comes from corn. Products thickened with cornstarch have a clearer, more translucent appearance than mixtures thickened with flour, which produces a more opaque look. It has twice the thickening power of flour, so when substituting cornstarch for flour, use half as much cornstarch. Cornstarch will keep up to 2 years in a cool, dry place.

 Glazed Cran-Apple Pie   *Yield: 6 servings*

4 cups peeled, chopped all-purpose apples

½ cup frozen cranberry-orange sauce, thawed

¼ cup sugar

¼ cup packed brown sugar

¾ teaspoon cinnamon

½ teaspoon nutmeg

⅛ teaspoon salt

¼ cup cornstarch

1 cup apple cider

2 teaspoons orange juice

2 teaspoons lemon juice

3 tablespoons butter or margarine

1 recipe (2-crust) pie pastry

1 tablespoon milk (optional)

Orange Glaze

Preheat oven to 400 degrees. Mix the apples, cranberry-orange sauce, sugar, brown sugar, cinnamon, nutmeg, salt, cornstarch, cider, orange juice, lemon juice and butter in a microwave-safe bowl. Microwave until mixture thickens and apples are partially cooked. Roll half of the pie pastry into a 12-inch circle on a lightly floured surface. Fit into 9-inch pie plate. Spoon the apple mixture into the pastry shell. Roll the remaining half of the pie pastry into a 12-inch circle on a lightly floured surface. Place over the hot apple filling, fluting the edge and cutting vents. Brush with milk. Bake for 10 minutes. Reduce the oven temperature to 350 degrees. Bake for 20 to 25 minutes longer. Cool on a wire rack. Drizzle Orange Glaze over the cooled pie.

Approx Per Serving: Cal 579; Prot 4 g; Carbo 83 g; T Fat 27 g; 41% Calories from Fat; Chol 17 mg; Fiber 4 g; Sod 486 mg

Orange Glaze

⅓ cup sifted powdered sugar

¼ teaspoon grated orange peel

⅛ teaspoon salt

¼ teaspoon almond extract

2 tablespoons half-and-half

Combine the powdered sugar, orange peel, salt, almond extract and half-and-half in a bowl and mix well.

Caramel Apple Pie *Yield: 8 servings*

1 cup sugar

¼ cup flour

1 teaspoon cinnamon

6 cups peeled, chopped all-purpose apples

1 (9-inch) unbaked pie pastry

Caramel Crumb Topping

⅓ cup caramel apple dip

Preheat oven to 350 degrees. Combine the sugar, flour and cinnamon in a bowl and mix well. Add the apples and toss to coat. Spoon into the pie pastry. Sprinkle with Caramel Crumb Topping. Cover the edge of the pie with a strip of aluminum foil. Place on a baking sheet. Bake for 30 minutes. Remove foil. Bake for 25 to 30 minutes or until bubbly. Cool on a wire rack for 10 minutes. Drizzle with caramel apple dip.

Approx Per Serving: Cal 561; Prot 4 g; Carbo 89 g; T Fat 22 g; 35% Calories from Fat; Chol 34 mg; Fiber 4 g; Sod 276 mg

Caramel Crumb Topping

2 tablespoons caramel apple dip

2 tablespoons milk

1 cup flour

½ cup packed brown sugar

½ cup butter

Combine the dip and milk in a bowl and mix until well blended. Stir in the flour and brown sugar. Cut in the butter until crumbly.

Caramel Cream Cheese Pie *Yield: 8 servings*

8 ounces cream cheese, softened

1 cup sweetened condensed milk

1 (16-ounce) container nondairy whipped topping

1 cup caramel ice cream topping

1½ cups flaked coconut, toasted

½ cup chopped pecans

1 (9-inch) graham cracker pie shell

Combine the cream cheese and condensed milk in a bowl and mix until smooth. Stir in the whipped topping. Layer the cream cheese mixture, caramel topping, coconut and pecans half at a time in the pie shell. Refrigerate, covered, until ready to serve.

Approx Per Serving: Cal 763; Prot 8 g; Carbo 89 g; T Fat 41 g; 49% Calories from Fat; Chol 45 mg; Fiber 2 g; Sod 449 mg

Ground Cherry Pie   *Yield: 6 servings*

1 cup water

3 tablespoons cornstarch

1 teaspoon tapioca

3 cups ground cherries

1 tablespoon lemon juice

¼ cup butter or margarine

1 recipe (2-crust) pie pastry

Preheat oven to 400 degrees. Combine the water, cornstarch and tapioca in a microwave-safe bowl and mix well. Microwave on High for 2 minutes; stir. Microwave on High until mixture thickens. Stir in the ground cherries. Add the lemon juice and butter, stirring until the butter is melted. Roll half of the pie pastry into a 12-inch circle on a lightly floured surface. Fit into the pie plate. Spoon the cherry mixture into the pastry shell. Roll the remaining half of the pie pastry into a 12-inch circle on a lightly floured surface. Place over the hot cherry filling fluting the edge and cutting vents. Bake for 15 minutes. Reduce the oven temperature to 350 degrees. Bake for 25 minutes longer or until browned.

Approx Per Serving: Cal 426; Prot 5 g; Carbo 40 g; T Fat 28 g; 59% Calories from Fat; Chol 21 mg; Fiber 4 g; Sod 391 mg

 ## Cherry-Berry Pie   *Yield: 8 servings*

1½ cups frozen red sour pitted cherries

1¼ cups frozen raspberries

1¼ cups sugar

3 tablespoons cornstarch

1 tablespoon quick-cooking tapioca

⅛ teaspoon salt

1½ tablespoons butter or margarine

1½ teaspoons lemon juice

⅛ teaspoon almond extract

1 recipe (2-crust) pie pastry

Thaw the cherries and raspberries in a colander over a bowl, reserving the juice. Preheat oven to 400 degrees. Add enough water to the reserved fruit juice to measure 1 cup. Combine with the sugar, cornstarch, tapioca and salt in a saucepan and mix well. Cook until thickened and bubbly, stirring frequently. Add the butter, lemon juice and almond extract, stirring until the butter melts. Stir in the cherries and raspberries. Cook for 3 to 5 minutes or until mixture has thickened, stirring constantly. Roll half of the pie pastry into a 12-inch circle on a lightly floured surface. Fit into 9-inch pie plate. Spoon the cherry mixture into the pastry shell. Roll the remaining half of the pie pastry into a 12-inch circle on a lightly floured surface. Place over the hot cherry filling, fluting the edge and cutting vents. Bake for 30 to 40 minutes. Cool.

Approx Per Serving: Cal 434; Prot 3 g; Carbo 68 g; T Fat 17 g; 35% Calories from Fat; Chol 6 mg; Fiber 4 g; Sod 293 mg

Sugar-Free Lemon Cloud Pie   *Yield: 8 servings*

1 small package sugar-free vanilla instant pudding mix

2 cups low-fat milk

1½ teaspoons aspartame sweetened lemonade drink mix

4 ounces nondairy whipped topping

1 (9-inch) graham cracker pie shell

Combine the milk and pudding mix in a bowl. Beat until thickened. Stir in the drink mix. Fold in the whipped topping. Pour into the pie shell. Refrigerate, covered, for 2 hours or longer.

Approx Per Serving: Cal 236; Prot 3 g; Carbo 29 g; T Fat 11 g; 44% Calories from Fat; Chol 5 mg; Fiber <1 g; Sod 333 mg

Sour Cream Lemon Pie   *Yield: 6 servings*

¼ cup plus 1 tablespoon cornstarch

1 cup light cream, divided

3 egg yolks

1 cup sugar

⅓ cup lemon juice

1 cup milk, warmed

1 cup sour cream

¼ cup butter, melted

3 tablespoons honey

1 (9-inch) baked piecrust

1 cup whipping cream, chilled

1 tablespoon powdered sugar

1½ teaspoons vanilla extract

Combine the cornstarch and ½ cup of the cream in a mixer bowl and mix until well blended. Beat in the egg yolks. Combine the remaining ½ cup cream, sugar and lemon juice in a saucepan. Cook over medium heat until the sugar dissolves, stirring constantly. Stir the warm milk into the egg yolk mixture. Pour into the cream mixture. Bring to a boil. Boil for 1 minute. Remove from heat. Stir in the sour cream, butter and honey. Cool. Spoon into the piecrust. Beat the whipping cream, powdered sugar and vanilla in a mixer bowl until stiff peaks form. Spoon over the pie. Garnish with lemon peel twists.

Approx Per Serving: Cal 811; Prot 8 g; Carbo 71 g; T Fat 57 g; 62% Calories from Fat; Chol 248 mg; Fiber 1 g; Sod 315 mg

Ground cherries, or more properly called Cape Gooseberries, grow wild throughout the United States, including northern Indiana, and are generally cultivated in tropical zones. With its inflated, papery skin (calyx), the ground cherry looks like a Chinese lantern. The bittersweet, juicy berries inside are opaque and golden in color. To use the berries, peel back the husk and rinse. Piquant in flavor, they make great pies, jams, and meat accompaniments.

Peaches and Plums Pie   *Yield: 8 servings*

2 cups peeled sliced fresh
  peaches
2 cups peeled sliced fresh
  purple plums
1 tablespoon lemon juice
¼ teaspoon almond extract
1½ cups sugar
¼ teaspoon salt
¼ cup quick-cooking tapioca
½ teaspoon grated
  lemon peel
1 recipe (2-crust) pie pastry
2 tablespoons butter

Combine the peaches, plums, lemon juice and almond extract in a bowl and mix well. Combine the sugar, salt, tapioca and lemon peel in a separate bowl and mix well. Stir into the fruit mixture. Let stand for 15 minutes. Preheat oven to 450 degrees. Roll half of the pie pastry into a 12-inch circle on a lightly floured surface. Fit into 9-inch pie plate. Spoon the fruit mixture into the pastry shell. Dot with butter. Roll the remaining half of the pie pastry into a 12-inch circle on a lightly floured surface. Place over the fruit filling, fluting the edge and cutting vents. Bake for 10 minutes. Reduce oven temperature to 350 degrees. Bake for 35 to 40 minutes longer or until lightly browned and filling is bubbly. Cool on a wire rack.

Approx Per Serving: Cal 446; Prot 3 g;
Carbo 70 g; T Fat 18 g; 36% Calories from Fat;
Chol 8 mg; Fiber 3 g; Sod 336 mg

No-Sugar Frozen Peanut Butter Pie   *Yield: 8 servings*

4 ounces cream cheese,
  softened
12 ounces nondairy whipped
  topping
½ cup peanut butter
1½ tablespoons aspartame
  sweetener
1 teaspoon vanilla extract
1 (9-inch) graham cracker or
  chocolate crumb piecrust

Beat the cream cheese in a mixer bowl until fluffy. Add the whipped topping and mix well. Add the peanut butter, sweetener and vanilla and mix well. Spoon into the piecrust. Garnish with chocolate sprinkles. Freeze, covered, for 1 hour or longer. Let stand at room temperature for 45 minutes before serving.

Approx Per Serving: Cal 434; Prot 6 g;
Carbo 36 g; T Fat 29 g; 60% Calories from Fat;
Chol 16 mg; Fiber 1 g; Sod 287 mg

192

Pecan Pie *Yield: 8 servings*

1/2 cup margarine
1 cup sugar
4 eggs
1/8 teaspoon salt
1 cup light corn syrup
1 teaspoon vanilla extract
1/2 teaspoon cinnamon
1 1/2 cups chopped pecans
1 (9-inch) unbaked pie pastry
Pecan halves (optional)

Preheat oven to 400 degrees. Beat the margarine and sugar in a mixer bowl until light and fluffy. Add the eggs, salt, corn syrup, vanilla and cinnamon and mix well. Stir in the pecans. Spoon into the pastry-lined pie plate. Arrange pecan halves around the edge. Bake for 10 to 15 minutes. Reduce the oven temperature to 350 degrees. Bake for 40 to 50 minutes longer or until center is set. Cover with aluminum foil if the top becomes too dark.

Variations: Substitute 1 1/2 cups hickory nuts for the pecans or use 3/4 cup chopped walnuts and 3/4 cup chopped pecans.

Approx Per Serving: Cal 614; Prot 6 g; Carbo 71 g; T Fat 36 g; 51% Calories from Fat; Chol 106 mg; Fiber 3 g; Sod 368 mg

Sugar-Free Pineapple Cream Pie *Yield: 6 servings*

1 large package sugar-free
    vanilla instant pudding mix
1 cup fat-free sour cream
1 (20-ounce) can unsweetened
    crushed pineapple, drained
1 envelope artificial sweetener
1/4 cup margarine, melted
1 (9-inch) baked piecrust or
    piecrust of choice

Combine pudding mix and sour cream in a bowl and mix well. Add the pineapple, sweetener and margarine and mix well. Spoon into the piecrust. Refrigerate, covered, until ready to serve. Garnish with light nondairy whipped topping.

Approx Per Serving: Cal 327; Prot 5 g; Carbo 37 g; T Fat 18 g; 50% Calories from Fat; Chol 0 mg; Fiber 1 g; Sod 672 mg

How to Prepare Fresh Pumpkin

It's easy to make your own pumpkin pulp if you have the time. Select a small to medium size pumpkin (4 to 6 pounds). Remove the stem. Use a large firm blade knife to cut the pumpkin into quarters; remove the seeds and fibers. Cut the quarters in half; arrange, skin side up, in a large shallow baking pan. Cover with aluminum foil; bake in a 375 degree oven 1 to 1½ hours or until tender. Scoop the pulp from the rind. Using a small amount at a time, place in blender or food processor; blend until smooth. Pour into cheesecloth-lined strainer; press out liquid. (Makes about 2 cups.)

Pumpkin Custard Pie   *Yield: 6 servings*

3 eggs

*2 cups cooked pumpkin, or
  1 (15-ounce) can pumpkin*

⅔ cup sugar

1 cup half-and-half

1 teaspoon cinnamon

½ teaspoon ginger

½ teaspoon nutmeg

½ teaspoon salt

1 (9-inch) unbaked pie pastry

*Sour Cream Topping or Streusel
  Topping*

Preheat oven to 425 degrees. Beat the eggs in a mixer bowl until pale yellow. Add the pumpkin, sugar, half-and-half, cinnamon, ginger, nutmeg and salt and mix well. Pour into the pastry-lined pie plate. Bake for 10 minutes. Reduce oven temperature to 350 degrees. Bake for 25 minutes longer. Spread the Sour Cream Topping over the pie. Bake for 10 to 15 minutes longer or until a knife inserted 1 inch from the edge comes out clean. Cool on a wire rack.

Tip: To make 2 pies, use 3½ cups cooked pumpkin or 1 (29-ounce) can pumpkin and double all other ingredients.

Approx Per Serving: Cal 441; Prot 8 g; Carbo 48 g; T Fat 25 g; 50% Calories from Fat; Chol 138 mg; Fiber 2 g; Sod 419 mg

Sour Cream Topping

1 cup sour cream

2 tablespoons sugar

1 teaspoon vanilla extract

Combine the sour cream, sugar and vanilla in a bowl and mix well.

Streusel Topping

¼ cup packed brown sugar

¼ cup flour

*2 tablespoons butter or
  margarine, chilled*

¼ cup chopped nuts

Combine the brown sugar and flour in a bowl and mix well. Cut in the butter until crumbly. Stir in the nuts.

Indiana Raisin Pie   *Yield: 6 servings*

2 cups seedless raisins

1½ cups water, divided

½ cup orange juice

½ cup packed brown sugar

2 tablespoons cornstarch

1 teaspoon cinnamon

1 teaspoon grated orange peel

⅛ teaspoon salt

1 tablespoon vinegar

2 tablespoons margarine or
   butter

1 recipe (2-crust) pie pastry

Preheat oven to 425 degrees. Combine the raisins, 1¼ cups of the water and orange juice in a saucepan. Bring to a boil. Reduce the heat. Simmer, covered, for 5 minutes. Add the brown sugar, cornstarch, cinnamon, orange peel, salt and remaining ¼ cup water. Bring to a boil, stirring constantly. Remove from the heat. Add the vinegar and margarine, stirring until margarine melts. Roll half of the pie pastry into a 12-inch circle on a lightly floured surface. Fit into 8-inch pie plate. Spoon the raisin mixture into the pastry shell. Roll the remaining half of the pie pastry into a 12-inch circle on a lightly floured surface. Place over the raisin filling fluting the edge and cutting vents. Sprinkle with additional sugar and cinnamon if desired. Bake for 25 minutes.

Approx Per Serving: Cal 571; Prot 5 g; Carbo 88 g; T Fat 24 g; 37% Calories from Fat; Chol 0 mg; Fiber 4 g; Sod 418 mg

Old-Fashioned Sugar Cream Pie   *Yield: 8 servings*

½ cup sugar

½ cup packed brown sugar

3½ tablespoons flour

2 cups whipping cream

2 tablespoons butter or
   margarine, melted

1 (9-inch) unbaked pie pastry

Preheat oven to 400 degrees. Combine the sugar, brown sugar, flour, cream and butter in a bowl and mix well. Pour into the pastry-lined pie plate. Bake for 10 minutes. Reduce the oven temperature to 350 degrees. Bake for 45 to 50 minutes longer or until filling bubbles in the center.

Approx Per Serving: Cal 457; Prot 3 g; Carbo 40 g; T Fat 32 g; 63% Calories from Fat; Chol 89 mg; Fiber 1 g; Sod 174 mg

Sugar-Free Fresh Strawberry Pie   *Yield: 8 servings*

1¼ cups hot water

2 tablespoons cornstarch

2 teaspoons sugar-free strawberry gelatin mix

½ cup artificial sweetener

1 pint strawberries

1 (9-inch) baked piecrust

Combine the water and cornstarch in a microwave-safe bowl and mix well. Microwave on High for 1 minute; stir. Microwave on High until thickened, stirring after each minute. Stir in the gelatin mix, sweetener and strawberries. Spoon into the piecrust. Refrigerate, covered, until ready to serve. Serve with whipped cream or whipped topping.

Approx Per Serving: Cal 161; Prot 2 g; Carbo 27 g; T Fat 8 g; 38% Calories from Fat; Chol 0 mg; Fiber 1 g; Sod 139 mg

Frozen Strawberry Margarita Pie   *Yield: 8 servings*

1¼ cups finely crushed pretzels

½ cup plus 2 tablespoons butter or margarine, melted

¼ cup sugar

1 (14-ounce) can sweetened condensed milk

1½ cups chopped fresh or frozen unsweetened strawberries, thawed, drained

⅓ cup lime juice

2 tablespoons tequila

2 tablespoons orange-flavored liqueur

Red food coloring (optional)

1½ cups whipping cream, whipped

Combine the crushed pretzels, butter and sugar in a bowl and mix well. Press firmly over the bottom and up the side of a buttered 9-inch pie plate. Combine the condensed milk, strawberries, lime juice, tequila, orange-flavored liqueur and food coloring in a bowl and mix well. Fold in the whipped cream. Spoon into the prepared crust. Freeze, covered, for 4 hours or until firm. Let stand at room temperature for 10 minutes before serving. Garnish with additional whipped cream, strawberries and lime or orange slices.

Margarita Pie

Omit the strawberries and red food coloring.

Approx Per Serving: Cal 556; Prot 7 g; Carbo 52 g; T Fat 36 g; 57% Calories from Fat; Chol 117 mg; Fiber 2 g; Sod 431 mg

Nutritional Profiles

The editors have attempted to present these family recipes in a format that allows approximate nutritional values to be computed. Persons with dietary or health problems or whose diets require close monitoring should not rely solely on the nutritional information provided. They should consult their physician or a registered dietitian for specific information.

Abbreviations for Nutritional Profiles

Cal — Calories	T Fat — Total Fat	Sod — Sodium
Prot — Protein	Chol — Cholesterol	g — grams
Carbo — Carbohydrates	Fiber — Dietary Fiber	mg — milligrams

Nutritional information for these recipes is computed from information derived from many sources, including materials supplied by the United States Department of Agriculture, computer databanks, and journals in which the information is assumed to be in the public domain. However, many specialty items, new products, and processed foods may not be available from these sources or may vary from the average values used in these profiles. More information on new and/or specific products may be obtained by reading the nutrient labels. Unless otherwise specified, the nutritional profile of these recipes is based on all measurements being level.

- Artificial sweeteners vary in use and strength so should be used "to taste," using the recipe ingredients as a guideline. Sweeteners using aspartame (NutraSweet and Equal) should not be used as a sweetener in recipes involving prolonged heating, which reduces the sweet taste. For further information on the use of these sweeteners, refer to the package.
- Alcoholic ingredients have been analyzed for the basic information. Cooking causes the evaporation of alcohol, which decreases alcoholic and caloric content.
- Buttermilk, sour cream, eggnog and yogurt are the types available commercially.
- Cake mixes which are prepared using package directions include 3 eggs and 1/2 cup oil.
- Chicken, cooked for boning and chopping, has been roasted; this method yields the lowest caloric values.
- Cottage cheese is cream-style with 4.2% creaming mixture. Dry curd cottage cheese has no creaming mixture.
- Eggs are all large.
- Flour is unsifted all-purpose flour.
- Garnishes, serving suggestions, and other optional information and variations are not included in the profile.
- Margarine and butter are regular, not whipped or presoftened.
- Milk is whole milk, 3.5% butterfat. Low-fat milk is 1% butterfat. Evaporated milk is whole milk with 60% of the water removed.
- Oil is any type of vegetable cooking oil. Shortening is hydrogenated vegetable shortening.
- Salt and other ingredients to taste as noted in the ingredients have not been included in the nutritional profile.
- If a choice of ingredients has been given, the profile reflects the first option. If a choice of amounts has been given, the profile reflects the greater amount.
- Profiles do not include variations.

Contributors List

Special thanks to those who tested recipes.

Albers, Natalie
Alderson, Madonna
Allbaugh, Erica
Andrews, Debbie
Andrews, Susan D.
Andruch, Donna
Anglin, Lorraine
Anglin, Norma J.
Armstrong, Tonya
Arvin, Grace L.
Ash, Paul
Bachert, Scott
Bailey, Carolyn
Bailey, Shirley
Baker, Barbara
Baker, Carol
Baker, Marilyn J.
Balmer, Clarice O.
Barbour, Danielle
Barge, Marie
Barnes, Teresa
Barnett, Sharon
Barnhart, Carla
Baumgartner, Barbara
Beard, Kayla
Beaver, Alicia
Becher, Amanda
Beckwith, Fran
Benham, Jackie
Benham, Libby
Berenda, Arnetta
Bergman, Abby
Berry, Beth
Bershell, Andrew
Bershell, Christine
Bershell, Nettie
Bickel, Helen J.
Blackford, Edna
Blackwell, Lois
Blankenship, Mary S.
Bluhm, Christy
Boggs, Carolyn

Boling, Andrea
Bonaguro, Nancy
Bonaventura, Betty
Boone, Ann
Bouse, Susan
Bowen, Joannie
Bowers, Cassie
Bozarth, Barb
Bozarth, Judy
Bradley, Mary
Bragg, Barbara
Branum, Linda
Bray, LaCinda
Bridges, Nita
Brooks, Mary Ethel
Brown, Diana
Brown, Jeroma
Brown, Phyllis
Brown, Ruth
Brubaker, Kari
Bruce, Louise S.
Budde, Lauren
Budreau, Kathy
Burns, Peggy
Burrus, Ruth M.
Busing, Jane
Butler, Loretta
Bylsma, Andrew
Byrd, Micki
Caffee, Cindy
Callis, Irene
Calloway, Phyllis
Carlisle, Jeannie
Carr, Sarah E.
Carter, Dorothy
Catlett, Sue
Chappell, Joan
Chase, Patricia
Cheetham, Becky
Cheetham, Cam
Cheetham, Cody
Chenette, Emily

Chestnut, Rachel
Clark, Rita
Clemons, Anna
Cline, Lucille
Cloncs, Annie Watts
Clutinger, Ashley
Coleman, Beverly A.
Coleman, Matt
Cook, Janet
Cook, Jeffrey
Cook, Linda M.
Cook, Veronica
Crabtree, Helen
Craig, Beth Ann
Craig, Jodi
Cramer, Elizabeth
Crane, Marianne
Crist, Julianne
Crites, Martha
Cullison, Kathleen
Cundiff, Phyllis
Curry Jr., R.H.
Cutter, Marcella
Cybulski, Susan
Darkis, Renee
David, Norma Jean
Davis, Marilyn
Dawson, Amy
Day, Marilyn
Decker, Katie
Decker, Kitty
DeGraff, Cathy
Demske, Jane
Deutsch, Elveria
Devore, Jean
Dietz, Paula
Dilger, Lisa
Dimmett, JeniRose
Dimmett, Lisa
Dingman, Karen L.
Dixon, Pauline
Dowden, Nancy

Downs, Esther
Downton, Paulette
Duke, Mary
Dunlap, Phyllis
Dye, Kelle
Dyer, Maxine
Earley, Erin
Early, Barbara
Early, Janet
East, Ivy Susan
East, Jeannie M.
Eaton, Sarah
Eckerty, Velma
Ehle-Newman, Karen
Eisenbeiss, Mary Ann
Eizinger, Amy
Ellerbusch, Helen
Eller, Kay
Ellis, Alice
Elzer, Veronica
Emigh, Jennifer
Emmert, Janelle
Endres, Vada
Engle, Barbara
Evans, Katie
Evers, Andrew
Fain, Margaret
Falls, Arbella E.
Farrer, Lisa
Fewell, Louise
Fife, Whitney
Finster, Sarah
Fischer, Mary Jane
Fitch, Joellen
Floyd, Linda
Fox, Erica
Franks, Susan
Freeman, Candace
Freyberger, Nicole
Friend, Brian
Friend, Kenda
Frischie, Susan

Froedge, Joni
Fry, Mindy
Fudge, Bev
Fullenkamp, Jenny
Gaier, Shirley
Gallagher, Karen
Gamble, Jean
Gamble, Marjorie
Gantt, Meredith
Gantt, Natalie
Gasaway, Jane
Gauck, Beth
Gaudard, Jason
Gaudard, Jordan
Gerber, Jennifer
Geswein, Jean
Gibbs, Brenda F.
Gillam, Frances
Giselbach, Leketta
Glotzbach, Helen
Gochenour, Susan
Goff, Elizabeth
Good, Adam
Good, Kelli
Goodspeed, Patricia
Grajewski, Rachel
Grandlienard, Letitia
Gray, Lisa
Green, Jack
Green, Vera R.
Greenwood, Ashley
Gretencord, Karen
Grider, Connie
Gumbel, James
Gumbel, Nancy E.
Guthridge, Joan
Hackett, Mary Ann
Hackett, Sue
Haddon, Amanda
Haley, Emily
Hall, Ashley K.
Hamilton, Libby

Hamilton, Lynn
Handley-Lynch, Donna
Hannon, Ashlee
Hannon, Erin
Hardesty-Jerrell, Wilma
Hardin, Gwen
Hardwick, Darcy
Harmon, Kathleen
Harner, Carla
Harper, Margaret
Harris, Jennifer
Hart, Grace
Hart, Kathryn
Hartman, Dorothea
Hauenstein, Sandra
Havel, Emalee
Hawes, Pam
Heald, Amy Jo
Hedge, Patricia J.
Hein, Velma
Heinz, Betty
Helfrich, Ericka
Hemmerlein, Terri
Hensley, Jennifer
Hensley, Marthanna
Hibschman, Donna
Hight, Charlotte
Hight, Justin
Hill, Debi
Hines, Heather
Hinkle, Sandra
Hodge, Alice
Hoeing, Mandy
Hoffman, Mary
Hoffmann, Carla
Hood, Karen
Hoopengarner, Sue
Hopf, Joyce A.
Hostetler, Esther
Hubbard, Diana
Huber, Lysiane
Hubster, Violet
Huff, Maxine
Huff, Pam
Hugg, Aileen
Hulsey, Shylah

Hungerford, Betty
Hunnicutt, Lisa
Hunt, Rosalie
Hutchinson, Margaret
Hutson, Christine
Ice, Annabelle
Iles, Geneva
Illyes, Leeanna
Indiana Soybean
   Development
   Council
Ingerson, Kati
Ingle, Kim
Inman, Sarah
Irvin, Pamela
Isaacs, Helen
Jackman, Cathryn
Jackson, Florence
Jacobs, Wilma
Jahn, Megan
Jarrett, Hazel
Jaskowiak, Gail
Jaworski, Kathy
Jean, Carmelita
Jeffers, M. Marcia
Jernas, Vicki
Johnson, Ann
Johnson, Helen
Johnson, Kylie
Johnson, Leah
Johnston, Carolyn
Johnston, Thelma Lou
Jones, Caitlyn
Jones, C. Britt
Jones, Stephanie
Kaiser, Carolyn
Kaiser, Doris J.
Kaser, Georgianna
Kaufman, Lois M.
Keller, Amy Jo
Keller, Anne
Keller, Gwen
Keller, Mary Ann
Keller, Mary Elisabeth
Keller, Patsy
Kelley, Angela

Kellum, Joan
Kerr, Rebecca
Kiefer, Kimela
Kingery, Carole
King, Nancy
Kitchel, Mary
Klefeker, Sharlee
Klosterman, Amy
Knight, Mary Rose
Kobelt, Pam
Koehler, Andrea
Komendo, Pam
Kottkamp, Kacey
Krom, Ivy
Kunkler, Leona
Kurtzhals, Shirley A.
Lackey, Karen
Larsen, Erin
Lawler, Elna Mae
LeCount, Emily
Leffel, Kathryn A.
Lenderman, Sarah
Lengerich, Mary
Lidrbauch, Sharon
Lienhart-Cross,
   Mary Ann
Lockett, Melba
Loehr, Betty
Lonabaugh, Katie
Loude'n, Jennifer
Lowe, Fayetta
Lowes, Bernice
Loyd, Melba
Lucas, Mickey
Lueken, Dolores
Lumpkin, Renea
Magnus, Wilma
Manier, Brandon
Manlief, Jerilyn
Mann, Carmel C.
Mann, Linda
March Beginnings
   Homemakers
Mark, Lorelei
Marriberon,
   Mary Anne

Marshall, Marah
Martin, Letha
Martin, Ruth
Mason, Lucille
Mast, Fanny
Matteson, Paul
Mattingly, Barbara J.
Mauck, Patricia A.
Maynard, Ethylean
McAfee, Dana
McClatchey, Robert
McCollum, Robin
McCorkle, Marie
McCutchan, Mindy
McDonald, Dorothy J.
McGrady, Meredith
McKee, Joanna
McMurray, Mary C.
Menchhofer, Della
Menzie, Ruth A.
Merkley, Brenda
Merlau, Curtis
Merlau, Kelly J.
Metzger, Kathryn L.
Meuser, Matt
Meyer, Janeie
Meyer, Marilynn
Meyer, Scott
Michel, Phyllis
Miller, Brian
Miller, Stephanie
Million, Elaine
Mills, Lena
Mitchell, Charlotte S.
Mohr, Carolyn
Mohr, Margaret L.
Molt, Trudy
Moore, Penny
Moore, Rosemary
Morgan, Suzan
Morin, Andre
Morrow, Norma
Mottweiler, Betty
Mulder, Janet
Mundy, Virginia
Murray, Caroline

Musselman, Helen
Myers, Mallory
Myers, Robin
Nannenga, Donna
Nelson, Dean
Nelson, Loretta
Nelson, Lorrie
Nichols, Aaron
Nickander, Joan
Nicodemus, Holly
Nix, Shirley
Nold, Alexis
Ogden, Jackie
Olin, Amy
Oliver, Jayne
Orr, Heather
Oudghiri, Stephanie
Owens, Alita
Paden, James
Parnell, Mary Ann
Parsley, Karen
Pearcy, Marthalyn
Pearson, Carol
Pearson, Robyn
Pelz, Evelyn
Pennington, Margie
Perkins, Ila
Persinger, Kendra
Peterich, Barbara
Peters, Estella
Petty, Dee
Petty, Linda
Petty, Regina
Phillippi, Barbara
Phillips, Amy
Pickel, Barbara
Pickens, Kimberly
Pickett, Gerry
Piety, Joy
Poe, Carol
Pontius, Sydney
Prue, Nancy Jo
Puckett, Sarah
Pullen, Dawn
Pulver, Lisa
Pund, Alexander

Pund, Paulita
Quinzer, Mary
Raderstorf, Peg
Rainey, Melanie
Ramirez, Raquel
Ratliff, Riley
Rauchmiller, Joan
Rausch, Rebecca
Ray, Anna
Ray, Barbara
Reedy, Linda
Reimer, Jacqueline
Reinhard, Carleen
Rentchler, Carla
Rentchler, Christa
Rentchler, Joann
Resler, Fancheon
Resler, Kathryn
Resler, Kraig
Rettinger, Jeanette
Reynolds, Nancy J.
Rhodehamel, Cathy
Rhudy, Carol
Rice, Leslie
Richard, Rosemary
Richardson, Nancy
Richter, Nicolas
Richwine, Beth Ann
Riggles, June
Rinker, Tiffany
Robenhorst, Jared W.
Roberts, Esther
Roberts, Mary Helen
Robertson, Tabitha
Robinson, Mary Jo
Robison, Molly
Rodrick, Lucinda
Roelle, Rosemarie
Roesner, Earl
Rogers, Joshua
Rogers, Pat
Rompf, Katherine
Rooze, Helen
Rose, Joyce
Rosenberger, Karen
Rush, Peggy

Rusk, Angela
Rusk, Brian
Rusk, Vera
Ryan, Jill
Sachs, Betty
Sala, Nancy
Sallee, Sue
Salmon, Kim
Sandefur, Katherine
Schentrup, IdaAnn
Schmidt, Vicki
Schmitt, Dwayne
Schmitt, Mary Ann
Schopmeyer, Bayleigh
Schuble, Theresa
Schwartz, June
Scott, Lucy
Scott, Mary D.
Scott, Sheila
Seffel, Kathryn
Seffel, Robert
Sendmeyer, Betty
Senter, Lu
Sergesketter, Cheryl
Sergesketter,
    Christina
Sergesketter, Lauren
Sergesketter, Natalie
Shackleton, Suzann
Shapland, Janette
Sharp, Michael A.
Sharp, Terry
Sheridan, Deanna
Shields, Alta
Shields, Jane
Shindler, Janet
Shock, Jill
Shoemaker, Kris
Sholtey, Mary
Shull, Virginia
Shultz, Jilann S.
Shumaker, Trina
Sickman, Jane
Sickman, Minerva
Silver, Alice
Sinclair, Regina

Slabaugh, Rosalind
Slagal, Connie
Small, Alma
Smith, Angilee
Smith, Devota
Smith, Kae
Smith, Kayanna
Smith, Marissa
Smith, Nancy
Smith, Stephanie
Smith, Wanda K.
Sneed, Katti J.
Snoeberger, Kathy
Snyder, Cindy
Soladine, Christina
Sommers, Sharon
Spaulding, Andrea
Speedy, Clara
Spitznogle, Nora
Sriver, Judith
Stackhouse, Shae
Stafford, June
Stahly, Patricia
Stam, Heidi
Standiford, Donald
Standiford, Maria
Standiford, Yvonne
Steiner, Alice
Steiner, Ann
Steiner, Jane
Stippler, Jan
Stokes, Barbara
Stoner, Hazel
Street, Cornelia
Street, Jamie
Streich, Marge
Stroup, Linda L.
Stuart, Marla J.
Sueberkrop, Patti
Sula, Laurie
Sureck, John
Sureck, Kate
Swaim, Delores
Swank, Ruth
Sweeney, Alice
Swisher, Jean

Swisher, Joan
Sylvester, Judit
Tanselle, Barbara
Taylor, Jayne
Taylor, Joanna
Taylor, LouAnna
Temme, Doris
Thacker, Rita
Theisen, Kristyne
Thomas, Jill
Thomas, Katherine
Thomas, Linda
Thomas, Marsha
Thompson, Lucille
Thompson, Rachel
Thornburg, Sue
Tikijian, Nancy
Towne, Marian
Trent, Sue
Trevarthan, Inez
Tweedy, Dorothy
Uhlmansiek, Janice
Ulmer, Trisha
Ummel, Phillip
VanHook, Helen
VanKirk, Irene
VanMeter, Pamela
Vargo, Diana
Vaskowiak, Gail
Veen, Laurie
Verkamp, Mary
Vermillion, Frances
Wade, Linda
Wainwright, Jenessa
Waite, Beatrice
Walker, Janet
Walker, Jeremy
Walker, Marge
Walston, Jacob
Waltz, Jane
Ward, Rita
Washington County
    4-H Council
Watterson, Kathy
Watts, Laura
Waymire, Virginia

Weaver, Olive
Weiss, Mary Anne
Welp, Angie
Westfield Cloverleaves
    4-H Club
Whitaker, June
White, Barbara
Whitehorn, Abby
White, Jeannette
Whitlow, Heather
Widawski, Apryl
Wiggins, Wilma
Wilder, Ruth
Wild, Lisa
Wild, Steffi
Wilfong, Linda
Willcox, Joyce
Wilson, Betty
Wilson, Jennifer
Winters, Mary
Wise, Mary
Wood, Dorothy
Wood, Elizabeth
Woosley, Shirley
Wright, Joann
Wright, Marilyn
Yes Mobile
    Catering, Inc.
Yoder, Evelyn
Yoder, Jean
Yoder, Tyler Craig
Yoeman, Kim
Yohey, Marilyn
Youngblood, Samantha
Young, Linda
Young, Stella
Yundt, Phyllis
Zeck, Staci
Zieseniss, Frances
Zmyslony II, Robert

Index

Order Information

The
Indiana
4-H
Foundation

225 S. East St., Suite 760
Indianapolis, IN 46202
317-692-7044

Please send _____ copies of *Picnics • Potlucks & Prizewinners* $18.95 each $ _____

Postage and Handling $3.00 each $ _____

TOTAL $ _____

Name _____

Address _____

City/State/Zip _____

Telephone Number _____

Method of Payment: ☐ Check or Money Order   ☐ VISA   ☐ MasterCard

Card Number _____ Expiration Date _____

Signature _____

Please make checks payable to Indiana 4-H Foundation.

This page may be photocopied.

The 4-H Pledge

I pledge:

My HEAD to clearer thinking,

My HEART to greater loyalty,

My HANDS to larger service, and

My HEALTH to better living,

for my club, my community,

my country, and my world.

Indiana 4-H is a partnership of adults and youth working together to develop important life skills through "hands on" learning experiences. Through 4-H clubs and other 4-H activities, 4-H members develop lifelong friendships and have fun while learning to recognize self-worth, relate to others, communicate well, develop a work ethic, accept responsibility, deal with change, and expand their horizons.

Indiana 4-H is open to young people from urban, suburban, and rural communities. Each county has 4-H clubs and other 4-H activities to provide opportunities and experiences that can be an important factor in "growing up."

To find out more about 4-H membership, or the advantages of being an adult volunteer leader, or just to help with a 4-H activity or event, call your county Cooperative Extension office.

The 4-H Motto:
"To Make the Best Better"